This book offers the first in-depth study of Aristotle's theory of the sense-organs. It aims to answer two questions central to Aristotle's psychology and biology: why does Aristotle think we have sense-organs, and why does he describe the sense-organs in the way he does? The author looks at all the Aristotelian evidence for the five senses and shows how pervasively Aristotle's accounts of the sense-organs are motivated by his interest in form and function. The book also engages with the celebrated problem of whether perception for Aristotle requires material changes in the perceiver. It argues that, surprisingly to the modern philosopher, nothing in Aristotle's description of the sense-organs requires us to believe in such changes. The book should appeal to readers specifically interested in Aristotle's philosophy of mind and biology as well as to those generally interested in sense-perception.

CAMBRIDGE CLASSICAL STUDIES

General Editors

M. F. BURNYEAT, M. K. HOPKINS, M. D. REEVE,

A. M. SNODGRASS

ARISTOTLE ON THE SENSE-ORGANS

＾ARISTOTLE ON THE SENSE-ORGANS ／

T. K. JOHANSEN
Lecturer in Classics and Ancient Philosophy
University of Bristol

CAMBRIDGE
UNIVERSITY PRESS

PUBLISHED BY THE PRESS SYNDICATE OF THE UNIVERSITY OF CAMBRIDGE
The Pitt Building, Trumpington Street, Cambridge CB2 1RP, United Kingdom

CAMBRIDGE UNIVERSITY PRESS
The Edinburgh Building, Cambridge CB2 2RU, United Kingdom
40 West 20th Street, New York, NY 10011-4211, USA
10 Stamford Road, Oakleigh, Melbourne 3166, Australia

First published 1998

Printed in the United Kingdom at the University Press, Cambridge

Typeset in 11/13 pt Times

A catalogue record for this book is available from the British Library

Library of Congress cataloguing in publication data
Johansen, T. K.
Aristotle on the sense-organs / T. K. Johansen.
p.   cm. – (Cambridge classical studies)
Based on the author's thesis (Ph.D.) – Cambridge University, 1994.
Includes bibliographical references and index.
ISBN 0 521 58338 1 (hardback)
1. Aristotle.   2. Sense and sensation – History.   3. Perception
(Philosophy) – History. I. Title. II. Series.
B491.P38J64 1997
121'.35 – dc21   96-46730 CIP

ISBN 0 521 58338 1 hardback

AO

Til mor og far

CONTENTS

ACKNOWLEDGEMENTS

This study is based on a PhD thesis submitted to Cambridge University in 1994. In writing the thesis and revising it for the Cambridge Classical Studies Series I have incurred a number of debts which it is a pleasure for me to acknowledge here.

By far my greatest debt is to my PhD supervisor, Myles Burnyeat. He first suggested the sense-organs in Aristotle as a topic for my thesis. He directed its execution with a philosophical understanding and an interpretative genius for which my admiration and gratitude are still growing. Whatever merit this study may have is due largely to his influence.

David Charles and Geoffrey Lloyd examined the thesis and made comments which have been invaluable in revising it for publication. My debt to Geoffrey Lloyd's writings will be apparent on most pages. Conversations with him on Aristotle's explanatory strategies and biological detail have been equally vital for this work.

I would like to thank the editors of the Cambridge Classical Studies for accepting this work for publication. Numerous improvements to the final draft were due to their incisive comments.

I am grateful to Sarah Broadie, Nicholas Denyer, Richard King, Fraser MacBride, Christopher Rowe, David Sedley and Christopher Williams for many helpful comments, to Bob Sharples for advice on the sections of chapter 5 that appeared in *Phronesis* 1996 as 'Aristotle on the sense of smell' and to Brill Academic Publishers for permission to reprint.

I owe thanks also to Christian Wildberg for his help during my stay in 1991–2 at the Free University, Berlin, to my former colleagues at the University of Aberdeen for the excellent work conditions that allowed me to finish the revisions sooner than I could have hoped for, and to present and past colleagues at Bristol University, Richard Buxton, Catharine Edwards, Charles Martindale and, above all, Christopher Rowe, for much theoretical and practical assistance.

Finally, a personal thanks to my parents, to whom I dedicate this book, and to my wife, Frisbee Sheffield, for their support.

ABBREVIATIONS OF ARISTOTLE'S WORKS

Abbreviation	Latin title	English title
APo	*Analytica Posteriora*	Posterior Analytics
APr	*Analytica Priora*	Prior Analytics
Cael.	*De Caelo*	On the Heavens
Cat.	*Categoriae*	Categories
De an.	*De Anima*	On the Soul
De Div.	*De Divinatione per Somnum*	On Divination through Sleep
DI	*De Insomniis*	On Dreams
EE	*Ethica Eudemia*	Eudemian Ethics
EN	*Ethica Nicomachea*	Nicomachean Ethics
GA	*De Generatione Animalium*	Generation of Animals
GC	*De Generatione et Corruptione*	On Generation and Corruption
HA	*Historia Animalium*	History of Animals
IA	*De Incessu Animalium*	Progression of Animals
Int.	*De Interpretatione*	On Interpretation
Juv.	*De Iuventute et Senectute*	On Youth and Old Age
MA	*De Motu Animalium*	Movement of Animals
Mem.	*De Memoria*	On Memory
Metaph.	*Metaphysica*	Metaphysics
Mete.	*Meteorologica*	Meteorology
PA	*De Partibus Animalium*	Parts of Animals
Ph.	*Physica*	Physics

Resp.	*De Respiratione*	*On Respiration*
Rh.	*Rhetorica*	*Rhetoric*
Sens.	*De Sensu*	*On Sense*
Top.	*Topica*	*Topics*

INTRODUCTION

Why do we have sense-organs? We have ears, intricate structures composed of membranes, bones, channels, etc., a nose
with two nostrils and a mucous membrane which covers a
nasal cavity. We have taste buds, a range of tactile sensors
under our skin, not to mention the eyes. Why?

The simple answer is that we have sense-organs because
they enable us to perceive. A sense-organ, as Aristotle would
say, is an *organon*, a tool or instrument of perception. But to
understand why the sense-organ is instrumental in perception
we must understand something about perception. Just as we
must understand something about gardening before we can
appreciate the usefulness of a rake, so we must understand
something about sense-perception before we can see the point
of having a sense-organ. An explanation of the sense-organs
must therefore start with an understanding of what sense-
perception is. Once we understand what sense-perception is,
we can explain how the sense-organs help bring about sense-
perception as we have understood it.

In modern science it can be taken for granted that the
explanation of perception will refer to physical processes.[1] For
example, vision is said to be the process whereby the eyes 'feed
the brain with information coded into neural activity – chains
of electrical impulses – which by their code and the patterns of
brain activity, represent objects'.[2] Vision is understood as a
physical process in a physical system: reference is made to
'light energy', 'electrical impulses' and 'the brain'. Particular
stages in the process of vision are located in particular parts
of the body. The conversion of light energy into electrical

---

[1] By 'perception' I shall throughout this study mean 'sense-perception'.
[2] Gregory (1966) 7.

I

impulses is something that happens in the eye, whereas the decoding of the electrical impulses is something that happens in the brain. The eye is a sense-organ of vision in this way: the eye is a part of the body in which the physical process which defines vision takes place.

The question why we have sense-organs thus shows up a particular view of how perception is to be explained. An explanation such as Gregory's explanation of the eye goes hand in hand with understanding perception to be a physical process. The assumption here is that if we are to have more knowledge about perception then that knowledge is to come from a greater understanding of the physical processes involved in perception, that is to say a greater understanding of which part of the body does what and when. Perception as a physical process is something that we can observe and measure in the sense-organs. It is here already assumed that if there is perception then there are parts of the body which realise that process. If we call these parts 'sense-organs' then we can see why we must have sense-organs if we are to have perception.

If this is the assumption behind scientific explanations of sense-perception and its organs today, then what are we to make of a philosopher who held that perception is not a physical[3] process but who (nevertheless, as we might say) held that sense-organs are necessary for perception? According to some interpreters, Aristotle is just such a philosopher. If they are right, Aristotle must have had other ways of explaining the presence of the sense-organs than modern scientists. Aristotle cannot have held, like modern scientists, that we have sense-organs because (i) perception is a physical process, (ii) a physical process must be realised in some parts of the body, that is in sense-organs. For perception is not, as it is

---

[3] That is, not 'physical' in the modern sense. As a first approximation, read 'material' in Aristotle for 'physical' in a modern context. Explaining the difference between 'φυσικός' in Aristotle and 'physical' in a modern context in itself gets one far into Aristotle's theory. As a first intimation of the difference the following may serve: whereas 'physical' and 'φυσικός' both contrast with 'immaterial', 'φυσικός' in Aristotle never means *just* 'material', cf. pp. 7–10, below.

for modern scientists, a physical process. Why, then, *would* Aristotle have held that the sense-organs are necessary for perception? The present study tries to give an answer.

The view that for Aristotle there are or need be no material processes (κινήσεις) in perception goes back to the ancient commentators.[4] More recently, Friedrich Solmsen noted that in Aristotle's theory 'it is doubtful whether the movement or the actualisation occurring when the eye sees or the ear hears has any physical or physiological aspects'.[5] Solmsen's comment has been most prominently developed by Myles Burnyeat. Burnyeat argues that in 'Aristotle's theory of perception there is no physiological process which is related to the perception of a colour or a sound as matter to form'.[6] Perception for Aristotle is not a physiological or material process but a cognitive change. In perception the perceiver changes only insofar as he or she becomes aware of a sense-object of which she was previously unaware. Saying that there is no material process which is related to the perception of a colour as matter to form means that the cognitive change which defines the perception of the colour is not necessarily realised in some material change. Contrast the case of building a house. Here the changes that the materials, the bricks, timber, etc., undergo whilst the house is being built are necessary material changes if there is going be a house. You cannot build a house without changing some materials. On Burnyeat's interpretation of Aristotle, there need be no similar material changes that happen in the perceiver when he or she perceives.

The main rival to Burnyeat's interpretation is the view that Aristotle was a precursor of modern functionalism.[7] The debate between defenders of the two interpretations has

---

[4] On the history of this interpretation, cf. Sorabji (1991).

[5] Solmsen (1961), as quoted by Burnyeat (1993) 263.

[6] Burnyeat (1993) 263. Note again that by saying that there is no physiological or physical aspect of seeing or hearing we should take Solmsen to mean that there is no *material* change in the eye or the ear. As we shall see, this need not mean that Aristotle thinks there is no material basis of perception.

[7] Cf. Burnyeat (1992).

produced a number of insights into Aristotle's views on the relationship between the soul and the body. The debate is also largely responsible for the renewed interest in Aristotle amongst modern philosophers of mind.[8] The issues involved in the debate provide an excellent introduction to the study of Aristotle's sense-organs. And, as I hope to show in the Conclusion, the study of the sense-organs can in return instruct us on a number of these issues. Let me start therefore by briefly sketching the basis of a functionalist interpretation.[9]

Functionalism understands mental states as analogous to computer or machine states. Machine states are functional states. That is to say, they are defined in terms of their relations to a causal input and a causal output. Compare the case of a cash machine. You insert your card in the slot, enter your code, and the machine issues some money. Whilst waiting for the money to come out, the machine displays the text 'processing your request'. You can define this state of the machine as the state brought about by inserting the card (causal input) which causes the machine to issue the money (causal output).[10] Similarly, functionalism suggests, we can define mental states in terms of their causal input and output. For example, we can define 'seeing red' as the state, say, that an animal is in when its visual centre is affected by the light reflected from pillar boxes, traffic lights, blood, etc. (causal input) and which causes the animal to believe that or to say that or to behave as if there is a red object in front of it (causal output). Defining mental states in terms of their causal input and output allows functionalists to say something about the relationship between mental states and physical states which neither reductionists nor dualists can say: a mental state can, as a functional state, be realised by a number of different physical states. The

---

[8] Cf. Ostenfeld (1986) ch. 5; Burnyeat (1992) 16.

[9] Since the drafts of Burnyeat (1992) and Nussbaum and Putnam (1992) first appeared, a range of more sophisticated functionalist interpretations has appeared. I cannot hope to do justice to these within the scope of this study. But I hope that by focusing on the multiple realisability claim I have addressed a claim that is central to any functionalist interpretation.

[10] Cf. Block (1980) 173–5.

functions of a machine can be realised in all sorts of gadgetry. Similarly, a mental state can be realised by any number of physical states. A mental state cannot therefore be defined as identical with any particular type of physical state. For example, pain is not identical with the firing of one's C-fibres, even though firing of one's C-fibres may be *one* of the physical states that realise a feeling of pain. Functionalists may here agree with identity theorists that each token, each occurrence, of feeling pain is identical with a *token* of some type of physical state, for example my feeling pain at this moment is identical with my C-fibres firing at this moment. But functionalists will disagree with those identity theorists who claim that a type of mental state can be identified with any one *type* of physical state, for example that feeling pain is always identical with the firing of one's C-fibres. They will disagree with this claim because mental states as functional states are in principle 'multiply realisable' or 'compositionally plastic', that is they can in principle be realised by any number of different types of physical state. In this sense mental states cannot be reduced to physical states.

Avoiding reductionism, however, does not mean agreeing with dualism. Dualists may argue that mental states are not identical with physical states because mental states have properties that cannot be properties of physical states. Descartes, for example, held that awareness defined mental states and could not be shared by physical states. Mental states were therefore different from physical states. The dualist will say not only that no types of mental and physical states are identical but also that no token of a mental state is identical with any token of a physical state. No instance of, say, feeling pain is identical with any physical state. Dualists and functionalists therefore agree to reject type-type identity but disagree about token-token identity: functionalists accept it, dualists do not.

Functionalism seems therefore to steer a middle course between reductionism and dualism. Modern philosophers have tried to find such a middle course because they want to avoid problems in both positions. On the one hand, they want to avoid the problems that dualists have in explaining the interaction between the mental and the physical. On the other hand, they want to avoid the problems that reductionists face in accounting for features that are considered characteristic of 'the mental', features such as subjectivity, intentionality and privacy.[11]

So if functionalism did offer a 'third way' that avoided both sorts of problem, then that was clearly welcome. If Aristotle could be seen as a functionalist *avant la lettre*, then that too was clearly welcome.[12] Thus Putnam wrote that he 'was pleasantly surprised to find that my view was substantially the same as Aristotle's, although stated a bit more precisely with the aid of the vocabulary of contemporary scientific methodology and cybernetics'.[13] But was Putnam's surprise justified? Was Aristotle really a proto-functionalist? The discussion that followed focused on one point in particular: to what extent, if any, Aristotle believed (A) that mental processes are realised by material processes. For the specific functionalist claim (B) that the same mental states according to Aristotle can be realised by many different types of material process would of course only be relevant if mental states are realised by material processes in the first place.

In defence of A, Nussbaum related Aristotle's philosophy of mind to his general hylomorphism.[14] Hylomorphism is the theory that natural beings are composites of form and matter. Natural beings are in this respect similar to artefacts. A

---

[11] The irreducibility of intentional states to computational states was one reason why Putnam gave up his earlier functionalism, cf. his (1988) 73–4; Nussbaum and Putnam (1992) 48–9.

[12] Cf. the acute comments by Wardy (1990) 260–1 on this use of Aristotle:

> at least in this instance [sc. Aristotle's anti-reductionism] Aristotle speaks the truth directly to us, conveying a message that is not essentially antique, or couched in a philosophical language that we can no longer speak. This approach is seductive ideologically, as it were: ancient and modern thinkers become mutually supportive, the Greek icon lending a sort of authority to his supposed philosophical descendants, while the moderns conversely ensure that Aristotle continues to play an active role in contemporary discourse.

[13] Putnam (1975) xiv.

[14] Nussbaum and Putnam (1992).

bronze sphere, for example, is a composite of some matter, the bronze, and a spherical shape or form. Similarly, a human being, for example, is made up of blood, bone, tissue, etc., materials that have a certain form, namely the structure and organisation characteristic of a human being. So both artefacts and natural beings are essentially composites of form and matter. They are essentially composites in the sense that the form is always realised in some matter. The form does not come without some matter.

In living beings the form is the soul and the matter the body. It follows, so the functionalists argue, that the states of the soul are realised by states of the body. If the states of the soul change, so should the states of the body. We should expect, then, on general hylomorphic grounds that perception as a change of state of the soul is realised by a change of state of the body. This would give us claim A.

However, Nussbaum and Putnam pressed the analogy between living beings and artefacts even further towards functionalism, towards claim B. They argued that just as a sphere can be made out of different materials, so the soul and its states can be realised in different materials. The sphere, for example, can be made of plastic or wood or bronze. Seeing, similarly, can be realised not just by changes in a human eye, but by changes in different material structures such as the eye of a frog, a bird, etc. This seems to give us B, the thesis that mental states for Aristotle are multiply realisable. So the functionalists argue that Aristotle's understanding of living beings as hylomorphic wholes by analogy with artefacts supports both the claim A, that the changes in the soul are realised by material changes, and the specifically functionalist claim, B, that the changes in the soul could be realised in different sorts of material change.

Let me briefly try to characterise the explanatory procedure of Aristotle's psychology and then ask whether it supports the functionalist interpretation. Aristotle introduces *De Anima* by suggesting that the study of the soul or psychology (ἡ περὶ τῆς ψυχῆς ἱστορία) is part of the study of nature in general.

Indeed, one of the reasons for studying the soul is that it contributes greatly to our understanding of nature.[15] The reason for this is that the soul is like a principle (ἀρχή) of animals.[16] One thing that is meant by a 'principle' is 'what you need to understand *first* if you are going to explain other things'. *Physica* tells us that animals are prime instances of natural beings, beings that exist by nature.[17] So if you have understood the principle of animals, you can start to explain other things about some paradigms of nature. That is why studying the soul as the principle of animals will contribute to our understanding of nature.

In his psychology, Aristotle borrows the explanatory procedure from his physics. Physics, as he understands it, explains things by reference to 'the four causes' (ἀρχαί/αἰτίαι).[18] They are: (i) form (εἶδος), (ii) matter (ὕλη), (iii) moving cause (ἡ ἀρχὴ ὅθεν) and (iv) goal (τέλος) or final cause (τὸ οὗ ἕνεκα).[19] For example, if you ask 'Why is this a frog?' I can answer you in different ways, pointing to different explanatory and causal factors.[20] I can say that this is a frog because: (i) it has a certain shape, arrangement and structure characteristic of a frog (formal cause); (ii) it is made of flesh and bones and skin without which there would not be a frog (material cause); (iii) its parents, and in particular its father, created it (moving cause); and (iv) it is able to do certain things characteristic of a frog, for example leap and croak (final cause).

When Aristotle says that living beings are to be explained in the manner of physics he means that they are to be explained by reference to all of the four causes. Living beings are ex-

---

[15] *De an.* I.1 402a4–6.

[16] *De an.* I.1 402a6–7: ἔστι γὰρ οἷον ἀρχὴ τῶν ζῴων.

[17] *Ph.* II.1 192b9–12; cf. *De an.* II.1 412a13.

[18] *Ph.* II.7 198a22–3: 'Since there are four causes, it is the job of the φυσικός to know about all of them. If he leads back the 'why' question to them all he will give a "physical" account (ἀποδώσει φυσικῶς).'

[19] *Ph.* II.3.

[20] 'αἰτία' covers both cause and explanation in Aristotle. The moving cause is what comes closest to what we would call a 'cause' or a 'Humean cause'; cf. Sorabji (1980) 40.

plained in terms of the four causes by being analysed in terms of soul and body. In *De Anima* II.4 Aristotle says that the soul is the cause and principle (αἰτία καὶ ἀρχή) of the living beings in three senses: as the cause of motion, as the cause of being or substance (οὐσία) – and here Aristotle is thinking of the formal cause – and, as the final cause, that for the sake of which living beings live.[21] The body, in contrast, provides the material cause. Living beings are thus explained φυσικῶς by being explained as composites of a soul, which is a cause in the first three of the four required senses, and a body, which is a cause in the fourth sense.[22]

The changes that the soul gives rise to and suffers cannot be analysed in isolation from the body, for the soul is a cause of living beings that are essentially composites of form and matter. Physics studies 'destructible things that change'.[23] Physics studies these things *qua* changing and that means that the accounts that physics gives have to mention matter, for matter is a principle of change. Ὕλη is what underlies any sort of change.[24] Without matter there would be no change.[25] Hence physics tries not just to give a formal account of its subject matter. It tries to give an account that shows the formal features as instantiated in matter. Physics here differs from mathematics, since mathematics studies the formal features of changeable objects in abstraction from the matter of these objects and so in abstraction from their changeability. *De Anima* I.1 thus contrasts the φυσικός who is concerned with 'everything that is a function or affection of such and such a body and such and such matter'[26] with the μαθηματικός who treats properties of bodies that are not separable from bodies as if they were separate from bodies, for example he treats the

---

[21] *De an.* II.4 415b9–12; cf. *Metaph.* V.1 1013a16–17: 'cause' (αἰτία) is said in as many senses as principle (ἀρχή).

[22] The soul thus provides an example of how the final, formal and efficient causes often coincide; cf. *Ph.* II.7 198a24–6.

[23] *Ph.* II.7 198a31.

[24] Cf. *GC* I.4 320a2–3.

[25] *Metaph.* XII.2.

[26] *De an.* I.1 403b11–12.

geometrical shape of a body in abstraction from the body whose shape it is. Explaining a living being φυσικῶς means accounting for its functions and affections as enmattered and not treating them as functions and affections in abstraction from the matter in which they are realised.[27]

As an example of this physical mode of explanation, Aristotle in *De Anima* I.I mentions the explanation of anger. Anger, he says, when defined in the physical mode is 'a certain change of a body of such and such a kind or of a part or of a potentiality of it as a result of this and for the sake of this'.[28] The explanation mentions, first, the material cause of anger. This is the boiling of the blood around the heart. But the explanation mentions also the reason for or principle of (λόγος) anger, namely, a desire for retaliation. Here, giving the λόγος provides the formal explanation of anger.

The explanation of anger follows the example of 'snub' in *Physica* II.2. 'Snub' is defined as 'concave nose', where 'concave' gives the form and 'nose' the matter in which the form is realised. A physical explanation is like 'concave nose'. By mentioning both the form and the matter, the explanation reflects the fact that the *explanandum*, what is to be explained, is an enmattered form or λόγος.

The important question as concerns the functionalist debate is whether the claim that the affections of the soul are λόγοι ἔνυλοι, and should be defined as such, implies that each mental change is realised in a material change. When I see red, for example, is there then necessarily a material change of some sort in my eye? The example of anger seems to imply that mental changes are realised by such material changes. For it was said to be necessary that the desire for retaliation be realised in a particular sort of matter such as boiling of the blood around the heart.[29] And the passage seems to imply that similar material changes are necessary in the case of all

---

[27] *Ibid.* 403a25: δῆλον ὅτι τὰ πάθη λόγοι ἔνυλοί εἰσιν.
[28] *Ibid.* 403a26–27: τὸ ὀργίζεσθαι κίνησίς τις τοῦ τοιουδὶ σώματος ἢ μέρους ἢ δυνάμεως ὑπὸ τοῦδε ἕνεκα τοῦδε.
[29] *De an.* I.I 403b2–3: ὁ μὲν γὰρ λόγος εἶδος τοῦ πράγματος, ἀνάγκη δ' εἶναι τοῦτον ἐν ὕλῃ τοιᾳδί, εἰ ἔσται.

affections of the soul. If so, material changes are clearly also necessary in perception.[30]

However, the text is not as clear-cut as the functionalists or Sorabji might wish. Aristotle need not be taken to say that '*every* mental process...requires a physiological process'. He need only be taken to say that there is no mental process, with the possible exception of thought, which is not a process of the body. On Burnyeat's interpretation, this claim is easily accommodated. Seeing red will be an affection of the eye insofar as seeing red actualises the potentiality of the eye to see. Seeing is an affection of the eye simply because the eye is understood as a potentiality to see. But this is different from saying that the eye undergoes a material change when we see. The eye is affected in the sense that its potentiality to see is affected. In this sense, the affection is an affection of the eye, of matter. But it is not an affection in the sense that the eye materially changes. In short, an affection of the sense-organ need not be a material change once we have understood that the sense-organ is a potentiality and a potentiality can be realised without a material change.

That this is how we should understand what happens when somebody sees red seems to be confirmed by *De Anima* II.5 417b2–5, where Aristotle says that 'being affected' (πάσχειν) is said in two senses.[31] It is said in one sense when something is affected in such a way that one of its attributes is replaced by an opposite attribute. Aristotle has in mind here what happens for example to the colour of my milk when I pour cocoa into it. It goes from white to its opposite, dark. But 'being affected' is said in another sense when a potentiality is preserved and brought to actuality. Aristotle's example is what happens to a builder who starts building. He already was a builder and now simply actualises his potentiality to build. So there is no change of attribute to an opposite attribute (cf. ch. 6, sec. 3).

---

[30] Cf. Sorabji (1992) 211: 'We have already encountered the illustrative example that anger requires the boiling of the blood around the heart. And perception is explicitly included in the theory' (at *De an.* I.1 403a7).

[31] Book II here, as we might expect, revises the aporetic statements of Book I.

Now perception is said to be an affection in this second sense, involving no change of attributes in the perceiver. But if the functionalists and Sorabji are right, we would expect perception to be a change of attributes. For if perception necessarily involves a material change, then how is that material change to be described if not as a change of attributes? On Sorabji's interpretation the material change that, for example, the eye undergoes in vision is a literal coloration of the eye jelly inside the eye. But this coloration seems to be just the kind of change that would illustrate a change of attributes. The change in the eye jelly would be like the change in the milk when I pour cocoa into it.[32] But Aristotle says that all the changes of this sort that are required in order to perceive have been completed by the time we are born.[33]

Whether or not we accept this line of argument, Burnyeat seems right in saying that Sorabji's interpretation provides an essential piece of support for the functionalist interpretation.[34] If perceiving does not involve a material process in the sense-organs, then a fortiori perceiving is not a functional state that can be realised by a number of different material processes. Sorabji provides the only clear proposal as to which material processes perception, according to Aristotle, would necessarily involve. The key notion here is that perception is a way of making the sense-faculty like a sensible form, F.[35] In perception, the sense-faculty receives the form of the sense-object without its matter. The sense-faculty thereby comes to have the same form as the sense-object. On Sorabji's account, the sense-faculty becomes like F insofar as the sense-organ literally becomes F. In seeing red, the eye jelly literally becomes red, in smelling cheese the nose becomes cheesy, in feeling heat the body literally becomes hot, and so on and so forth.[36] If the notion of the sense-faculty's becom-

---

[32] Sorabji (1992) 221 deals with this objection by denying that the De an. II.5 passage is about a contrast between being physically and non-physically affected.

[33] De an. II.5 417b16–18.

[34] Burnyeat (1992) 15.

[35] De an. II.5 417a18–21; III.4 429a13–18.

[36] Cf. Sorabji (1992) 209–23 and Sorabji (1974) 52.

ing like the sense-quality is to be cashed out in terms of material processes, then it is difficult to see what these material processes could be other than the ones Sorabji points to. This weakens Putnam and Nussbaum's response to Burnyeat that 'it is one thing to argue against a particular story of what the physiological change is [i.e. Sorabji's], quite another to establish that there need be no physiological change [as would be required to refute Nussbaum and Putnam]'.[37]

Who is right, then, Sorabji or Burnyeat? Much of the language in which Aristotle describes the processes of perception would *prima facie* suggest that Sorabji was right. Terms such as κίνησις, πάθος, ἀλλοίωσις, δύναμις, ἐνέργεια, ὕλη and εἶδος are all borrowed by Aristotle from his physics to form the conceptual framework of his psychology. They are terms which have initially been introduced to explain ordinary material changes. In psychology, however, the terms are frequently stretched to deal with other sorts of change in the soul. So, for example, thinking becomes either a ἕτερον γένος ἀλλοιώσεως or not an ἀλλοίωσις at all.[38] In such cases it is difficult to know when to stress the continuity between the explanations of psychology and physics and when to stress the abnormality of the psychological uses of the terms. In certain cases, whether one favours Sorabji's or Burnyeat's interpretation may depend on how one reads a claim such as 'τὸ γὰρ αἰσθάνεσθαι πάσχειν τι ἐστίν' (*De an.* II.11 423b32–424a1). Is this a claim that includes perception amongst the sorts of change that we know from the physics, which would make us think of perception as an ordinary material change? Or is it a claim that, by means of the word τι, distances perception from such ordinary changes, making perception a change only in a very tenuous sense?[39]

As Sarah Broadie has suggested, it may be that 'in the absence of conclusive textual evidence either way, the debate on [whether perception for Aristotle involves physiological pro-

---

[37] Nussbaum and Putnam (1992) 36.
[38] *De an.* II.5 417b6–7.
[39] Cf. Burnyeat (1993) 274.

cesses] may never be closed'.[40] Following Broadie's strategy, I shall not try to argue for either position from the ground up. My primary concern in this study is with the composition of the sense-organs and the account that I present of the sense-organs is one that ought to be acceptable on both positions.

However, if Aristotle's account of the sense-organs is acceptable on both positions, then that in itself might be considered remarkable, for the fact that we have sense-organs and the fact that the sense-organs in Aristotle are apparently structured with some complexity are facts with which we might expect Burnyeat's interpretation to have particular difficulties. The present work may provide an indirect contribution to the functionalist debate in that it takes on one of the potentially most embarrassing aspects of Aristotle's theory for Burnyeat's interpretation, the fact that we have sense-organs. On modern accounts of perception and on Sorabji's interpretation of Aristotle, the reason why perception requires a material basis is straightforward. Perception itself is a material change and the sense-organs provide the matter in which the material change occurs. On Burnyeat's interpretation, the fact that we have sense-organs appears much more problematic. Why do we have eyes in our heads rather than simply holes, for why should the senses have a material basis if there is no material change in perception? If perception is just a 'cognitive' change, why does perception require a sense-organ? If, however, as I try to show, the sense-organs in Aristotle's theory can be explained sufficiently without the assumption of material changes in perception, then that must count as indirect support of Burnyeat's interpretation.

This study follows Aristotle through his explanations of each of the sense-organs. The intention is to fill a gap in the literature, for there is to my knowledge no work that systematically sets out Aristotle's account of the sense-organs in detail. Most of the work on the sense-organs in Aristotle is to be found in piecemeal form in commentaries and editions, such as G. R. T. Ross (1906), W. D. Ross (1955) and (1961), R. D.

---

[40] Broadie (1993) 145.

Hicks (1907), W. Ogle (1882) and A. L. Peck (1953), (1961) and (1965–70). In J. I. Beare's (1906) we do have a full-length study of the senses and their organs in Aristotle. The study is valuable in bringing the sources together, but offers no philosophical analysis of the sources. It relates Aristotle's views on the sense-organ but shows no interest in why he held them. The present study tries to make amends. It asks not only how Aristotle thought the sense-organs were composed but also why he thought as he did.

One of the great advantages for the person who sets out to write on Aristotle's views about the sense-organs today is the growing attention of scholars to the way in which Aristotle's psychological views affect his biological views.[41] In an important recent study, G. E. R. Lloyd shows the extent to which Aristotle's zoology is determined by his psychological doctrines.[42] Lloyd argues that '[g]iven that zoology is a study of living creatures and that what makes them the living creatures they are falls under the rubric ψυχή, [that zoology is largely devoted to a consideration of ψυχή] should occasion no surprise'.[43] Aristotle's zoological writings require the bodily parts of animals to be seen as organs or instruments that serve the faculties of the soul, as defined in the psychological writings.

As Lloyd shows, a central example is perception. Animals are in *De Anima* defined as living beings with perception.[44] This definition leads Aristotle in the biological works to suggest that the entire body must have the potentiality to perceive if it is going to be the body of an animal. The flesh (or its analogue), for example, is composed in such a way that it will be able to perceive or mediate all the tangible qualities.[45] The other parts of the body, 'bones and skin and tendons and blood-vessels, etc.',[46] are said to be for the sake of the flesh.

---

[41] Cf., for example, Gotthelf and Lennox (1987).
[42] Lloyd (1992).
[43] *Ibid.* 149.
[44] *De an.* II.2 413b2–4.
[45] Cf. ch. 4, secs. 7–8.
[46] *PA* II.8 653b30–654a31; Lloyd (1992) 151.

15

Though these parts do not themselves have the ability to perceive or mediate perception, even they can be explained as parts of the animal body since they are related, as supportive structures, to the flesh, which does have the ability to perceive or mediate perception.

One consequence of Aristotle's use of psychological definitions to define the parts of animals is, as Lloyd points out, that 'there can be no question of the souls/forms of living creatures being realisable in matter other than the matter in which they are found, and what has been called the "compositional plasticity" of ψυχή is minimal, if not zero'.[47] Lloyd's point here against the functionalist interpretation relates to a point emphasised by Wardy: the functionalists fail to see how radical Aristotle's teleology is.[48] The point is not so much that the same form perhaps could be realised by different sorts of matter, though there are particular difficulties with this idea when we go from artefacts to living beings (cf. ch. 1, sec. 2). The point is rather that the different sorts of matter could not be identified and described without describing it as the matter of a particular form and function (cf. ch. 1, sec. 5). Talk of 'boiling of the blood around the heart' is already talk of a potentiality to feel anger. Saying, therefore, that anger could be realised in different sorts of matter from boiling blood around the heart is to miss the point that those different sorts of matter are different sorts of matter because they are potentialities for sorts of function different from anger. When Aristotle talks about the flesh *or its analogue* as what has the potentiality to perceive or mediate tangibles he is not making a functionalist point about the compositional plasticity of perception.[49] He is making the point that whatever matter serves the same function in perception as flesh is to count as the same matter. As Aristotle says in *Physica*,

---

[47] Lloyd (1992) 165.

[48] Cf. Wardy (1990) 261–2. Other important recent studies on Aristotle's teleology include: Cooper (1982) and (1985); Charles (1984) ch. 5, (1988) and (1991); Sedley (1991) (with which cf. Wardy (1993)); Sorabji (1980), esp. part III.

[49] *PA* II.1 647a19–21; contrast the functionalist interpretation of this passage in Marc Cohen (1992) 59.

matter is relative: matter is matter *of*.[50] In particular, matter is relative to form and function. Hence 'there is different matter for different forms'.[51]

Having made this fundamental point, we should acknowledge that there are limits even to Aristotle's teleology. The limits are set by the necessity of matter. If you make a house out of wood, then some of the attributes of the wood, the shape and length of the planks, for example, are going to be dictated or necessitated by the fact that the wood is part of *a house*. But the wood will still have some attributes that wood has as such, irrespective of the fact that it has been turned into a house, for example it will be inflammable. These attributes are said to be necessitated by the matter as such. One such case of 'material necessity', which I explore in chapter 4, section 9, is eye colour.

This work tries to show that Aristotle's explanations of the sense-organs can be seen as teleological. I treat the sense-organs here as a specific test case of teleology in Aristotle. I do not argue extensively for the basic claim that Aristotle is a teleologist. This would require a much more comprehensive investigation of Aristotle's biology, physics and metaphysics. Instead, I try to strengthen the teleological claim by showing how much of the detail of what Aristotle says about the sense-organs makes best sense if understood in the context of a teleological theory.

However, 'teleology' can mean many things. Aristotle's account of the sense-organs is worth studying also because it illustrates the point that Aristotle's teleology is no monolithic theory. Aristotle's teleology is remarkably flexible because it employs different strategies in different cases. A teleological explanation explains something by referring to its *telos*, its goal or end.[52] But there are different sorts of goal. The goal may be the ability to do something, to function in a certain way. I shall argue that this is the basic sort of explanation of the sense-organs. The sense-organs are composed

[50] *Ph.* II.2 194b8–9.   [51] *Ibid.*   [52] Cf. Charles (1991).

the way they are so that we may be able to perceive. But in Aristotle's zoology the goal may also be the ethical character or life-style of the animal (ch. 4, sec. 10), its well-being or survival (ch. 4, sec. 6) or what is appropriate or to be expected (ch. 4, sec. 7). However, even where the sense-organ is explained by its contribution to perception, perception is not a simple goal. Often we have to take into account other facts about the animal to explain the composition of the sense-organs. For example, the goal of perception will often explain the composition of the sense-organs only if perception is seen in the context of the animal's natural environment (ch. 3, sec. 5; ch. 4, sec. 10; ch. 5, sec. 8). And often we need to consider how perception has to be accommodated together with the animal's other characteristic activities, such as respiration, or flying, or swimming. As is now commonly recognised,[53] Aristotle's teleology comes in different guises. The sense-organs provide a specific test case for this point.

Of all the sense-organs in Aristotle the eye is perhaps best served by the secondary literature. An article by G. E. R. Lloyd analyses the information available on the composition of the eye and underlines the difficulty of interpreting this information.[54] What Aristotle says about the eye and, to generalise Lloyd's argument, about the other sense-organs is often tantalisingly vague. Though trying to find precision where possible, I have frequently had to acknowledge vagueness in Aristotle's description of the sense-organs. However, I argue that the vagueness is philosophically pointed (ch. 1). It shows something about Aristotle's attitude to the explanation of the sense-organs. My thesis is that Aristotle is primarily interested in the composition of the sense-organs to the extent that the composition shows the presence of key functional attributes. In the case of the eye, for example, the key functional attribute is transparency (cf. ch. 1, secs. 6–11). It is the transparent that has the ability to be changed by colour as such, which for

---

[53] Cf. e.g. Sorabji (1980) ch. 10; Cooper (1982); Charles (1991); Sedley (1991).
[54] Lloyd (1978).

Aristotle defines the ability to see. My general strategy is first to identify the key functional attribute and then to identify the parts of the sense-organ that realise this attribute. The description of the sense-organs stops when Aristotle thinks that he has shown the material parts required for the presence of the functional attribute. His account of the sense-organs is in agreement with his declared policy in *De Partibus Animalium*: 'Just as in any discussion of parts or equipment we must not think that it is the matter to which attention is being directed or which is the object of the discussion, but rather the form as a whole.'[55] Vagueness is relative to our interpretative demands. I argue that we find vagueness in Aristotle if we expect empirical precision of a sort that is not envisaged by his functional approach to the sense-organs.

Another interpretative issue, beside vagueness, is the question of the unity and consistency of Aristotle's account of the sense-organs. Does Aristotle have one way of accounting for all the sense-organs? Or does his account of one sense-organ sometimes differ in kind from his account of another? This is a question that particularly arises when we compare the sense-faculties of sight and touch. There is a discrepancy between these two senses on at least two points. First of all, Aristotle will mostly define a sense-faculty in terms of its proper sense-objects. This is what he does in the case of the 'distance' senses, sight, hearing and smell. But in the case of the contact senses Aristotle seems to be more impressed by the fact that we feel things by direct contact with our skin and flesh (ch. 4, secs. 1–2). Here what singles out the sense of touch is not so much what we perceive by touch but how we perceive by touch. However, sometimes Aristotle will also try to define touch in terms of its objects. But here he comes across the problem that there are too many objects of touch for them to deliver a neat definition of touch in terms of its proper object. Aristotle's instinct here is to press for consistency by showing

---

[55] *PA* 1.5 645a30–3.

that in the case of the distance senses, too, the proper objects are more varied than was at first thought.[56]

The wavering in definitional procedure is reflected in a wavering as regards the location of the sense-organ of touch. If we are said to perceive something by touch because we perceive it by touching it with our skin and flesh, then that suggests the organ of touch is the skin and flesh. But again Aristotle is concerned with the consistency of this claim with his analysis of the distance senses, for he has already argued forcefully against Democritus that there is no perception when you put a sense-object directly on the sense-organ. This datum leads Aristotle to reconsider the sense-organ of touch, locating it now inside the body in the area around the heart (cf. ch. 4, sec. 8).

If we can generalise from these two examples, the impression is that he tries, as he proceeds, to account for the characteristic features of the different senses. But when these features significantly diverge he tries to maintain a consistent overall theory of the senses. He seems therefore to aim at relative consistency within a single theory of the sense-faculties. My policy has accordingly been to show consistency where possible; where not, to explore the theoretical pressures that give rise to the inconsistencies.[57]

As shown recently by Richard Sorabji, the question of the consistency of Aristotle's accounts of touch and sight goes back at least as far as Themistius (4th cent. AD).[58] There is a tendency in the ancient commentators on Aristotle to make touch a corporeal sense and vision an incorporeal sense. When you feel something as hot, your sense-organ of touch becomes literally hot. But when you see something as red there is no literal coloration in the eye. As Sorabji says, 'the diversity of the five senses in respect of their corporeality' is 'a subject mentioned, but certainly not emphasised, by Aris-

---

[56] *De an.* II.11 422b28–35. On Aristotle's definitional procedure, cf. Sorabji (1971).
[57] Cf., for example, the discussion of Aristotle's mixed methodology in his treatment of smell in ch. 5, sec. 4.
[58] Sorabji (1991).

totle'.[59] However, the ancient commentators, to varying degrees, did emphasise the diversity. Should we follow them on this point, that some senses necessarily undergo material changes in perception while others do not? Could Burnyeat, then, be right about vision and Sorabji right about touch?

I argue not.[60] When Aristotle raises the subject (in *De an.* II.12), he does so in terms of the effects that different sorts of sense-objects can have. He asks, 'Are the only effects that sense-objects can have to make themselves perceived?' When asking this question, Aristotle is apparently assuming that there is a fundamental difference between having a corporeal effect on something and being perceived. He then suggests that at least tangible qualities have to be able to affect bodies that do not perceive, for otherwise no body can change its qualities other than by perceiving them. Here it seems, for a while, that a fundamental difference between the effect of tangible qualities as bodily and the effect of other sense-qualities as merely perceptual has opened up, making touch more corporeal than the other senses. But again Aristotle at the end presses for consistency and suggests that all sense-qualities may have bodily effects but that these effects are not what we call smelling, seeing, hearing, etc.: the effects of sense-qualities that we call smelling, etc., are forms of perceiving or being aware of something (αἰσθάνεσθαι). In other words, though Aristotle mentions the subject of the diversity of the senses in terms of their corporeality, he tends to try also in this case to maintain the overall unity of his account of the senses.

Aristotle may also seem liable to a charge that has been raised against Western philosophers from Plato to Husserl. The charge is that they base their theories of perception (if not entire philosophies of mind) on the model of vision.[61] As D. M. Armstrong says, '[w]hen we think of sense-perception, we

---

[59] *Ibid.* 231–2. The attempt to distinguish the five senses in degrees of corporeality may in some cases reflect the Neoplatonic tendency to look for a hierarchy of higher and lower stages within each of the parts of the soul; cf. Blumenthal (1976).

[60] Cf. especially ch. 6, sec. 7.

[61] Cf. Stigen (1961).

have a strong impulse to think of *sight*'.[62] The reason is that 'our eyes yield us remarkably detailed and precise impressions of the world'. Aristotle would agree, for he repeatedly stresses that vision is the most important of the senses. It is the most important exactly because it reveals to us more differences in the world than any other sense.[63]

Add to this Aristotle's practice of beginning most discussions of the senses with sight,[64] and an analysis of the senses biased towards sight might be expected. This would be an analysis in which essential differences between the senses were ignored and the other senses forced into a single pattern applicable only to sight. However, the more characteristic feature of Aristotle's analyses of the sense-faculties is that they are conducted on the basis of a single causal theory. Bias towards one sense is greatly reduced by the fact that a single causal framework, taken from outside the theory of perception, is applied to all the senses. Aristotle's first move in *De Anima* II.4 before he starts his discussion of perception in II.5 is to discuss nutrition. He picks up the key causal scheme from the *Physica* and *De Generatione et Corruptione* and applies it to nutrition. He thereby sets an example for how the other faculties of the soul are to be analysed. He only then applies the causal scheme to the sense-faculties, of which sight is first. One could say that sight is here modelled on nutrition. Placing all the senses within the same basic causal scheme leaves relatively little scope for sight to dominate over the other senses. With this in mind, I shall now, like Aristotle, begin the investigation of the sense-organs with the organ of sight.

[62] Armstrong (1962) 118.
[63] *Metaph.* I.I 980a24–6; *Sens.* I 437a5–9; cf. *PA* II.10 656b3–4.
[64] For example, in *De an.* and *Sens.*

1

SIGHT

I. The argument

This study aims to answer two questions in Aristotle. First, why do we have sense-organs? Second, why are the sense-organs composed the way they are? Aristotle's theory of the sense-organs, I shall argue, is briefly this. We have five so-called special senses: sight, hearing, touch, taste and smell. The five senses are powers or potentialities (δυνάμεις) that animals have to perceive certain objects – for example sight is the power to perceive colour while hearing is the power to perceive sound. The power to perceive a sense-object consists in the ability to be changed by the sense-object. When an animal perceives a sense-object, its sense-faculty is changed by the sense-object so as to become like the sense-object, for example when I see a red pillar box then my faculty of sight becomes red in a certain way. This ability that the sense-faculty has to be changed by a certain sense-object is what defines the sense-faculty, for example the faculty of sight is defined as what has the ability to be changed by colour. The faculty of hearing is defined as what has the ability to be changed by sounds, and so on.

The ability to be changed by a sense-object is something that is only found in matter. That is why we need sense-organs which provide the matter that is required for the presence of the ability to be changed by sense-objects. This answers the first of the two questions, why we have sense-organs. But the matter has to be matter of a certain sort because it is not in all sorts of matter that the ability to be changed by a certain sense-object is present, for example the ability to be changed by colours is found only in transparent matter, such as water, and the ability to be changed by sound is found only in matter

23

that is resonant, such as air. The first stage of explaining how the sense-organs are composed is therefore to find out in what kind of matter the ability to be changed by a certain sense-object is present.

The second stage of explaining the composition of the sense-organs is to show why certain other features of the sense-organs are required. If the sense-organ of sight is transparent water, for example, why is it that the sense-organ of sight, the eye, has a number of other parts? The eye has a membrane, an eyelid, an iris, a white part and various channels. How are we to make sense of these other features of the eye? If the eye is simply there to provide the necessary transparent matter for the ability to be changed by colours, could it not simply consist of water? Similarly, if the sense-organ of hearing is resonant air, why is it that the ear has a membrane and certain other external and internal features? This study aims to answer these questions by showing how the further features of the sense-organs can all be seen as necessary or useful for the fundamental function of the sense-organs, which is to help us perceive.

2. How to explain the sense-organs

In *De Anima* II.1 Aristotle says that the sense-organs stand to the senses as matter to form or as potentiality to actuality. Thus 'the eye is the matter of sight' (412b20). The sense of sight is the form or first actuality of the eye. This claim about the relationship between the sense-faculty and its organ emerges out of a discussion of the relationship between the soul and the body as a whole. Aristotle says that the relationship between the parts of the body and the parts of the soul is analogous to the relationship between the entire body and the entire soul.[1] The bodily parts stand to the psychic parts as matter to form or potentiality to first actuality. Let us see what he means by this.

---

[1] *De an.* II.1 412b22–5.

To illustrate the relationship between the soul and the body Aristotle uses the example of an axe. Aristotle (412b11–12) says that if an axe were a natural body, then what it is to be an axe (τὸ πελέκει εἶναι) would be its substance (οὐσία) and soul. He then says that the substance and the soul are also the form and the definition of the axe. The form and definition of an axe are its ability to cut (412b29). The ability to cut is what defines what it is *for an axe* to be. It is what makes an axe an axe, rather than a hammer or a spoon, etc. If you take away its ability to cut, for example by removing its blade, the axe also ceases to be an axe. So being able to cut is what being an axe is about or, as Aristotle puts it, what it is for an axe to be. The axe's ability to cut is a potentiality (δύναμις) rather than an actuality (ἐνέργεια/ἐντελέχεια). For the axe has the ability to cut even when it is not actually being used in cutting. Hence what it is for the axe to be, its definition and substance, is a potentiality of a certain sort.

Aristotle focuses on the potentiality as what defines what it is to be an axe because he wants to make a similar point about the soul. He wants to say that what defines the soul is the presence of an ability to do certain things, in this case not the ability to cut but the ability to do certain things which are characteristic of living beings. This is an ability that living beings have even when they are not actually exercising it. For example, we want to say that an animal has a soul and is alive even when it is asleep, when it is not actually digesting, or perceiving, or actually doing any of the other things that characterise an animal. Similarly, we said that the axe was able to cut even when it was not actually used in cutting. The soul is therefore, like the definition of the axe, a potentiality.

Aristotle's analogy with the axe enables him to distinguish the potentiality by which we define the soul from its actuality. It also allows him to distinguish the soul from the body. The soul stands to the body as the ability of the axe stands to the matter of which the axe is made, the wood and iron. That is to say, the soul stands to the body as form to matter, for the ability to cut is the form of an axe and the wood and iron of which the axe is made are its matter.

Aristotle says in general that matter is potentiality and form is actuality.[2] However, in the example of the axe we can see that something can be an actuality and a potentiality in different ways. Whether we call something an actuality or a potentiality is relative to what we are comparing it with. In comparison with actual cutting the ability to cut is a potentiality, but in relation to its matter the ability to cut is an actuality. You could imagine that the materials of which the axe is made were not part of an axe and did not have the ability to cut, for example the wood and the iron could have been part of a fishing rod. Wood and iron as such are matter that *can* be made into something with the ability to cut. But if the matter has not been made into an object with the ability to cut, the matter is as yet a *mere* potentiality for cutting. You cannot go and chop wood with any old wood and iron. The wood and iron get the ability to be used in cutting only if you give them the right shape and form. You need to collect the wood and iron, shape the iron into a blade by making it sharp, cut the wood into the shape of a handle, and put the two together. Once you have in this way given the right form and shape to the matter, you can straightaway go and chop wood with your product. So it is really the form and shape that gives the axe its ability to cut, not the matter as such, the mere wood and iron. The form is therefore also more closely related to actual cutting than the matter and, because of this, it deserves to be distinguished as more of an actuality than the matter. The matter as such is a *mere* potentiality, but the form compared with the matter as such is more like an actuality. That is why Aristotle calls the form a 'first actuality'.[3]

The example of the axe gives us three levels of potentiality and actuality: potentiality, first actuality and second actuality.

---

[2] *De an.* II.1 412a9–10.   [3] *De an.* II.1 412a27.

We find these three levels also in living beings. We can set them out as follows:

	An animal	*An axe*	*An eye*
Second actuality	Being awake	Cutting	Seeing (ὅρασις)
First actuality	Being alive	Being an axe	Ability to see
Potentiality	The body of a man, a dog, etc.	The material of an axe (iron, wood)	The eye jelly (κόρη)[4]

At the level of potentiality we are talking about living bodies and their parts. It is not dead bodies, nor amputated eyes nor things like that, that we are referring to, for a dead body cannot really be said to be a human body and an amputated eye cannot really be said to be an eye. A severed eye is more like a replica of an eye. Aristotle says that a dead body is a human body only *homonymously.*[5] He explains what he means by 'homonymous' by saying that two things are called 'homonymous' when they have the same name but the definitions of what they are differ. In this way you could call both Michelangelo's painting of Adam and a living man 'a human body'. But if you try to say what makes each of them a human body, then you will have to say different things about each of them. For the body of the living man is called a human body because it is able to take part in the activities that are characteristic of a human being – eating, drinking, dancing, etc. But Michelangelo's painting can do none of these things. That is why talking about a human body in the case of living humans is not talking about the body in isolation from the activities that define a human being. Talking about the human body is rather talking about the body as a potentiality for these activities. Stripped of this potentiality, the body ceases to be the body of a human being. That is of course what happens when the human being dies. The body ceases to be able to

---

[4] For 'κόρη' meaning 'eye jelly', see below, sec. 8.   [5] *Cat.* I 1a1.

take part in human activities. If it is then still right to call the body of a dead man a 'human body', then that must be because the term is being used to refer to different attributes from those potentialities which defined the living body. According to our definition, this will be a homonymous use of the term. The same applies to parts of the human body as to the whole. In the case of the eye, for example, the defining potentiality is the ability to see. Take away its ability to see and the eye becomes an eye in name only.

When Aristotle uses the analogy with tools in *De Anima* II.1 he places living beings and their parts within the general causal and explanatory framework of the *Physica*. Art, Aristotle says, imitates nature.[6] In art we can find the same four αἰτίαι – form, matter, moving cause and final cause – which operate in nature, though their manner of operation sometimes differs. It is because the same causes are present in art and nature that Aristotle often thinks he can use artefacts to illustrate a particular point about the causes of natural beings.[7] Since living beings are a subset of natural beings, the point extends to living beings. We would expect that if the analogy with tools and artefacts can illustrate the relationship between form and matter in natural beings in general it can also illustrate the relationship between form and matter in living beings in particular.

There are at least two related reasons why Aristotle uses artefacts to illustrate the relationship between the soul and the body in living beings. The first is that matter can be seen as a distinct cause in the production of an artefact. When a craftsman makes an artefact he imposes a form (εἶδος) or shape (μορφή) on some matter according to the rules of his craft. A builder is given some bricks and timber. He arranges them in the shape of a house according to the rules of architecture. We can see here that the matter is something distinct from the form. For the form of a house is something the matter only gets in the process of building. It did not have that form before. The matter can be described independently of the

---

[6] *Ph.* II.2 194a21–2, II.8 199a15–17.   [7] Cf. *PA* I.1 642a9–13 and Introduction.

particular sort of artefact it is going to be turned into. We could talk about what the bricks and timber were, and still are, as such before they were put into the house: they are mixtures according to certain ratios of more basic elements – earth, water, etc.; they have a certain hardness, weight and durability, and so on. Some of these are attributes that make the materials suitable *building* materials. That is why the bricks and timber can be called a potential house. But the materials might also be suitable for other purposes than to build houses with. Whether or not they are in fact used to build a house depends on what the craftsman has in mind, what he intends to do with them. The matter has certain attributes that will make it suitable for this or that artefact. But whether the matter is turned into one particular sort of artefact rather than another depends not on the matter itself but on the form that the craftsman imposes on it. The matter can therefore be talked about independently of its potentiality to become a house, or a bridge, or a wall. In other words, the matter of artefacts can be talked about independently of the particular form it is going to gain in the production of a particular sort of artefact. That is why we can see clearly in the production of artefacts that matter is a distinct causal factor from the form.

In the creation of living beings, by contrast, it is not often, if ever, possible to find matter that in this way appears distinct from the form.[8] Look, for instance, at the way in which a frog develops from an embryo into an adult frog. Here there seems

---

[8] The analogy between living beings and artefacts can therefore also be seen as problematic. Cf. Lloyd (1992) 164:

> in the case of artefacts the bricks or stones have the characteristics they have (as bricks and stones) whether or not they are incorporated in a house. But that is not true of the material parts of living creatures ... As Aristotle says in so many words at *PA* 645a35ff., the material the biologist has to deal with are things 'that do not even occur separated from the being itself'.

For the classic statement of the problem of specifying the matter of living beings independently of the form, cf. Ackrill (1972) 69–70. Wilkes (1992) 112, with reference to *Metaph.* VII.11 1036b3–7, stresses the complementary point that in living beings *the form* is always found in a certain sort of matter, e.g. man is always found in flesh and bones. The matter therefore enters into the definition of man; cf. also Marc Cohen (1992) 68.

to be no stage at which we can say that the matter of the frog could develop into anything other than a frog. Aristotle says that a frog is produced when the menstrual blood of a female frog receives the semen of the male frog.[9] The semen of the male frog stands to the menstrual blood of the female frog as form to matter. But all this means is that the menstrual blood is at a lower level of actuality in terms of what it is to be a frog than is the male semen. Considered on its own, the menstrual blood is already well on its way to becoming a frog. Both the menstrual fluid and the male semen are purified blood, but the male semen is more purified than the menses. The menstrual blood has already been 'cooked up', to use Aristotle's analogy, in the particular cooking process that produces frogs, but the male semen has been even more cooked up and is hotter. Because of this, it is required to continue the cooking process in the menstrual blood that develops it into a frog. The menstrual blood needs to be acted upon by the male semen in order to *carry on* developing into a frog. The matter that the female provides is already in quite an advanced state of potential froghood, but requires the higher-level actuality of the male semen to develop this potentiality further. What constitutes the matter in the generation of a frog is already endowed with the form of froghood to a considerable degree.

The menstrual blood of a female frog is neither just any old blood nor even any menstrual blood nor is it the same menstrual blood as that of a female cat or any other animal. The menstrual blood is therefore not the potential matter of a frog in the same way that the bricks, timber, etc., were the potential matter of a house. The bricks, etc., *could* be turned into a house. But they could equally well be turned into something else, say a wall or a bridge. The menstrual blood of a female frog, however, is already so endowed with the form of froghood that it can *only* be used to create a frog and no other animal. That is why it is difficult to see the menstrual blood as a clear example of matter contrasting with form. To be sure, the menstrual blood is less informed by the form of froghood

---

[9] Cf. for the following *GA* I.19–22.

than the male semen. That is why we can say that it stands as matter to the semen's form. But it is also so informed by froghood that it is not so easy in this case to distinguish the matter from the form.

Another reason why artefacts are a good illustration of natural beings is that artefacts have an end. A chair is made so that one can sit on it, an axe so that one can cut wood with it, a house so that it may give us shelter, and so on and so forth. Aristotle is keen to show the goal-directedness of nature. He believes that animals are born in order to live a typically animal life of smelling, hunting, eating, etc., and that human beings are born to live a typically human life of thinking, talking, being friends, etc. These activities are all thought of as the end of the living being in question. The analogy with artefacts is supposed to spell this idea out.

The two reasons for choosing artefacts as an example of the relationship between matter and form are connected because the end towards which the artefact is produced coincides with the form of the artefact. When you make an axe, you provide it with the ability to cut by giving the matter a certain form and arrangement. The form and arrangement of the axe enable the axe to cut and cutting is the end towards which the axe is produced. There is no difference between creating something out of the material which has the form and arrangement characteristic of an axe and creating something which we can use to cut with in the way an axe cuts. Endowing some matter with the form and arrangement of an axe also makes the instrument able to cut and cutting is the activity that is the end of an axe. That is why the two features of the analogy with tools, goal-directedness and being composites of form and matter, are connected.

Now one might agree with Aristotle that *if* living beings are analogous with tools, *then* living beings are composites of form and matter and have an end. But we might also want to deny the antecedent here because we hold that living beings in fact are not analogous with tools. We might agree with Aristotle about the implications of the analogy between tools and nature but deny that the analogy holds.

To understand why *Aristotle* thinks that the analogy holds, we should remember that for him living involves a range of functions and functioning requires tools. The bodies of living beings and their parts are the tools (ὄργανα) with which living beings live. In *De Generatione Animalium* I.2 Aristotle says that male and female are differentiated by a potentiality and function and 'since instruments are needed for all functioning and since the bodily parts are the tools that serve the faculties, it follows that certain parts must exist for the union and production of offspring' (716a23–6). Aristotle is making the point that all functioning requires tools. Therefore the functions of the soul in particular require tools and it is the bodily parts that provide these tools. The bodily parts are not just understood by analogy with things in other domains such as art which really are tools. They are themselves understood literally as tools within the general domain of things that have a function. Just as the function of cutting requires a tool such as a saw, so the functions of the soul require bodily parts as their tools.[10]

3. Explanation from the top down

The text to turn to for more information on form as an end in nature is *Physica* II.9. Here Aristotle discusses the relationship between form and matter from the point of view of necessity. He argues against the position of the 'materialists' who hold that form is necessitated by matter. By materialists Aristotle has in mind people like Democritus and Empedocles. We need not take Aristotle's description of the materialist position as necessarily being historically accurate or fair to any of these philosophers.[11] What is important for present purposes is how *Aristotle* sees a basic contrast between his own way of explaining nature and the way these other philosophers explain nature. The materialists say that natural beings come into be-

---

[10] Cf. *De an.* II.I 415b18–20: πάντα γὰρ τὰ φυσικὰ σώματα τῆς ψυχῆς ὄργανα, καὶ καθάπερ τὰ τῶν ζῴων, οὕτω καὶ τὰ τῶν φυτῶν, ὡς ἕνεκα τῆς ψυχῆς ὄντα.

[11] On the question of Aristotle's fairness to the materialists, cf. Wardy (1990) 256–8 and Sorabji (1980) 178–9.

ing because of certain attributes that their matter has. Again, Aristotle uses the analogy with artefacts to make his point about the causes of natural beings. The materialists, he says, explain natural beings as if they were explaining the construction of a wall by referring exclusively to the attributes of the wall's materials.[12] If the wall has a foundation of stone, a middle structure of earth and some wooden posts on top, the materialists will say that the foundation is of stone because stone is the heaviest material and therefore sinks to the ground, whereas the earth is on top of the stone because it is lighter, and the posts come on top of all because wood is the lightest element of all.

In this way, the arrangement of the materials in the wall would be explained from the point of view of the attributes that the materials have as such. Stone is always heavier than earth and wood is always lighter than earth. So these are attributes that the materials have irrespective of their presence in the wall. It is accidental that the materials come together in the form of *a wall*. For the attributes that cause them to come together, namely the different weights of wood, earth and stone, are attributes that the materials would have anyway. The attributes are not specific to wood, earth and stone *as the materials of a wall*. They are specific to wood and earth, etc., *as such*. For the materialists it is necessary that the materials arrange themselves in the shape of a wall because of their attributes *qua* stone, earth and wood.

For Aristotle, however, it is necessary that the materials are arranged the way they are because that is the arrangement that will serve the function or end by which we define a wall. The materials have been put there in order to provide shelter, or some such function. It is this function that defines what it is to be a wall. The function makes the materials necessary because if the function is to be realised then it must be realised in certain sorts of material. *If* you want a wall that protects you, then you need a foundation for it that consists of heavy materials, such as stone, which make the wall stable. You then

---

[12] *Ph.* II.9 200a1–5.

also need a middle structure that is made of lighter material than the foundation, such as earth, so that the middle structure does not push the foundation down, and so on and so forth. The matter is hypothetically necessary. It is necessary only *if* a certain form is to be realised. It is not necessary that there should be a wall. But it is necessary, if there is going to be a wall, that it should consist of such and such materials.

Contrast the materialist explanation, where it is necessary that if the materials are present, a wall comes about. The conditional here goes in the opposite direction. That makes the presence of the materials a sufficient condition for the presence of a wall. On Aristotle's notion of hypothetical necessity, there are no such sufficient material conditions of a wall. For whether the materials are present in a wall depends on whether there is a wall in the first place and *that* is a question of there being a certain form present, not a question of there being wood, stone and earth around.[13] That is why he says that the materials are necessary, only *if* a certain form is to be present.

There is a good example of Aristotle's criticism of the materialist explanation of living beings at *De Anima* II.4 415b28–416a8. The question is, Why do plants grow? Empedocles says that plants take root because they have earth in them. Earth naturally tends to move downwards. So too does the earth that plants have in them. Plants' taking root is the expression of this downward movement. By contrast, plants grow upwards because they also contain fire, for fire tends naturally to move upwards. The growth of plants in both directions, upward and downward, is explained in terms of the attributes that the material components of plants, earth and fire have as such. As Aristotle would put it, plants move upwards *qua* fiery and downwards *qua* earthy, but not *qua* plants.

Aristotle's objection to Empedocles' explanation of plant growth is symptomatic. Aristotle says that which part of the

---

[13] Aristotle himself in certain cases explains features of living beings by reference to the attributes that their matter has as such. I consider one such case in sec. 11 below, namely, eye colour.

plant counts as being up and which part counts as being down depends on the function that the part serves in the plant. The function of the roots is to take in nourishment. The roots therefore correspond with the head in an animal. For this is the part of the animal body where the mouth is situated.[14] This part, Aristotle says, is naturally the upper part of the organism. So the roots in the plant too should be thought of as being up, not down, as Empedocles says.[15]

The objection is symptomatic because it shows that for Aristotle it is the function and form of an organism that decides how we should describe its body and its parts. It is not the attributes that the body has insofar as it is composed of material elements. Thus we describe the plant's roots as being up because they have the function of taking in nourishment and not as down because they are composed of earth. The function and form takes precedence over the matter. Nor can we derive the function and the form from the attributes of the matter as such. If the composition of the plant was determined by the attributes of its material components as such, then the roots would count as down, for they are made of earth and the natural direction of earth as such is downwards. But in fact the roots count as being up because of their function and form.[16]

4. The application of top-down explanation to sight

The contrast between the Aristotelian and the materialist explanations is a contrast between what are now commonly known as explanation from the top down, that is to say, explanation from the point of view of the form and the end, and explanation from the bottom up, that is to say, explanation from the point of view of the material attributes.

---

[14] Cf. *IA* 705a28–b8; *Juv.* 468a1–12; *PA* 686b34–687a1.

[15] Similarly, the front of an animal is defined as the direction in which it moves and perceives; cf. *PA* 665a10–15.

[16] This argument develops a passage in *Ph.* II.8 where Aristotle argues that plants grow leaves for the sake of their fruits and send roots down (not up) for the sake of nourishment. It is worth noting that the prime examples for goal-directedness in nature as a whole are living beings.

Towards the end of *Physica* II.9, Aristotle again uses the example of a tool.[17] Again, the purpose of the example is to explain the notion of top-down explanation and the way in which matter can be said to be necessary from the point of view of the form. A saw is an instrument with a certain function and end, cutting wood or some such thing, but this end cannot be realised unless the saw consists of a certain material that is rigid and hard. Since only iron is adequately rigid and hard, it is necessary that the saw be made of iron for it to fulfil its function and end. In other words, the matter, the iron, is necessary from the point of view of the end or form of the saw, its ability to cut. So this is how we explain the fact that a saw is made of iron, from the point of view of its form.

In this book I shall try to show that the account in *Physica* II.9 of the relationship between form and matter underlies Aristotle's account of the sense-organs. The sense-organs are understood as the matter of the sense-faculties. They are to be explained, like other natural bodies and artefacts, from the point of view of their forms and ends. That is to say, Aristotle explains the sense-organs from the top down just as we explain the material of the saw and other tools from the point of view of *their* forms and ends.

In this first chapter, I try to show how the definition of the form and end of the sight for Aristotle determines the composition of the eye. In outline, Aristotle's explanation of the organ of sight goes like this. We start out by considering sight from the point of view of its highest actuality. This is the end or function of sight. The highest actuality of sight, actual seeing (ὄρασις), is to be changed by colour so as to become actually like it. This is what Aristotle calls the second actuality of sight. Sight (ὄψις) itself is an ability, the first actuality, to be so changed. This ability requires transparency, but transparency is realised only in certain sorts of body, water or air.

If this outline of Aristotle's explanation of the eye is correct, then his explanation follows the pattern of top-down expla-

---

[17] 200a28–b8.

nation recommended in the *Physics*. It is *thus* necessary that the sense of sight be realised in water or air or some such transparent material if it is going to be able to see, *just as* it is necessary that a saw be realised in iron or some such rigid and hard material if it is going to be able to saw.

Let me now consider the account in more detail. We understand perception in general as a way of being changed (κινεῖσθαι) or affected (πάσχειν) by something.[18] What happens in all change is that an agent acts on a patient. The agent is actually something, say actually hot. The patient is not yet like the agent but it is able to become like the agent. For instance, it is not yet hot but it is able to become hot. When the agent changes the patient, the patient is made to be like the agent. When it is exposed to an agent which is already hot, the patient acquires the heat from the agent. It becomes hot itself like the thing that causes it to become hot.

When we say that an object has the ability or potentiality to be hot, we explain what this potentiality is by first defining what it is actually to be hot. For the potentiality to be hot consists in being able to become like something that is actually hot. That is why we look first towards what is already actually hot to explain the potentiality to be hot. What is actually hot also has the ability to make something else hot. So by looking towards what is actually hot in order to explain the potentiality to be hot we are also finding out about the cause or agent that is able to actualise the potentiality to be hot.[19]

Aristotle applies the same method of definition to perception.[20] In perception it is the sense-object which is the agent and the sense-faculty which is the patient. The sense-faculty is potentially like the sense-object. In perception the sense-object acts on the sense-faculty so as to make the sense-faculty actually like it. As with other potentialities, we need therefore to look first at the actuality for which the sense-faculty is a potentiality. That is to say, we need to look first at the sense-object. The sense-object will tell us what kind of potentiality

---

[18] Cf. *De an.* II.5 416b33–5. [19] Cf. *Ph.* III.2. [20] Cf. *De an.* II.5 418a3–6.

the sense-faculty is.[21] The sense-object of sight is the visible as such.[22] The faculty of sight has the potentiality to be changed by the visible as such so as to become actually like it. The visible as such is colour, which has the ability to change (κινεῖν) what is actually transparent as such.[23] But the actuality of the transparent as such is light. That is why colour is only visible in light. We do not see colours in the dark, though we do sometimes, for other reasons, see phosphorescent things in the dark.[24]

So far we have been told that transparency is a condition of something's being visible. But what does Aristotle mean by 'transparency'? He explains that:

> I call transparent what is visible, not what is visible in itself speaking without qualification [ἁπλῶς] but because of the colour of something else. Of such a sort are air and water and many of the solid bodies. For it is not *qua* water or *qua* air that they are transparent but because a certain nature is present in them which is the same both in those two and in the eternal body above. Light is the actuality of this, the transparent *qua* transparent. (*De an.* II.7 418b4-10)

The occasion for this account of transparency is the claim that vision requires a medium. Aristotle wants to show that colour is the visible as such but, since it is only visible in a

---

[21] Cf. *De an.* II.4 415a14-22; *De an.* I.1 402b14-16; Sorabji (1971) 77. The point that Aristotle defines the sense-faculties by reference to their objects has been disputed by Hamlyn (1959) 10, 14-15. He distinguishes the case of vision where there is no internal connection between colour and vision from the case of hearing where it is impossible to define the sense-object, sound, without referring to the sense of hearing. It is difficult to see how this can work as an interpretation of Aristotle, for, apart from *De an.* II.4's insistence that we define the sense-object before the sense-faculty, *Metaph.* v.15 1021a34-b3 shows that there are general explanatory grounds for not accepting a definition of the sense-object that involves mentioning the sense-faculty. Aristotle says here that we should not explain sight by saying that it is relative to what is visible, for 'visible' itself means 'what sight is of'. So saying that sight is of the visible would be like saying that sight is of what sight is of. Aristotle admits that it is true to say this. The problem is that it is trivially true. That is why it does not *explain* what sight is to say that it is of the visible. It is better, Aristotle says, to say that sight is of colour. The point seems to be that it is better to explain sight with reference to colour because we can define colour independently of sight. *Mutatis mutandis*, the point applies to the other senses also. Cf. also Everson (1995) 281-2.

[22] *De an.* II.7 418a26-7.

[23] *Ibid.* 418a30-b2.

[24] *Ibid.* 419a2-7.

organs aims at establishing what kind of material composition is necessary for the realisation of their sense-faculties' forms and ends. It aims to show what matter is necessary if a certain form is to be realised. That is to say, it explains the matter from the top down in the way prescribed by *Physica* II.9. If this is Aristotle's aim, then it also suggests a terminus of how far we need to describe the sense-organs. For once we have described the matter of which the sense-organs are composed to the degree that we can see how they are apt or necessary for the realisation of the form, there is no incentive to describe the matter any further because this is just the degree to which we as natural students of the soul are interested in matter. We have explained why 'this form in this matter' when we have shown how this matter is the right matter if this form is to be realised.

I return to the introduction to *De Sensu* 2. Aristotle accepts that the composition of the sense-organs can be analysed in terms of the four elements. This is the analysis that he himself offers at the end of the chapter (438b17–439a5). He says that the organ of sight is made of water, the organ of hearing of air, that of smell is made of fire, that of touch of earth. Finally he mentions taste as a form of touch, with the implication that its sense-organ too consists of earth. Otherwise, the five senses would not match up with the four elements.

We may also recall here the discussion in *De Anima* III.1 where the composition of the sense-organs is also discussed in terms of the four elements. However, here the assignments of the elements come out differently. Water is the matter of the eye, air of the organ of hearing, and the organ of smell is composed of either water or air. But fire is said to be the matter either of none of the sense-organs or common to all of them insofar as there is no ability to perceive without heat. Earth is said to be the matter of none of the sense-organs or especially mixed with the sense-organ of touch.

There is some doubt here whether the elements can be assigned especially (ἰδίως) to some of the organs or whether they belong commonly to all of them or perhaps to none of them. So whether the assignment of the elements to the sense-organs can be achieved on a one-to-one basis is doubtful. But it is clear that Aristotle thinks that the way to understand the composition of the sense-organs is through some assignment (or other) of the elements to them.

There are two initial points to be noted about the claim that the sense-organs are composed of simple elements. The first is that when Aristotle assigns an element to a sense-organ we should probably understand him to mean something like this: the sense-organ of touch is 'earthy' rather than simply made of earth; the eye is watery rather than pure water; the organ of smell is fiery, etc. For in Aristotle, something is called 'water' even when it is not pure H_2O but is merely wet or liquid. 'Water' often seems to mean no more than 'the wet' or 'the liquid'.[27] Aristotle defines water in *De Generatione et Corruptione* II.2 as the cold and wet, a definition which is broad enough to include a range of substances that we would not think of as water (H_2O). In this vein, Aristotle describes the organ of sight alternately as made of 'water' (ὕδωρ) and 'the wet' (τὸ ὑγρόν).[28] Saying that the organ of sight is made of water is therefore vague enough to allow for any sort of liquid composition of the eye. Correspondingly, saying that the organ of touch is made of earth need not mean it is made of the sort of stuff we get when digging our gardens. It need mean no more than that the organ of touch is solid, this being the characteristic attribute of earthy substances.[29] As we shall see the sense-organ of touch is in fact made of flesh. Again, if the organ of smell is said to be made of air, it can probably consist of any gaseous substance.[30]

Vagueness attaches to the project of describing the sense-

[27] Cf. Williams (1982) 178, *ad GC* 334b31.
[28] Cf. *Sens.* 2 438b19 with *HA* 1.9 491b20–1.
[29] There might seem to be a contradiction between the *Sens.* passage saying that the organ of touch is made of earth and *PA* (discussed in ch. 4, sec. 7), which says that the sense-organ of touch is flesh (or its analogue) because it is a mixture of all the four elements. If flesh may be considered 'earthy' simply because it is solid, however, the contradiction disappears.
[30] Cf. Lloyd (1968) 166: 'If we bear in mind that we are not dealing with pure chemical elements, it is not too misleading or inaccurate to associate three of the four simple bodies with the three primary states of matter, "earth" with the solid, "water" with the liquid, and "air" with the gaseous.'

organs from the very beginning because the terms used to describe the basic composition of the sense-organs – 'water', 'earth', 'fire' and 'air' – are taken from a physics that uses 'water' as a generic term for substances as different as iron and H_2O.[31] We cannot determine the exact character of the composition of the sense-organs merely on the basis of being told what element they are made of. It is only when we are told in addition that the eye is made of 'water' because 'water' is *transparent* that H_2O begins to appear a more plausible candidate for the composition of the eye than certain of the other substances referred to as 'water'. But even then we have to remember that there is a range of transparent oily substances that Aristotle might equally well have in mind.

The second point to notice is that, though the elements are supposed to provide the matter for the sense-organs, the elements are themselves already understood functionally.[32] In *Mete.* IV.12 Aristotle explains the nature of simple (homogeneous) bodies:

For each of these elements has an end and is not water or fire in any and every condition of itself, just as flesh is not flesh nor viscera viscera, and the same is true in a higher degree with face and hand. What a thing is is always determined by its function: a thing really is itself when it can perform its function; an eye, for instance, when it can see. When a thing cannot do so it is that thing only in name, like a dead eye or one made of stone, just as a wooden saw is no more a saw than one in a picture. The same, then, is true of flesh, except that its function is less clear than that of the tongue. So, too, with fire; but its function is perhaps even harder to specify by physical inquiry than that of flesh. (*Mete.* IV.12 390a7–16, trans. Barnes (1984))

To find out what is meant by saying that the eye is made of water we need to find out what the function of water is because it is the function that defines it and that function differs in different contexts. The function of water in the eye is not going to be the same as the function of water in the sea. Because the function determines the nature of the water, it is not

---

[31] Plato in *Timaeus* 58d–59c takes metals to be a sort of water because they can melt and so are found in liquid as well as solid form. Aristotle follows suit in *Mete.* IV.10 389a7–9, as does Theophrastus in *De Lapidibus* I.

[32] Cf. Marc Cohen (1992) 70.

the same water that we find in the eye and in the sea. To explain the kind of stuff that the eye is made of we cannot therefore point to the stuff we find in the sea and say that this is the matter of the eye. Saying that the eye is made of water does not give us an external reference point for our understanding of the matter of the eye. We cannot point to other specimens of water and say that we understand the composition of the eye because we have already understood the composition of those specimens. By contrast, when told today that the eye is made of water, we can use our previous general understanding of the composition of water as H_2O and infer on that basis that if the eye is made of water, it must be made of H_2O. But for Aristotle the function of water determines its composition. That is why it is only when we have understood the particular function of water in the eye that we can understand what it means to say that the eye is made of water.

6. Aristotle versus Democritus

As we have seen, Aristotle does not wish to criticise the idea that the four elements can be assigned to the sense-organs. He agrees with that. Rather he wants to address the particular ways in which the assignments should be made and have been made by other philosophers. His own account of the composition of the eye is integrated into a critique of other accounts. Two of these are picked out for special treatment, those of Democritus and Empedocles, Empedocles being treated in tandem with Plato in the *Timaeus*.

The first thing to notice about Aristotle's criticism of these philosophers is that it deals with more than just the question which organ is composed of which element. Aristotle is not just interested in the correct assignment of an element to a sense-organ. That is why it is not enough for Democritus to say, for example, that the eye consists of water, even though it is right. Democritus is criticised for not having understood correctly the *function* that water has in vision. Democritus said that the watery composition of the eye enables objects to cast reflections or mirror images in it, vision being a sort of reflection (ἔμφασις).

It is this claim by Democritus about the function of the water in vision that occupies Aristotle. To understand Aristotle's objection, we need first of all to keep in mind the origin of the word *korē*. The word has its origin in the little image of oneself that appears in another person's eyes when one looks into them. The image that appears looks like a miniature or 'puppet' (*korē*) of oneself. Socrates in *Alcibiades* I 132e7–133a3 asks, 'Have you thought about the fact that the face of the one who looks into the eye appears (ἐμφαίνεται) in the eye (ὄψις) of the person opposite as if in a mirror, which we actually also call a *korē* because it is a kind of image (εἴδωλον) of the person who looks into the eye?'[33] The little puppet seen in the eye of the person opposite is a reflection of oneself.

The real explanation of this phenomenon, Aristotle argues, is not one that lends support to a reflection theory of vision:

Δημόκριτος δ' ὅτι μὲν ὕδωρ εἶναί φησι, λέγει καλῶς, ὅτι δ' οἴεται τὸ ὁρᾶν εἶναι τὴν ἔμφασιν, οὐ καλῶς· τοῦτο μὲν γὰρ συμβαίνει ὅτι τὸ ὄμμα λεῖον, καὶ ἔστιν οὐκ ἐν ἐκείνῳ ἀλλ' ἐν τῷ ὁρῶντι· ἀνάκλασις γὰρ τὸ πάθος. (*Sens.* 2 438a5–9)

The detail of the text is open to interpretation.[34] But the general meaning, I take it, is clear. When I look into somebody's eye I see a little picture of myself formed on his eye. This is the ἔμφασις. Democritus says that it is this little picture of me on that person's eye that allows *him* to see me. This, Aristotle says, is mistaken, for the little picture of myself that I see in his eye is only a picture that appears to me. It is only I

---

[33] LSJ notes *s.v.* κόρη that the change of sense in 'γλήνη' (pupil, eyeball) is exactly the converse of the change of sense in 'κόρη'. That is to say, where 'κόρη' first meant 'puppet' or 'girl' and then came to mean also 'pupil, eyeball, eye', 'γλήνη' originally meant 'pupil, eyeball' and then came to mean 'puppet, girl'. There is evidence of this semantic expansion of 'γλήνη' already in Homer *Il.* 8.164 (cf. *Od.* 9.390). So perhaps the semantic expansion of 'κόρη' in the opposite direction was influenced by that of 'γλήνη'. In any event, the author of *Alcibiades* I is not making a new point when he says that the κόρη is so called because of the reflection of puppet image. He is making a point that is already well established through common Greek usage of the term.

[34] Cf. G. R. T. Ross (1906) *ad* 438a8.

who see this picture not he (καὶ ἔστιν οὐκ ἐν ἐκείνῳ ἀλλ' ἐν τῷ ὁρῶντι). I see the picture because I am mirroring myself in his eye. This mirroring is possible because his eye is smooth and all smooth surfaces can throw back mirror images. This is the phenomenon called 'ἀνάκλασις'.

But the case of me seeing myself in his eyes as in a mirror is different from the case of him seeing me. In fact my ability to mirror myself in his eyes has nothing to do with what it is for him to see me. I could mirror myself in his eyes even if he were dead just as I can mirror myself in all sorts of inanimate smooth surfaces.

This is where the connection lies with the other objection that Aristotle makes: 'It is also strange that it never occurred to Democritus to ask why only the eye sees but none of the other things in which images are reflected see' (*Sens.* 2 438a10–12). The little image (ἔμφασις) of me formed on somebody else's eye is not what enables that person to see me. It is what I see when I use that person's eye to see a mirror image (ἀνάκλασις) of myself in. The fact is that I can use all sorts of smooth surfaces to mirror myself in, not just eyes. But none of these other smooth surfaces can be said to see me just because they display an image of me when I look at them.

Theophrastus in a criticism similar to Aristotle's gives the good Aristotelian reason why these other smooth surfaces cannot be taken to see me. He says that even soulless things contain reflections.[35] The point is too fundamental for him to require spelling out. But the point is that soulless things by definition would be without perception. For perception belongs only to a living animal and without a soul the animal is dead.[36] So no soul, no perception.

An eye cannot, then, be taken to see me just because there is a reflection of me in it, and so the reflection does not explain how we see. The fact that there are images formed in our eyes does not explain how we come to see things. So the reflection theory of vision has to be wrong.

Aristotle goes on to present his own side of the story. 'It is

---

[35] *De Sensibus* 36.   [36] Cf. *De an.* II.2 413a21–2.

not insofar (ᾗ) as the eyes are made of water that they see but insofar as it is transparent, which it has in common also with air' (438a13–15).[37] Water is not alone in being transparent. It is an attribute that air and other things also have. It is being transparent, rather than being watery, that is the attribute relevant to the eye's ability to see, for sight is understood as the ability to be changed by colour and this is an attribute of the transparent. Transparency is the condition of the sense-organ that meets the definition of sight as the faculty to perceive colour. So when the eye is described as transparent it is described by the only term that is directly relevant to its power to see.

There are reflections in things that are not transparent, for instance in mirrors, but these things are not said to perceive even though they cast reflections. It follows that the eye's taking on a reflection cannot be a sufficient condition of its seeing something. We can put Aristotle's case against the reflection theory of vision more strongly than this, however, for it seems that if the eye sees *qua* transparent, then the occurrence of a reflection in the eye is not even a necessary condition of vision.

For a start, let us consider what 'transparent' means. If you look into some water, what makes the water transparent is that you are able to see through it. If the water is transparent, you can see what is on the other side of the water. That is what it means for something to be transparent. Reflection, in contrast, is something that appears on the surface or just beneath the surface of the object that you look into. So insofar as you look at the water and see a reflection, say of yourself, you are not seeing through the water. You are seeing something just behind the surface of the water. Therefore insofar as you see a reflection in the water, you are not treating the water as transparent.[38]

---

[37] 'ὄψις' is used here and elsewhere, in the singular, as a term for the eyes. For other instances of this usage in Aristotle, cf. LSJ *s.v.* ii.c.

[38] There are further questions here about what transparency is if we take it, as I do here, to mean primarily 'that which something can appear through'. I try to answer these questions in ch. 2.

That is also why it is important that Aristotle insists exactly on this point against Democritus, that what enables the eye to see is the transparent inside the eye, not a reflection on the surface of the eye. The reflection that Democritus' theory is based on is an image that occurs only on the surface of the eye opposite to the perceiver. In the *Alcibiades* I 133a5–7 the idea is that when you look into another eye and see an image you see that by which (ᾧ) the eye sees. 'That by which my eye sees' is for Aristotle not an image on the surface of my eye which I can see reflected in your eye. 'That by which my eye sees' is something inside my eye, the transparent eye jelly in my eye. By identifying the reflection not as part of the process of the seeing but as what is seen, Aristotle excludes reflection from his account of seeing. Reflection for him is something that happens in certain conditions on the object side rather than what happens always in the perceiver when she sees something. Reflection is not a condition, sufficient or necessary, of seeing. It is a special sort of object of vision.

For Aristotle, as a special sort of object of vision, 'reflection' is a phenomenon that belongs less to the theory of vision proper than to optics.[39] Reflection is most commonly brought in to explain meteorological phenomena, that is, the phenomena that take place in the region around the stars. These phenomena include the Milky Way, comets and the motions of meteors, as well as such affections of the four elements as bring about winds, earthquakes, haloes, rainbows, etc.[40] Haloes and rainbows are caused by reflections.[41] Reflection occurs when a ray of light (ὄψις) hits a smooth surface and is sent back to the eye. For instance, a rainbow happens when a ray of light from the sun strikes a cloud in which the particles of air and water have been condensed so as each to form a

---

[39] Aristotle puts the confusion about reflection in Democritus' theory of vision down to the insufficient development of optics at Democritus' time, *Sens.* 2 438a9–10. Aristotle gives his own explanation of reflection in *Mete.* III.3 372b34–373a19.

[40] *Mete.* I.I.

[41] *Ibid.* III.2–4.

little mirror. When all the particles are continuous they make up one large mirror.[42]

Aristotle's emphasis on transparency as that by means of which you see is inconsistent with a reflection theory of vision in two respects. First, as mentioned, reflection is to be understood in terms of the conditions of the object of vision, not as one of the conditions of vision itself. Reflection happens whenever vision, as already understood in Aristotle's way, comes across a certain kind of smooth surface. Second, an object is exactly *not* treated as transparent insofar as it reflects the ray of light. By analogy, the eye is not treated as transparent insofar as it reflects an image.[43]

7. The significance of Aristotle's criticism of Democritus

What does the criticism of Democritus reveal about Aristotle's approach to the composition of the sense-organs? What Aristotle criticises is not the view that the eye consists of water. He agrees with that. It is the way in which Democritus uses the fact that the eye consists of water to explain how we see. Most of Aristotle's criticism is taken up with refuting the view that vision happens because of a reflection in the eye. At first blush, we might say that this view had already been ruled out because we began the discussion having already defined vision, and in this definition reflection played no part. So why focus on the reflection theory, which is a faulty theory of vision, when what we are trying to establish is how the eye is composed?

What is shown here is Aristotle's unwillingness to discuss the composition of the eye in isolation from the actuality of sight. He determines the composition of the eye from the point of view of its ability to realise the actuality of sight, from the top down. If we have misunderstood the actuality of

---

[42] Cf. Beare (1906) 65–8.
[43] Aristotle accepts the use of ὄψις as a ray of light to account only for reflection, but he rejects this use of ὄψις to account for all vision. The two uses of ὄψις should not be confused.

sight, however, as Democritus has, then having 'understood' the composition of the eye is like having 'understood' what a dead eye is. Recall *De Anima* II.1 412b20–2: 'The eye is matter for sight, and if this fails it is no longer an eye, except homonymously, just like an eye in stone or a painted eye.' Similarly, if *we* fail to understand what sight is, then whatever we may say about the eye will apply only homonymously to it. If we define the eye as a smooth, watery object that has the ability to reflect objects, then our talk about the eye will have no more to do with a live eye than a dead eye has to do with a live eye. We need to have the right definition of the eye, we need to understand its ability to see, before we can understand the matter of the eye. The matter of the eye can only be understood in relation to the definition of sight. This is why it is such an insignificant achievement for Democritus to have said correctly that the eye consists of water, for he has not understood what the matter is the matter *of*. Therefore he has understood no more about the material composition of the eye than somebody who has made an accurate painting of the eye has understood about a live eye.

It is worth keeping the imagery of the painted eye in mind when we talk about different theories of the eye. From Aristotle's top-down point of view, a theory of the eye, such as the reflection theory, that applies equally well to a dead eye and a living eye tells us nothing about the matter of the eye,[44] for this matter can be understood only in relation to the actuality of the eye. This actuality reveals itself not to anybody who looks into the eye or removes the eye and dissects it. It reveals itself only to the person who understands the eye as part of a living animal with the ability to see.[45] The matter of the

---

[44] Cf. again Theophrastus' point that even soulless objects cast reflections.

[45] Cf. *PA* I.1 640b33–641a5:

> Now a corpse has the same shape and fashion as a living body. And yet it is not a man. Again, it is impossible for a hand to be constituted in such a way, for example of bronze or wood, except homonymously, just as a doctor in a drawing. For it will not be possible for flutes made of stone to perform their proper function, nor will it be for a doctor in a drawing. Equally, none of the parts of a corpse is one of such things. I mean, for instance, an eye or a hand. So it is said too simply and in the same way just as if a carpenter were to say about a

eye can only be understood by somebody who has already understood the potentiality of the eye for sight *as Aristotle defines it.*[46]

8. Aristotle versus Empedocles and the *Timaeus* on the *korē*

A similar conclusion, I want to argue, is borne out by Aristotle's discussion of Empedocles.[47] Unlike Democritus, Empedocles gives a plainly wrong answer to the question what the eye is composed of. He says that the inside of the eye is made of fire.

The fire inside the eye lights up its surroundings. Empedocles explains this by analogy with a lantern in the following passage which Aristotle cites:

And just as when somebody planning a journey through the stormy night prepares a lamp, a flame of blazing fire, fitting to it lantern-sides as shields against the various winds, and these scatter the blowing winds' breath, but the finer part of the light leaps out and shines across the threshold with its unyielding beams; so at that time did she [sc. Aphrodite] bring birth[48] to the round-faced[49] eye [κούρην], primeval fire wrapped in membranes and in delicate garments ⟨penetrated by divine channels⟩. These held back the sea

wooden hand [sc. that it was really a hand]. In this way the *phusiologoi* speak about the formations and causes of the shape.

[46] The functional attitude to anatomy in Aristotle is also suggested by his attitude to vivisection; cf. Lloyd (1975) 128: '[Aristotle's] use of vivisection was generally confined to observing the effects that maiming had on an animal's vital functions.' The interest in the result of maiming on an animal's vital functions is of course not exclusive to Aristotle. It is an interest that would be shared by modern medicine. For instance, a good way of finding out what function the pineal gland had in an animal would be to observe the result upon the animal's functions of its removal.

[47] For the view that this does not do justice to Empedocles, cf. Archer-Hind (1888) 156–7; O'Brien (1970). For the opposite view, cf. Taylor (1928) 278–80.

[48] Reading 'λοχεύσατο' ('gave birth') for 'λοχάζετο' ('entrapped'), following Förster's emendation; cf. W. D. Ross (1955) *ad loc.* Lloyd (1966) 325, n. 2 retains 'λοχάζετο' and translates 'so then did the primal fire, enclosed in membranes, trap the round pupil in delicate tissues'. The advantage of Förster's emendation is two-fold: (a) 'gave birth to' highlights the double sense of 'κούρη' as 'eye' and 'daughter'; (b) 'gave birth to' allows us more clearly to introduce Aphrodite as the subject of the verb and thereby link up fr. 84 with fr. 86, 'From these divine Aphrodite made the unfailing eyes', as argued by Sedley (1992) 22. 'Gave birth to' gives us a more direct reference to Aphrodite or Love as the generative principle in Empedocles; cf., for example, frs. 20 and 21.

[49] Or, 'round-eyed' (κύκλοπα).

of water that flowed around, but the finer part of the fire penetrated to the outside. (*Sens.* 2 437b26–438a3 = DK84 = fr. 88 Wright (1981))[50]

The eye, the *korē*, is constructed like a lantern. The lantern is made up of a light inside fitted with screens around it. The light inside the lantern seems to correspond to the fire inside the eye and the screens to the membranes composed of earth and air. Outside the lantern blow winds which are compared to water trying to get to the fire. If the water managed to get to the fire it would, presumably, put it out. Similarly, if the winds could blow inside the lantern they would put out the light inside the lantern. Just as the screens of the lantern protect its internal fire from gusty winds, so the membranes of the eye protect the fire inside the eye from the water surrounding the eye.[51]

Now Aristotle could refute Empedocles' theory that there is fire inside the eye simply on the basis of the empirical evidence which Aristotle uses later in the chapter.[52] When the eye decays, it exudes water (*Sens.* 2 438a17–18). So the eye must consist of water, not fire. However, this is not what interests Aristotle here. If it were, he could have dismissed Empedocles without further ado. What interests Aristotle is the way in which Empedocles uses his idea of the internal fire in the context of his theory of *vision*. Aristotle is interested not in the fact that Empedocles thinks there is fire in the eye but in the function that Empedocles supposes this fire to have in vision.

It has been argued that Empedocles did not take the emission of light from the eye as playing a role in vision.[53] If so, fragment 84 presents a theory of the eye but not a theory of vision. It is clear, however, that Aristotle does take fragment

---

[50] Translation from Sedley (1992) 21. I have added the words '⟨penetrated by divine channels.⟩' (⟨αἳ⟩χοάνῃσι δίανατα τετρήατο θεσπεσίῃσιν, line 9 in DK) in brackets simply to be able to refer to the possibility of this reading later in my argument. Sedley excludes them on the same grounds as Wright (1981) 241.

[51] Cf. Sedley (1992) 21–2.

[52] Cf. *GA* v.1 779b20.

[53] Cf. O'Brien (1970) 143–6 and Barnes (1979) 308, n. 13. Contrast Long (1966) 263–4, Wright (1981) 242 and Sedley (1992) 25, who, in different ways, argue that the emission of light does play a role in vision.

84 as presenting a theory of vision,[54] for he introduces the quotation by saying that 'Empedocles seems sometimes to think that vision takes place when light leaves [the eye], as was said earlier' (*Sens.* 2 437b24–5). He also sums up the quotation by saying 'sometimes he says that vision happens in this way' (438a4). It does not occur to Aristotle that Empedocles might be describing the eye for any other reason than as part of a theory of vision. If Empedocles did not intend fragment 84 as a theory of vision, then the fact that Aristotle does take it as presenting a theory of vision says more about Aristotle than about Empedocles. It suggests that when Aristotle is describing the eye he is describing it from the point of view of his theory of vision because he thinks that the natural philosopher should describe the eye as an organ of vision, as the matter necessary for the sort of activity that the natural philosopher takes vision to be. If this is what Aristotle expects of a natural philosopher, it might explain his inability to see Empedocles' theory of the eye as innocent of any theory of vision.

Because Aristotle takes fragment 84 to be presenting a theory of vision he is also puzzled by the fact as he puts it 'that he [sc. Empedocles] sometimes says vision happens in this way and sometimes by the effluences from the things that are seen' (*Sens.* 2 438a4–5). The comment suggests that Aristotle thinks that effluence theory and an emission theory are inconsistent. The reason why Aristotle thinks the two theories inconsistent is likely to be his own preoccupation with the question of the causal direction in perception. The question is whether the sense-faculty is the patient in perception, as Aristotle holds and as the effluence theory might suggest, or the sense-faculty is the agent, as the emission theory might suggest. According to Aristotle, it seems Empedocles ought not to believe both in the visual ray and in effluences for general causal reasons, because if sight enabled us to see both by emitting light and receiving effluences, then that would *per*

---

[54] Notice, however, that Aristotle's language at 437b23–5 (ἔοικε νομίζοντι; λέγει γοῦν οὕτως) suggests that he is not quite sure how to take fr. 84; on the possible implications of this language, cf. Ross (1955) 190 and O'Brien (1970) 142.

impossibile make sight both the agent and the patient of perception. In sum, the reason why Aristotle thinks that what Empedocles says in fragment 84 is incompatible with the effluence theory is that he recognises in fragment 84 the visual ray theory, and the causal direction in vision according to the visual ray theory appears to him to be opposite to the causal direction according to the effluence theory.

Aristotle expects then that a theory of the eye must express a theory of vision. There is another reason, however, why he takes fragment 84 as presenting a theory of vision: he is reading Empedocles together with Plato's *Timaeus*.[55] The *Timaeus* says that the light that the eye sends out is part of what happens in vision. Aristotle identifies the light that leaves the eye in Empedocles fragment 84 with the light that leaves the eye in vision according to the *Timaeus*. To understand Aristotle's criticisms of Empedocles, we should try, then, to read Empedocles with Aristotle's eyes as the philosopher who said what Plato also said in the *Timaeus*. In what follows, I shall therefore by 'Empedocles' refer to the holder of the theory of vision that Aristotle finds both in fragment 84 and the *Timaeus*.

Aristotle wants to show that fire will not serve the function given it by Empedocles since it will not enable the eye to see, and he tries to do this by reducing Empedocles' theory to absurdity. Empedocles' theory is that vision takes place when fire springing from the eye lights up the surroundings. This theory implies, Aristotle argues, that the eye is able to light up an object even in the dark, so that we ought to be able to see even in the dark. Empedocles cannot say that darkness extinguishes the fire coming from the eye, for if anything were to extinguish the fire coming from the eye, then it would have to be the opposite of fire, namely, what is wet and cold. The wet and the cold are not attributes of darkness, however, just as the dry and the hot are not attributes of light. So darkness cannot extinguish fire and the internal fire ought to be able to

---

[55] Cf. *Sens.* 2 437b11–13: 'if the eye was actually made of fire, as Empedocles says and as is written in the *Timaeus,* and vision happens when the light leaves the eye just as from a lantern ... '.

light up objects even at night. On Empedocles' theory, therefore, we ought to be able to see at night,[56] but we are not and so his theory is wrong.

Strictly speaking, Aristotle does not argue against the claim that the eye is composed of fire. He argues against the claim that the internal fire can function so as to light up an object of vision. As with Democritus, Aristotle is primarily interested in function when he discusses the physiological theories of Empedocles.

Now Aristotle himself goes on to use the image of a lantern to describe what *he* calls the *korē*, namely, the transparent inside the eye. Aristotle says that:

> The soul or the perceptive part of the soul is not at the surface of the eye, but it is clear that it is inside. That is why it is necessary that the inside of the eye is transparent and receptive to light. And this is clear also from what actually happens. For to those who have been struck on the temple in battle and who have thereby had the *poroi* of the eye severed [ἐκτμηθῆναι] it has seemed dark just as if a lamp [λύχνου] had been extinguished. For the transparent, what is called the *korē*, has been cut off [ἀποτμηθῆναι], like a lantern [λαμπτῆρά].[57] (438b8–16)

In this passage Aristotle uses the lantern metaphor to present his own theory of the transparent, the *korē*. His use of the metaphor follows close upon Empedocles'. It seems likely therefore that Aristotle is consciously appropriating the metaphor from Empedocles. In other words, he is adapting the metaphor to fit his own theory of the eye as opposed to that of Empedocles.

How does Aristotle appropriate the metaphor? To answer this question let us look at the two most prominent elements of the metaphor, the *korē* and the 'membranes'. I shall ask first what these terms mean in Empedocles, then what they

[56] *Ibid.* 437b11–438b23.
[57] In the Greek of W. D. Ross's edition:

> οὐ γὰρ ἐπὶ ἐσχάτου τοῦ ὄμματος ἡ ψυχὴ ἢ τῆς ψυχῆς τὸ αἰσθητικόν ἐστιν, ἀλλὰ δῆλον ὅτι ἐντός· διόπερ ἀνάγκη διαφανὲς εἶναι καὶ δεκτικὸν φωτὸς τὸ ἐντὸς τοῦ ὄμματος. καὶ τοῦτο καὶ ἐπὶ τῶν συμβαινόντων δῆλον· ἤδη γάρ τισι πληγεῖσιν ἐν πολέμῳ παρὰ τὸν κρόταφον οὕτως ὥστ' ἀποτμηθῆναι τοὺς πόρους τοῦ ὄμματος ἔδοξε γενέσθαι σκότος ὥσπερ λύχνου ἀποσβεσθέντος, διὰ τὸ οἷον λαμπτῆρά τινα ἀποτμηθῆναι τὸ διαφανές, τὴν καλουμένην κόρην.

mean in Aristotle, and finally how the two uses differ. My argument will show that we understand Aristotle's description of the eye best if we see it as redefining his predecessor's descriptions in the light of Aristotle's own theory of vision.

First the *korē*. The word *korē* is standardly used in Greek literature to refer to the eye as a whole.[58] The use of *korē* to refer to the 'pupil' in particular occurs in the Hippocratic corpus.[59] Also, *korē* almost certainly means 'pupil' in the *Alcibiades* passage that I discussed earlier, for the pupil is the part of the eye in which you would see the mirror-image. In Empedocles, however, *korē* seems again to refer to the entire eye, the 'primeval fire wrapped in membranes and delicate garments'.[60] The *korē* is compared with a lantern as a whole, that is, to the entire structure of a lantern including both the internal fire *and* the protective screens. It is not just compared with a particular part of the lantern. This leaves it rather indeterminate from the outset what *korē* may refer to in Aristotle: it does not have a cut-and-dried reference that he need subscribe to.

For Aristotle *korē* does not refer to what we call the 'pupil' but to liquid inside the eye,[61] which is transparent and receptive to light.[62] It is the definition of *korē* as the transparent that does the job of distinguishing the use of *korē* in Aristotle from its use in Empedocles. The transparent, according to *De Anima*, is what has the potentiality to be changed by colour as such and is therefore that which has the potentiality of sight. As *De Sensu* 2 shows, what Aristotle understands by sight is different from what Empedocles understands by sight. This

---

[58] Aristophanes *Vesp.* 7; Sophocles fr. 710; Euripides *Ion* 876, *Hec.* 972 (I owe these references to Sedley (1992) 22, n. 6); cf. also Euripides *Bacch.* 1087.

[59] For example, in *Internal Affections* 7.284.16, where the *korai* are said to be *dilated* because of an excess of bile in the medical condition called the 'thick disease'; cf. also *Carn.* 8 606.7; Sedley (1992) 22, n. 7.

[60] On the meaning of the 'garments', cf. Taillardat (1959).

[61] Cf. Sorabji (1974) 49, n. 22. *HA* IV.8 533a8–9 says, more specifically, that the *korē* is the liquid inside the iris (τὸ μέλαν), on which more below.

[62] *Sens.* 2 438b6–8.

difference is implied in the reference to 'the transparent'. The implication of a different theory of vision in 'the transparent' makes the comparison of the transparent with a lantern sufficiently unlike that of Empedocles as to dispel any suggestion for Aristotle that he is involved in the same theory of how the eye is composed. The meaning of *korē* is for Aristotle fixed by the definition of its potentiality *qua* transparent. It is this definition of *korē* that Aristotle refers to when he says that the inside of the eye is the transparent, for the transparent is what can be changed by colour and this is how we understand sight, as a potentiality to be changed by colour. But where the definition of its potentiality differs, there is no problem about a superficially similar description of its material composition. Again the case is like the case of a picture of an eye and a living eye. They may look similar and have the same name, but their definitions are different. Aristotle's appropriation of the *korē* from Empedocles' lantern metaphor does not occur to him as problematic, for Aristotle has redefined the term in the context of his own theory of vision.

There is a parallel here to the argument against Democritus. Aristotle agreed with Democritus that the eye consists of water, but this agreement was trifling for him for he disagreed with Democritus about the reason why the eye consists of water. The water served a very different function in Aristotle from the function it served in Democritus. Similarly, Aristotle now agrees with Empedocles that the sense-organ of sight is like a lantern and that it involves a *korē* that somehow lights up, but he disagrees about the function of the *korē*. Aristotle's use of the lantern metaphor is therefore only superficially similar to Empedocles'. For Aristotle, his own and Empedocles' uses of the metaphor represent completely different notions of the eye because they represent completely different notions of what the eye does in vision.

Aristotle's ability to re-use his rivals' description of the eye, be it the eye's watery composition or similarity to a lantern, is founded in his own method of describing the eye from the point of view of its function in vision. Where in his view the eye works in a different way from how his rivals thought, Aristotle takes this difference in function to be sufficient to differentiate his description of the composition of the eye from his rivals' apparently similar descriptions.

9. The membrane of the eye

At *De Sensu* 2 438a25–b2, Aristotle raises the following objection to any theory (ὅλως, 438a25) that says that we see by means of a visual ray (ὄψις) which is emitted by the eyes:

> In general it is unreasonable that the visual ray sees by something going out of [the eyes] and that it [*sc.* the visual ray] extends as far as to the stars, or that the visual ray goes out to a certain point where it coalesces [συμφύέσ-θαι], as some people say. It is better than this [to say] that it coalesces in the starting point [ἀρχή] of the eyes. But this too is naive. For what is the coalescence of light with light, or how is it able to occur? For not any chance thing coalesces with any chance thing. And how does the light inside coalesce with the light outside? For the membrane [ἡ μῆνιγξ] is in between.

This highly condensed passage raises a number of questions. Who are the people that talk about a coalescence of light with light? What did they mean by 'coalescence'? What does Aristotle mean by saying that it would be better to say that the coalescence occurred in the 'starting point' of the eye? And finally, what is the membrane he is talking about and why does he think it provides evidence against the coalescence of light inside with light outside the eye?

There are two emission theories mentioned in the passage. One says that the visual ray extends as far as to the stars. The authorship of this theory is uncertain. Alexander of Aphrodisias says it is the theory of certain mathematicians. These mathematicians argued that the visual ray is like a cone with its apex in the eye and its base at the objects. We can perhaps compare the visual ray again to a lantern. The lantern spreads light on a wide area in the direction in which it shines. The wide area lit up by the lantern is like the base of the cone. The source of the light inside the lantern is only a small flame, however, and is like the apex of the cone. Aristotle has nothing specifically to say about this theory.[63] So let us leave it to one side.

The other theory says that the visual ray leaves the eyes and reaches a certain point where it coalesces with the light outside. This is the theory that Aristotle criticises with the *Timaeus* in mind. In order to explain why I think he has the *Timaeus* in mind let me briefly summarise what the *Timaeus* says about vision. There are two passages in the *Timaeus* where Timaeus explains what happens in vision: 45b–46c and 67c–68e. In the first passage, Timaeus says that vision takes place as follows. The eye contains pure fire. Because the eye is fine-webbed, the coarser elements are kept inside the eye. Being pure and smooth, however, fire can flow through the eyes. By day, when a ray of this pure fire exits the eye, it meets with the daylight outside. The ray and the daylight are akin, for they are both made of the same gentle fire. This fire does not burn. It only brings light. Since the ray and the daylight are akin, they form a single body of light when they meet. This body of light can then hit upon an object. When it does so, the object affects the body of light. The affection spreads from the object all the way through the body of light into the eyes and from there to the seat of the soul. When the affection reaches the soul vision takes place.

The second passage, 67c–68e, explains how we see different colours. Colour is 'a flame which flows from all bodies' (67c8–9). In colour vision the particles of this flame impinge on the visual ray that we described in the earlier passage. If the particles of the flame are of the same size as the particles of the visual ray, no vision is produced. We call objects that emit particles of this sort transparent. If the particles of the flame are larger than those of the visual ray, they compress (cf. συγκρίνοντα, 67d6) the visual ray. We perceive this as black. If the particles of the flame are smaller than the visual ray's particles, they disperse (cf. διακρίνοντα, 67d7) the visual ray. In that case we perceive white. All the other colours are

---

[63] Perhaps because he himself uses a similar theory at *Mete.* III.3 372b34–373a19 to account for reflection.

mixtures of black and white (68a9–e1). So we have to imagine that whenever we perceive the other colours the visual ray is to some extent dispersed and to some extent compressed.

Finally, there is a special sort of colour (67e6–68a8). This is a flame which produces a particularly keen motion. When this motion moves along the visual ray, it disperses the visual ray all the way up to the eyes. There, it forcibly breaks through and melts away the very channels (διεξόδους, 68a1) of the eyes. From the channels a body of fire and water then gushes out. This body is what we call 'a tear'. When again the fiery motion from the outside meets the fire coming out of the eye in this watery body, all sorts of colour arise in the mixture. This experience is called 'dazzling', and the 'colour' which produces the experience is called 'bright' and 'shining' (λαμπρόν τε καὶ στίλβον, 68a8).

Timaeus' talk in these two passages of light from within the eye merging with light outside the eye and his use of the term *opsis* to refer to the light emitted by the eye identify the *Timaeus* as the target of Aristotle's criticism. But Aristotle's criticism of Timaeus is surprising on a number of points. First of all, Aristotle said that it is not any chance thing that coalesces with any chance thing. If this was meant as an objection to Timaeus it ignores that Timaeus was at pains to establish that the eye contained a special sort of fire that was pure and gentle (45b). This fire was akin (cf. ξυγγενοῦς, 45d3; ξυμφυὲς, 64d6) to the daylight. *That* was why they could merge. So Timaeus, far from implying that any chance thing can merge with any other, stresses the need for kinship between the two sorts of fire if they are to coalesce. This is also shown by what happens when the light tries to leave the eye at night. The light meets with darkness but, because darkness is dissimilar to light, no coalescence between the two takes place and the light is extinguished (45d).

Second, Aristotle objects that there can be no coalescence between the light outside and the light inside because the membrane is in between. What is this membrane and why should it prevent the coalescence of the two sorts of light? There is no mention of a membrane separating the light inside from that outside the eye in the *Timaeus*. Timaeus said that the gods made the entire eye, and particularly the middle of the eye, 'fine-webbed' (ξυμπιλήσαντες). That was why the coarser elements were kept back whereas the pure and smooth fire was allowed to leave the eyes. Timaeus had therefore made explicit provision for the composition of the entire eye to allow for the light inside to leave the eye and coalesce with the light outside. How can Aristotle object against Timaeus' theory that the membrane prevents the light inside coalescing with the light outside when Timaeus (a) says that the entire eye allows for it, (b) does not seem to allow for any membrane as part of the eye's composition, and (c) certainly should not allow any membrane if it prevented the coalescence of lights?

Before we conclude that Aristotle is just an inept reader of the *Timaeus*, we should reflect on two other suggestions. The first reminds us again that Aristotle is reading the *Timaeus* together with Empedocles. The second suggests that when Aristotle refers to the membrane he has in mind his own description of the eye, not Empedocles' or Plato's. In the passage Aristotle quoted from Empedocles (fr. 84), Empedocles described the eye as 'primeval fire wrapped in membranes and in delicate garments'. As Aristotle is criticising the *Timaeus* in conjunction with Empedocles, is it possible that Aristotle has Empedocles' references to the membranes in mind when he says that the membrane prevents the coalescence of fires? No, for Empedocles went on to say that the membranes 'held back the sea of water that flowed around, but the finer part of the fire penetrated to the outside'. So Empedocles explicitly says that the membranes allow for the fire to leave the eye. Aristotle's criticism would have as little force against Empedocles as against the *Timaeus*.

The other suggestion, which I think is right, is that Aristotle, by the membrane, is referring to the membrane as a part of his own theory of the eye. At *De Generatione Animalium* v.2 781a18–20, Aristotle says that just as in the case of sight so in the case of hearing and smell the ability to differentiate differences in sense-objects requires that the sense-organ and the membrane (μῆνιγξ) around the sense-organ be pure (καθαρόν). Aristotle nowhere else uses the word 'membrane' (μῆνιγξ) when discussing the eye. Instead, he uses the word 'skin' (δέρμα). We can be fairly sure that for Aristotle the 'skin' of the eye corresponds to the 'membrane' or 'skin' of the other sense-organs, for the reason why Aristotle at *De Generatione Animalium* v.2 781a18–20 says that hearing and smell like sight require a pure *membrane* is that he has just explained how the *skin* of the eye determines accuracy of vision (780a26–36, b26). In addition, at *De Anima* II.8 420a14–15 Aristotle says that there is no hearing when the membrane (μῆνιγξ) of the ear is damaged, just as there is no vision when the skin (δέρμα) on the *korē* is damaged.

The function of skin, in general, seems to be to protect the body. The function of the skin of the eye, in particular, seems to be to protect the *korē*. The skin is located on the surface of the *korē* (780b25) and works together with the eyelids for the protection of the eye. Thus animals which have thick skin over their eyes need no eyelids to protect their eyes further. Animals, however, which have thin skin over their eyes, like humans, need eyelids for extra protection (*PA* II.13 657a25–b2). This ability of the skin and the eyelids to compensate for each other suggests that they do the same job.

Empedocles compared the membranes of the eye to 'fine garments' (λεπτῆσιν ὀτόνησι). The membranes of the eye, like the screens of a lantern, were fine to allow the fire to pass through. Like Empedocles, Aristotle stresses that the skin of the eye must be 'fine' (λεπτόν). Also like Empedocles, he explains the composition of the membrane by means of the lantern metaphor. At *De Generatione Animalium* v.1 780a27–36 he argues that the skin of the eye must be transparent.[64] If the skin of the eye must be transparent, it is necessary (hypothetically necessary) that the skin be composed in a certain way. It should be thin (λεπτόν), even, and light (λευκόν). It should be thin 'so that the change from the outside will pass straight through' (ἡ θύραθεν εὐθυπορῆ κίνησις, 780a29). It should be even so that there are no wrinkles that produce a

---

[64] On the passage, cf. also Lennox (1983) 150.

shadow on the eye. The vision of old people, Aristotle says, is worse because they have wrinkly eyes. The reason why a shadow on the eye impedes vision seems to be that it makes the surface of the eye darker and therefore less transparent. Similarly, the skin should be light. For the opposite of light is dark (μέλαν) and what is dark is not transparent. That is also why lanterns that are made of non-transparent skin are unable to shine.

Why will the skin only let the change pass straight through if it is thin? Because it is only if the skin is thin that it is also transparent. But why should the transparent let the change pass through? Here we have to keep in mind the reason why the medium of vision has to be transparent. The job of the medium is to allow the colour to reach the eye by first being affected by the colour and then in turn by affecting the eye. But since it is was only the transparent that could be changed or affected by colour as such, the medium had to be transparent. It is for the same reason that we are now told that the skin of the eye must be transparent for the skin lies in between the medium outside the eye and the *korē*. So if the skin was not also transparent there would not be a transparent medium all the way from the sense-object to the *korē*. If so, the colour of the sense-object would not be able to affect the medium all the way up to the *korē* in such a way that the medium in turn could affect the *korē*. The skin, then, like the medium outside, has to be transparent to allow the change going from the sense-object to 'pass straight through', as Aristotle puts it, to the *korē* inside the eye.

The other two requirements for accurate vision, that the skin must be both even and light, also refer to the need for transparency. Thus the skin must be light, for if it is not light, it is dark, and if it is dark it is not transparent. The skin must be even, for if it is not it casts shadows which, it seems, would also make the skin dark. Aristotle clinches this argument by saying that the skin must be transparent like the skin of a lantern, for a lantern that is made of non-transparent skin will not shine.

We were told earlier that the medium had to be not just

transparent but actually transparent. Actual transparency was light, whereas mere potential transparency was darkness. Similarly, we have to assume now that the membrane of the eye must be actually transparent, for if it were only potentially transparent it would be dark which, as we saw, would prevent the change from getting through to the *korē*. Another way of presenting the lantern metaphor would therefore be to say that the membranes of the eye have to be actually transparent because it is only if they are actually transparent that there will be *light* all the way from the coloured sense-object to the *korē*, and we can only see in light.

Let us stop at this point and ask what has happened to Empedocles' lantern in Aristotle's hands and, in particular, what has happened to Empedocles' fine membranes. First of all, in Empedocles the eye was like a lantern in that it allowed the fire to pass out of the eye. This was in order to illuminate the surroundings, just as a man on a dark night needed a lantern to illuminate the road. The eye needed fine membranes to let the fire out. In Aristotle, the membranes do not serve to let anything *out of* the eye. They serve to let the change from the coloured sense-object *into* the eye, to the *korē* inside the eye. Like the medium, the membranes can only let the change through if they are transparent, but they are transparent only if they are fine. So in Aristotle the membranes of the eye are fine in order to let something (the change from the sense-object) into the eye, not in order to let something (fire) out of the eye.

This difference in the function of the membrane nicely reflects how Aristotle sees his view of the causal direction of perception as differing from that of Empedocles. For Empedocles vision happens when the sight, that is the visual ray, affects the sense-objects in a certain way. For Aristotle vision happens when the sense-object affects sight, that is the sense-faculty, in a certain way. Correspondingly, the membrane in Empedocles lets the visual ray out of the eye where it can affect the sense-object, whereas the membrane in Aristotle lets the change from the sense-object into the eye where it can affect the sense-faculty.

This difference between the views of Aristotle and Empedocles about the function of membranes leads Aristotle to a different view of the composition of the membrane. In order fully to appreciate this point, we need to understand Aristotle's criticism of the view that light is a kind of fire. As we have seen, Aristotle's view of light is that it is the actuality of the transparent *qua* transparent.[65] He distinguishes this definition of light from any theory of light as 'fire or a body or an effluence of a body' (*De an.* II.7 418b14–15). When Empedocles/Timaeus says that light is fire, Aristotle takes him to hold that light is body. Aristotle agrees that some such thing as fire or the body above plays a part in the account of light.[66] But fire 'or some such thing' is not what light *is* in the sense that Aristotle is looking for here. Fire does not provide the answer to the request for a formal definition of light which Aristotle is making: it does not answer the question, What is light?[67] Fire (if, indeed, it is fire and not αἰθήρ or something else) does not answer the definitional question. However, fire is connected with light as that whose presence ('παρουσία', 418b20)[68] actualises the transparent *qua* transparent (418b12). It is this actuality which provides the formal definition of light.

We are now in a position to understand Aristotle's apparently inept objection to the visual ray theory. Aristotle objected that the fire inside the eye could not coalesce with the fire outside the eye because the membrane was in between. Now if light is a body, as Empedocles/Timaeus implies by saying that light is fire, then there is no way that the light inside the eye and the light outside the eye could coalesce as long as a membrane separated them. As Alexander says, if the two lights are bodies they have to be at least in contact with each other to coalesce.[69] But the membrane is in between

---

[65] *De an.* II.7 418b9–10.

[66] *Ibid.* 418b12–13: ὑπὸ πυρὸς ἢ τοιούτου οἷον τὸ ἄνω σῶμα.

[67] Cf. *ibid.* 418b3–4: περὶ φωτὸς πρῶτον λεκτέον τί ἐστιν.

[68] Cf. *Sens.* 3 439a20.

[69] Alexander, *in de Sensu* 34.21. Alexander also explains Aristotle's observation 'that it is not any chance thing that coalesces with any chance thing' as drawing our attention to the fact that it is bodies that coalesce, or in Alexander's and Aristotle's terminology 'mix'. In this way, the observation leads up to the difficulty

them and prevents them from being in contact. On Aristotle's theory, in contrast, there is no problem with the membrane being in between the light outside and the transparent *korē* inside the eye, for what is needed for vision to take place is not a coalescence of bodies but a continuity of transparent bodies. The membrane was not fine, as we saw, in order to let the fire inside out. It was fine so that it would be transparent. By being transparent, it ensured that there was transparency all the way from the sense-object to the *korē*.

However, a membrane of the eye that lets through corporeal fire to illuminate the outside is a functionally different part of the eye from a membrane of the eye that communicates a *kinēsis* of colour *qua* transparent. If it is a functionally different part of the eye, it is also a different sort of matter since the matter is only to be understood as relative to this function. So, again, the superficial similarity of Aristotle's description of the eye to that of Empedocles should not make us think that their theories of the eye are the same.

We have seen that the notion of light as fire plays an important part in Aristotle's criticism of the visual ray theory. Aristotle goes on in the next lines of *De Sensu* 2 to give his own account of the role of light in vision. He first (438b2–3) refers us to his earlier account of why light is necessary for vision. This is the account in *De Anima* II.7. Vision required light because vision required a medium that was actually transparent.[70] For the proper object of vision, colour, could only change what was actually transparent. Having referred back to this account, Aristotle then (*Sens.* 2 438b4–5) says that it is the change, that is the change brought about by the colour, through this medium that produces vision. Finally, he says that it is reasonable that the inside of the eye should be made of water since water is transparent. The inside of the eye must be transparent, for, just as there is no vision without

presented by the membrane. It is bodies that mix because mixture involves a mixture of matter and form. For more on Aristotle's notion of 'mixture', cf. ch. 4 on taste.

[70] *De an.* II.7 418b2–10.

light outside the eye, so there is no vision without light inside the eye.

This suggests that the reason why there must be actual transparency in the eye is the same as the reason why there must be actual transparency in the medium. It is only the actually transparent that can be changed by colour. However, notice also the way Aristotle puts this point: 'just as there is no vision without light outside so there is no vision without light inside the eye' (438a6–7). The light outside is required for mediation. It is required as that 'through which' the change can produce vision. If light is required inside the eye for the same reason, then it suggests that light is also required inside the eye as something through which the change produces vision. In other words, the light inside the eye too is a medium of the change from the sense-object.

If this is right, the transparent *korē* acts as a medium in vision. The *korē* is then a part through which the change from the sense-object produces vision rather than the part in which vision occurs. There is textual support for this notion elsewhere in Aristotle.[71] For the moment, I just note it as a suggestion.

10. The *poroi* of the eye

Aristotle in *De Sensu* 2 438b8–16 describes how soldiers become blind when the *poroi* of their eyes are severed by a blow to the temple. The example is part of Aristotle's argument against the reflection theory to establish that the seeing part of

---

[71] Cf. *De an.* III.7 431a17–20: 'Just as the air makes the *korē* of such a quality and it makes something else [of such a quality] and in the same way hearing, but the last thing [that is made of such a quality?] is one and one mean [μεσότης], though its being is many.' The sentence is grammatically difficult in that, as Simplicius noted, it has no apodosis. Nor is it very clear how the sentence fits into the general argument of the passage. However, it does make the point fairly clearly that the *korē* takes on the quality of the medium and conveys it to something else. In this way, the quality may affect a single mean whose being is many, by which most commentators take Aristotle to mean the central sense-faculty in the heart; cf. Rodier (1900) *ad loc.*; Kahn (1966) 12.

the soul cannot be at the surface of the eye. But what exactly are these *poroi*? What is their function and where are they located? As we shall see, these questions are of fundamental importance to our understanding of not just the eye and vision but of all the sense-organs and all perception.

Let us start again with Aristotle's citation from Empedocles (fr. 84). If we could be sure that it said that the membranes were 'penetrated by divine channels', then *perhaps* we could see a reference to *poroi* in these words. But the text is uncertain, so we had better not rely on this reading.

Nevertheless, Empedocles did operate with *poroi* both in his theory of perception and in his theory of change. Aristotle, as we saw, refers to Empedocles' 'other' theory that vision happens by means of effluences from the sense-object. He does not specifically refer to the role that the *poroi* play in this theory, but it must have been well known to him because he had read Plato's *Meno*.[72] Socrates at *Meno* 76c–d explains Empedocles' theory of vision as follows. There are effluences from objects. There are also *poroi*. Some effluences fit into some *poroi*, others are too big or too small for these *poroi*. The effluences that are symmetrical with the *poroi* of the eyes are called colour and are perceptible.

Furthermore, a comparison of fragment 84 with Theophrastus in *De Sensibus* 7 suggests that the *poroi* occurred in the context of fragment 84. So even though the *poroi* are not explicitly mentioned in the passage that Aristotle quotes they must have been mentioned in the text before him. At *De Sensibus* 7 Theophrastus first reports Empedocles' explanation of why the different senses cannot perceive each other's sense-objects. He then goes on to describe the structure of the eye:

... the passages [*poroi*] of some [of the sense-organs] are too wide for the object and those of others are too narrow. And consequently some [of these objects] hold their course through without contact, while others are quite unable to enter. Then he attempts to tell us the character of the organ of vision. Its interior, he says, is of fire; while round about this [internal fire] are earth and air, through which the fire, by reason of its subtilty, passes like

---

[72] As shown, for example, by *APo* I.I 71a1–b8.

the light in lanterns. The passages [of the eye] are arranged alternatively of fire and water: by the passages of fire we perceive white objects; by those of water, things black; for in each of these cases [the objects] fit into the given [passages].[73] (*De Sensibus* 7)

Theophrastus seems, like Aristotle, to have had fragment 84 in front of him when reporting Empedocles' theory. Aristotle and Theophrastus both mention the internal fire and the earth and air that surround the fire. Further, they both say that the fire can leave the eye because fire is subtle.[74] The structure of the eye as reported by Theophrastus and fragment 84 may therefore be seen, at least roughly, to be the same. *And* the eye is in both passages compared with a lantern.

But Theophrastus adds to the claims reported also by Aristotle an account of the role of the *poroi* of the eye. The account seems to go like this. The eye has *poroi*. Some of the *poroi* are made of fire. These *poroi* will let through white particles because white particles are like the *poroi*, that is they are both fiery. Other *poroi* are made of water and will let through black particles since black is the colour of water.[75] It is because we have *poroi* in the eyes that are like the sense-objects, like white and black, that we are able to see these objects with our eyes. For perception, like thought, according to Empedocles, occurs by the action of like on like.[76] It is because the *poroi* are made up of the same elements as the sense-objects that the sense-objects fit into the *poroi*.[77]

I have argued that Aristotle must have known of the role that Empedocles assigned to the *poroi* in vision. It is also clear

---

[73] Translation Stratton (1917)

[74] No mention, however, of the surrounding water as in fr. 84. This has led some scholars to emend the text to read ὕδωρ καὶ after περὶ αὐτό; cf. Stratton (1917) 163–4, n. 25. Sedley (1992) 24–5 solves the problem by identifying the surrounding water of fr. 84 with the liquid outside the eye (on the surface of the membranes or the cornea). The membranes are there to protect the internal fire from the external water, corresponding to the winds on the lantern metaphor. The water is not part of the structure of the eye but an element outside the eye. We should therefore not expect Theophrastus to mention the water as part of the structure of the eye.

[75] Theophrastus, *De Sensibus* 8.

[76] Cf. DK (B) 109; Theophrastus, *De Sensibus* 12; Aristotle, *De an.* 1.5 410a27–b2.

[77] Much is obscure and controversial in this account; cf. O'Brien (1970) 163–6 and Sedley (1992).

from *De Generatione et Corruptione* I.8 324b26–32 that Aristotle takes perception to be the most prominent case of alteration that has to be explained by the *poroi* theory or any other theory of alteration. However, Aristotle, unlike Theophrastus, does not criticise the specific role that Empedocles assigns to the *poroi* in vision. Instead, he criticises the role assigned to the *poroi* in alteration in general. This happens in *De Generatione et Corruptione* I.8. Let us analyse this general criticism of the *poroi* in this chapter. We shall then see how the general criticism could be applied to vision by looking at Theophrastus' specific criticism of the *poroi* in vision.

Empedocles' idea is that alteration in general (not just perception) happens by an agent moving through small channels or *poroi* into the patient.[78] The strategy of Aristotle's attack is to argue that the *poroi* are superfluous. His first argument (326b6–21) has the disjunctive form of a dilemma: either the *poroi* are full or they are empty. Whichever way, they are superfluous. If the *poroi* are full, the patient will be affected in the same way as it will be affected if the body of the patient is continuous, for if the passages are already full, they will block the entry of other bodies. So there will be no passage through them.[79]

Let us instead assume that the *poroi* are empty (326b15–20). But, Aristotle goes on to show, if there are *poroi* at all, they will not be empty. So the second disjunct has the same result as the first. The *poroi* must in fact be full and, if so, they are superfluous. If there were *poroi* in a body, Aristotle argues, then they would not provide a vacuum, for there is no reason why they should not already have been filled up by another body. It makes no sense for Empedocles to object that the *poroi* are too small to admit another body, that it is their

---

[78] διὰ τῆς τῶν πόρων κινήσεως, *GC* I.8 326b7. By 'an agent', Aristotle explains (324b27), is meant the last agent in the alteration. It is the agent that directly affects the patient. If the case had been locomotion rather than alteration, we would have been thinking of something like the javelin hitting the target rather than the man who hurls the javelin.

[79] As it stands this argument seems to have little merit. It is of course quite possible that the *poroi* are initially full and that their contents are then displaced by the impact of the agent.

size that ensures that they are empty. For 'vacuum' means, Aristotle says, just 'place for a body'. So calling something empty just means, whatever its size, that it will admit a body and stipulating *poroi* that are especially small and invisible to the eye to explain why they have not already been filled up by other bodies is an irrelevance. The size of the *poroi* has nothing as such to do with their ability or inability to be filled by another body. Insofar as they are empty, they will admit a body. If so, however, there is no reason why the *poroi* should not already have been filled, that is, there is no reason why the first disjunct should not be true, and in that case the *poroi* have again been shown to be superfluous. For these general causal reasons, then, Empedocles has got his *poroi* wrong.

Theophrastus uses parts of Aristotle's criticism of Empedocles' *poroi* in his theory of alteration to criticise their particular role in Empedocles' theory of vision. What Theophrastus has to say is therefore of interest to us. 'Furthermore', he asks, 'are these passages empty or full? If empty, Empedocles is inconsistent; for he says that there is absolutely no void. But if full, creatures would perceive perpetually; for it is evident that a [substance] similar [to another] – to use his own expression – fits [into that other]' (*De Sensibus* 13). Theophrastus' argument against the *poroi* of the eye has a disjunctive structure similar to that of Aristotle's argument. Either the *poroi* are full or they are empty. If they are empty, Empedocles is inconsistent, for he also says there is no void. This part of the argument obviously deviates from Aristotle's argument which relied on the idea that Empedocles might argue that the *poroi* exactly did provide a vacuum.

If, in contrast, the *poroi* are full, so Theophrastus argued, then they fail to explain how perception *arises*. Aristotle in *De Anima* II.5 had argued that the sense-faculty must be understood as a potentiality rather than an actuality to account for the fact that the senses do not perceive themselves. It is only when an external object acts on the sense-faculty that we perceive, where the sense-object actualises the sense-faculty's potentiality to perceive. But the people who say that there is fire, earth and other elements in the sense-organs and that it is by means of these elements that the sense-organs perceive elements like them cannot explain why the presence of these elements in the sense-organs does not give rise to perception without the action of an external object. If we already have fire in our eyes and it is by means of fire that we perceive fire, why do we not always perceive the fire in our eyes?

The problem is one for all theories of perception, such as Empedocles', that hold that we perceive like by like. For if we perceive like by like then we are already before actual perception, as Aristotle would put it, actually like the sense-object. But change happens when something that is potentially like another object is *made* actually like it. So the like-by-like theories fail to explain why it is a change that makes us perceive, why we do not already perceive, given that we already contain the fire, earth, etc., that are sufficient as objects to make us perceive.

Theophrastus also applies Aristotle's criticism of the like-by-like theory to the *poroi* of the eye. If we perceive white objects by means of *poroi* that are made of fire because white is the colour of fire and white objects fit into fiery *poroi*, why do we not always perceive the whiteness of our own fiery *poroi*? There is a strong similarity here between Theophrastus' argument and the first disjunct of Aristotle's argument in *De Generatione et Corruptione* I.8. Aristotle's argument ran: if the *poroi* are full, then the patient will already be affected. Theophrastus' argument runs: if the *poroi* of the eye are full of fire, water, etc., then the eye will already perceive (already be affected by) white, black, etc.

We have seen how Aristotle in general causal terms criticises Empedocles' *poroi* and how this criticism was specifically applied by Theophrastus to the role Empedocles assigned to the *poroi* in vision. The question now is: if this is the Aristotelian approach to *poroi*, how are we to understand *De Sensu* 2 438b14 where Aristotle himself says that the eyes have *poroi*? Are not *poroi* necessarily channels for bodies to travel through? Does Aristotle not therefore imply that the mediation of the sense-quality involves bodies travelling through to the seat of perception?[80] If so, does he not invite the same objections that he himself raised against Empedocles' theory? How can the *poroi* work for Aristotle given his criticism of Empedocles? The answer lies in *De Generatione et Corruptione* I.9, where Aristotle corrects Empedocles' use of the term '*poros*':

> Let us say in what way it belongs to the things that are to generate and to make and to be affected, taking as our principle the principle that has often been mentioned. For if there is, on the one hand, what is potentially such-and-such and, on the other hand, what is actually such-and-such, it is natural for it to be affected, not in this place rather than in that but everywhere, to the extent that it is such-and-such, though to a lesser and greater degree according to whether it is more or less such-and-such. And in this way, one might rather speak of *poroi*, just as continuous veins [φλέβες] of what is specially liable to be affected extend in ore. (326b29–327a1)

The 'rather' reveals that Aristotle is correcting Empedocles' account of the *poroi* that Aristotle criticised in the previous chapter of *De Generatione et Corruptione*. We should not speak of *poroi* as empty passages through which particles travel. We should rather call something a '*poros*' if it is especially likely to be affected by *a quality*, or as he puts it, what is 'such-and-such' [τοιοῦτον].[81] For Aristotle, then, a *poros* is not, as for Empedocles, restricted to, nor does it primarily refer to, something that allows for spatial change. By a '*poros*' we should understand primarily something that allows for qualitative change since it is especially likely to be affected by a quality. In other words, the *poroi* are here picked out by their ability to allow for alteration, qualitative change, rather than locomotion.

We can see, then, how Aristotle can assign a role to the *poroi* in his theory of change. Change comprises generation (change in the category of substance), locomotion (change in position), growth and decay (change in quantity) and alteration (change in quality). Aristotle has shown how we can talk about *poroi* in the case of alteration. We can also now see how Aristotle can assign a role to the *poroi* in his theory of

---

[80] Cf. *De an.* II.7 418b20–6; *Sens.* 6 446b27–447a11.
[81] Cf. Joachim (1922) *ad GC* I.9 326b31.

perception, since perception is a (rather special) kind of alteration. So if it is legitimate to talk about *poroi* in connection with alteration in general, there is no reason why we should not also talk about *poroi* in connection with perception in particular.

It should come as no surprise, then, that Aristotle refers to *poroi* in his own theory of the eye. But we need to ask now (a) what function exactly, if any, the *poroi* have in vision and (b) what part of the eye they are supposed to be. Let us start with (b): what part of the eye are the *poroi*? C. H. Kahn takes the *poroi* to be the optic nerves extending from the back of the eye to the brain.[82] G. E. R. Lloyd is more cautious. He argues that 'the πόροι referred to at 438b14 might be any of a number of different passages, channels or connections behind the eye'.[83] He supplies three possible candidates from *Historia Animalium* 1.16 495a11–18, where Aristotle speaks of three sets of *poroi* leading from the eye to the brain:

From the eye three *poroi* [*sc.* sets of *poroi*] lead to the brain, the largest and the medium-sized to the cerebellum [τὴν παρεγκεφαλίδα], the smallest to the brain itself, the smallest being the ones closest to the nose. The largest run parallel and do not converge, the medium-sized converge (this is clearest in the case of fish), for these are also closer to the brain than the large ones. The smallest are furthest removed from each other and do not converge.

Lloyd argues that, by the medium-sized *poroi*, Aristotle *may* be referring to the optic nerves and their chiasma, although he did know their function as *nerves*.[84] There is no evidence in this passage that Aristotle distinguishes between

---

[82] Kahn (1966) 18–19.

[83] Lloyd (1978) 220.

[84] Lloyd (1975) 175, discussing Alcmaeon's discovery of *poroi* behind the eye, says that

> it seems much more likely that they [*sc.* the *poroi*] were what we call the optic nerves than that they were, for example, the arteries, veins or muscles of the eye. The reason for this is simply that the optic nerves are by far the most obvious and distinct features that an observer would remark behind the eye.

Aristotle in *HA* 1.16 distinguishes the three sets of *poroi* by their size. So perhaps this helps us determine the largest *poroi* as what we would call the optic nerves. However, this does not help us identify which *poroi* Aristotle has in mind in *Sens.* 2, for there is no reason why *he* should have thought the largest *poroi* played a role in vision rather than the others.

the functions of the three sets of *poroi*, let alone that he thinks that any of them function as nerves.[85]

We cannot, then, pick out any of the three sets of *poroi* mentioned in *Historia Animalium* 1.16 as more likely to have a function in perception. As a consequence, when we turn to the *poroi* at *De Sensu* 2 438b14 it *may* be, as Kahn suggests, that Aristotle is thinking of what we would take to be the optic nerves. Equally, it may be that he is thinking of one or both of the other sets of *poroi*, what we would take to be the ophthalmic arteries and veins behind the eye.[86] As Lloyd says, the reference in *De Sensu* 2 to *poroi* is too vague for us be able to identify these *poroi* with any particular set of *poroi*. *Historia Animalium* 1.16 does not help because it does not distinguish between the functions of the various sets of *poroi* that could be referred to in *De Sensu* 2. So we do not know which of them, if any, have a function in vision.

To make matters worse, there are more *poroi* described at *Historia Animalium* IV.8 533a12–15. Aristotle says here that 'there are two strong and sinewy *poroi* extending from the brain, where they are connected with the marrow, alongside [παρά] the seats of the eyes and terminating in the upper projecting teeth'. It is not clear whether these *poroi* are amongst those mentioned in *Historia Animalium* 1.16, for none of those mentioned in 1.16 were said either to connect with the marrow or to run alongside the eyes or to end at the upper teeth. So it may be that, in *Historia Animalium* IV.8, we are dealing with a fourth set of *poroi* in addition to the three mentioned in 1.16.

The *poroi* at *Historia Animalium* IV.8 533a12–15 are brought in to explain why the mole has such peculiar 'eyes'. The process that generates the eyes in other animals is stunted in the mole with the result that the mole's iris, pupil and white part are too small to be serviceable for vision and only discoverable underneath a thick layer of skin.[87] That is why the

---

[85] Lloyd (1978) 220.
[86] Cf. also Solmsen (1961) 558.
[87] *HA* IV.8 533a3–12; cf. *HA* 1.9 491b27–35.

mole is blind. The process [γένεσις] seems to be the one that Aristotle describes in more detail at *De Generatione Animalium* II.6 743b32–744b11. Here the *poroi* have a role in the formation of the eyes. The eyes are produced as the last stage of a process whose first stage produces the brain as a concoction of cold fluid.[88] When the brain has been formed an especially pure part of its fluid is secreted (744a8–9). This fluid travels down through the *poroi* that after the formation of the eyes can be seen to connect the eyes with the membrane around the brain (744a9–12). At the end of the *poroi* the fluid settles and, through a process of further concoction, forms the eyes (744a16–24).

If these are the *poroi* referred to also in *Historia Animalium* IV.8, then we can see their relevance to the explanation of the mole's stunted eyes: Aristotle mentions the *poroi* because they provide the connection between the brain and the eyes that allow the eyes to be formed by passing fluid from the brain to the location of the eyes. It is this process of passing fluid from the brain to the eyes through the *poroi* that has been stunted in the mole.[89] That is why the mole has only imperfectly formed eyes.

These *poroi* thus play a role in the explanation of why the mole, congenitally, cannot see, for the *poroi* are necessary if the eyes are to be formed adequately. So at least we have now discovered *a* function for some of the *poroi* behind the eye. We have been given no reason to think that they should continue to serve any function in vision after they have contributed to the formation of the eyes, however, so there is no reason why the *poroi* involved in the generation of the eyes should be at all relevant to our ability to see now. However, it is our ability to see now that is at issue when we say that people cannot see when their *poroi* are cut off.[90] We have no reason to think

---

[88] This explains also why the eyes are the only other part of the head that is cold and fluid (744a11–13).

[89] Contrast Peck (1970) 61, who brackets this passage on the grounds that it is 'of general reference and has no special application to the mole'.

[90] In Book XXXI of the pseudo-Aristotelian *Problemata*, which deals with 'problems connected with the eyes', the author states at 957b23–32 that those who suffer

that the *poroi* involved in the generation of the eyes should be relevant to our ability to use our eyes in vision now. So we have no reason to think that these *poroi* are any more relevant to the case of the wounded soldiers than any of the other three sets of *poroi* mentioned in *Historia Animalium* 1.16.

So far, then, we have had no luck in determining the exact identity of the *poroi* of *De Sensu* 2 by using the evidence from the biological works. The crucial problem has been that there is no way we can identify different references to *poroi* before we know exactly what the function of the *poroi* referred to is. Perhaps, then, we should consider another approach, such as G. R. T. Ross's interpretation. He makes no use of the *poroi* mentioned in the biological works. His interpretation is based solely on a reading of *De Sensu* 2. Ross argues that the *poroi* mentioned at 438b14 lead from the surface to the inside of the eye and not, like the *poroi* we have considered so far, from behind the eye to somewhere further inside the body. That this is the correct identification of the *poroi*, Ross argues, is shown by the metaphor of the lantern: 'Aristotle is not here referring to such a serious wound as one which would sever the optic

from running eyes can have the veins round their temples cauterised, for in this way the *poroi* through which the liquid flows to the eyes are closed. The cauterising seems to close the *poroi* in such a way that the eyes do not get filled with the water that is secreted. This procedure is connected with the reason why some people are blind from birth. When there is too much water in the head during the development of the embryo, the formation of the eyes is prevented. The eyes are never formed because all the water is gathered in the head (as shown by their abundant hair) rather than descending through the *poroi* to form the eyes. Similarly, eyesight is damaged now if a large quantity of water gathers in the head, in other words, it seems, if there is not a sufficient flow of water from the head to the eyes. The problem here and with the people who are blind from birth seems to be the opposite of the problem of running eyes. In the case of running eyes there is too much water descending through the *poroi* so the *poroi* need closing. In the case of people whose eyesight is damaged the problem is that not enough water is descending through the *poroi* and so the water is accumulated in the head. It is interesting here that the same *poroi* that are involved in the formation of the eye can be involved in the explanation of damaged eyesight. Could an opening of the *poroi* through a blow to the temple, like the one mentioned in *Sens.* 2, cause such a gathering of water in the head and thereby bring about blindness? Does this suggest that the *poroi* Aristotle is talking about in *Sens.* 2 are the same as those posited in *GA* II.6 to explain the generation of the eyes? Unfortunately, the uncertain authorship of the *Problemata* prevents us from exploring these possibilities as genuinely Aristotelian.

nerve but to a more superficial injury to the eye. This is also borne out by the simile which follows. You cut the wick and the flame goes out: and so you destroy the channel communicating the external light to the pupil and sight is destroyed.'[91]

On G. R. T. Ross's interpretation, the light in the lantern metaphor corresponds with the lighted-up *korē* and the wick with the *poroi* which communicate the light from the surface of the eye to the *korē*. Aristotle's point would then be that the severing of the *poroi* from the surface to the inside of the eye shows that there is no vision when there is no light inside the eye. The light is admitted to the inside of the eye through the *poroi*. If one cuts off the *poroi*, the light does not pass through to the inside, so there is no vision. This shows that the seeing part is inside the eye, for if the seeing part was on the surface of the eye, there is no reason why one should not see as long as there is light on the surface of the eye. Therefore the part of the eye which does the seeing has to be located inside rather than on the surface of the eye.

W. D. Ross argues in favour of G. R. T. Ross' interpretation on the grounds 'that plainly Aristotle is not here contrasting the eye with something else [sc. the seat of perception in the heart], but the outer surface of the eye (ἐσχάτου τοῦ ὄμματος) with its interior (τὸ ἐντὸς τοῦ ὄμματος). It is true that Aristotle makes the heart the seat of κοινὴ αἴσθησις (*De Juv.* [= *DI*] 469a5–12) but he is not speaking of that here, but of the five senses.'[92]

W. D. Ross is not being quite fair here, however, for in an important passage at *De Partibus Animalium* II.10 656a27–657a12[93] Aristotle says that the area around the heart is the seat of perception *tout court*, not just perception of the common sensibles. The passage as a whole argues that it is the heart rather than the brain that is responsible for all perception. People only think it is the brain because they can see no other reason why some of the senses should be located in the

---

[91] G. R. T. Ross (1906) 143.
[92] W. D. Ross (1955) 192, *ad* 438b10.
[93] A passage Ross must have had before him, for he quotes 656b16 immediately afterwards in connection with the *poroi*.

head.[94] Aristotle starts by referring us back to *De Sensu* where,

it was determined that the principle [ἀρχή] of the senses is the area around the heart and why, on the one hand [μέν], two of the senses, the senses of tangibles and flavours, are clearly connected with the heart, and, on the other hand [δέ], of the other three the sense of smell is in the middle, and hearing and sight primarily in the head because of the nature of their sense-organs, and of these sight is in all animals [located in the heart].[95]

The reason why touch and taste clearly depend on the heart is given by the context. Only if the organ of these senses were in the head would there be reason to think that touch and taste took place in the brain rather than in the heart. So the problem is not with touch and taste but with the other three senses whose organs, mostly or always, are located in the head. What Aristotle has to explain is why these three senses are mostly or always located in the head without saying that the brain is the seat of perception. Aristotle first mentions animals that hear and smell even though they apparently have no sense-organs of hearing or smell in the head (656a35–7). This shows that one does not need a sense-organ in the head in order to hear and smell. The implication is that it is possible that the seat of hearing and smelling is always in the heart, even in animals that do have sense-organs in their heads.[96]

As far as sight is concerned (656a37–b6), Aristotle explains that animals that see always have eyes in the head. There are two reasons for this: because the eyes are of the same cold and wet material as the brain and because the cold area around the brain is more conducive to the more accurate perception

---

[94] *PA* II.10 656a23–7; cf. *Juv.* 3 469a22–3: 'some of the senses are in the head, which is also why some people think that the animals perceive because of the brain'.

[95] *PA* II.10 656a27–33:

ὅτι μὲν οὖν ἀρχὴ τῶν αἰσθήσεών ἐστιν ὁ περὶ τὴν καρδίαν τόπος, διώρισται πρότερον ἐν τοῖς περὶ αἰσθήσεως, καὶ διότι αἱ μὲν δύο φανερῶς ἠρτημέναι πρὸς τὴν καρδίαν εἰσίν, ἥ τε τῶν ἁπτῶν καὶ ἡ τῶν χυμῶν, τῶν δὲ τριῶν ἡ μὲν τῆς ὀσφρήσεως μέση, ἀκοὴ δὲ καὶ ὄψις μάλιστ' ἐν τῇ κεφαλῇ διὰ τὴν τῶν αἰσθη-τηρίων φύσιν εἰσί, καὶ τούτων ἡ ὄψις πᾶσιν, κτλ.

[96] Cf. *Juv.* 3 469a13–14: 'we see that two of the senses, taste and touch, clearly extend to the heart: so it is necessary that the others also do so'; cf. Lloyd (1978) 222.

performed by sight. Both reasons explain why the eyes should always be near the brain. Neither says anything about the head being the area in which perception naturally takes place and, most importantly for Aristotle's argument, neither says that the eyes are located near the brain because this is the seat of perception. The eyes are located in the head not because the brain is the seat of perception but, as Aristotle puts it, 'because of the composition of their sense-organs' (656a33).

Aristotle goes on in the next lines (656b13–657a12) to give specific reasons why also the sense-organs of hearing and smell should be located in the head. For example, the head has a space called the 'vacuum' (τὸ κενόν) which is full of air. Since the organ of hearing is composed of air, it is natural that this organ should be in the head. This is shown also by the fact that there are *poroi* connecting the ears with the back of the head, where, presumably, the vacuum is located. Similarly, as we have seen, it is suitable that the eyes are in the head because the eyes are made of the same material as the brain. Again this is shown by the fact that there are *poroi* connecting the eyes with the brain. The *poroi* in both cases serve as testimony to a compositional affinity.

In short, there are reasons why each of the sense-organs that are located in the head should be located there. None of them says that the sense-organ is located in the head because the brain is the seat of perception. We have shown therefore that the best reason for saying that the seat of perception is the brain, namely, that some of the sense-organs are located in the head, is in fact not a reason for saying that the seat of perception is the brain. So there is no longer any good reason for preferring the brain as the seat of perception. Since the only acknowledged alternative to the brain is the heart, this suggests the heart rather than the brain is the seat of all perception.

The passage shows that W. D. Ross cannot say that Aristotle must be referring to a contrast between the surface of the eye and the inside of the eye (rather than the heart) *because* Aristotle is speaking of the five (special) senses and not the common sense for, as we have just seen, even where Aristotle is talking about all perception, including the perception of the proper objects of the five senses (and therefore not just about perception of the common sensibles),[97] he claims that the seat of perception is in the heart rather than in the proper sense-organs.

However, G. R. T. Ross and W. D. Ross had another argument in support of their claim that the *poroi* lay between the surface and the inside of the eye. They mentioned the contrast between the outer surface of the eye (ἐσχάτου τοῦ ὄμματος) and its interior (τὸ ἐντὸς τοῦ ὄμματος). Does this not show that Aristotle is contrasting the surface of the eye with the seeing part inside the eye? If so, must not the *poroi* lie in between the surface and the inside of the eye? For if the *poroi* lay behind the eye, their severing would not in itself provide a reason for the interruption of vision. As long as there was light in the transparent inside the eye, the sense-quality could be received and seen by the eye. Whatever happens further inside the body need not be relevant to vision. In other words, there is no reason why *poroi* behind the eye should be relevant to vision for vision takes place when the sense-quality is received by the transparent inside the eye.[98]

---

[97] For the distinction between special and common sensibles, cf. *De an.* II.6 418a12–25, III.1 425a14–30.

[98] It might also seem that Aristotle's reference to the blinding of soldiers who receive a blow across their temple should make us decide in favour of locating the *poroi* behind the eye. If you visualise a blow across the temple, the blow must surely cut behind the eye. Whichever features the blow severs must therefore lie behind the eye. However, the evidence is not so conclusive. A blow to the temple may well cut across the eye. It all depends on the angle of the blow, about which we are told nothing. Nor is there any reason to think that Aristotle himself necessarily knew the precise nature of the injury, for there is no need to suppose that he himself inspected such injuries. Case histories that tell of the blinding effect of head wounds occur in the Hippocratic corpus; cf. *On Wounds in the Head* 14.38ff.; *Epidemics* 7.32. It is possible that Aristotle obtained his evidence second-hand from sources such as the Hippocratic and adapted it to his own ends. If so, Aristotle need not himself have a had a very clear idea as to the exact nature of the injury mentioned in his sources. What is important is that *he* thought it provided evidence in favour of the point that the inside of the eye is transparent. For the influence of the Hippocratic writings on Aristotle's biology, cf. Byl (1977) 313–26.

To meet the challenge we need to look more carefully at the text:

> The soul or the perceptive part of the soul is not at the surface of the eye, but it is clear that it is inside. That is why it is necessary that the inside of the eye is transparent and receptive to light. And this is clear also from what actually happens. For to those who have been struck on the temple in battle and who have thereby had the *poroi* of the eye severed [ἀποτμηθῆναι] it has seemed dark just as if a lamp [λύχνου] had been extinguished. For the transparent, what is called the *korē*, has been cut off [ἀποτμηθῆναι], like a lantern [λαμπτῆρά].[99] (*Sens.* 2 438b8–16)

In the context it may initially look more likely that Aristotle is talking about the transparent *korē* as the place of the perceptive soul, that is the place where the sense-faculty of sight is located. As W. D. Ross says, Aristotle is interested in the five senses, and particularly in the composition of their sense-organs. In this context, Aristotle wants to show that the eye is composed of water because water is transparent. He also wants to show that this transparent seeing part is situated inside *the eye* (τὸ ἐντὸς τοῦ ὄμματος, *Sens.* 2 438b11), not on the surface of the eye as the reflection theorists say. Also, the story I told suggested that if the eye jelly goes dark when you cut off the *poroi*, then we experience darkness because the seeing part in us is no longer in a state in which it can be affected by sense-qualities. Since it is the eye jelly that is cut off surely that shows that the eye jelly is the seeing part.

Aristotle appears to say first that the perceptible soul is inside and then that the perceptible soul is, specifically, inside the eye. For 'the inside of the eye' (τὸ ἐντὸς τοῦ ὄμματος) looks like an expansion of what was said in the previous line, namely, that 'it is clear that the perceptive part is inside' (ἀλλὰ δῆλον ὅτι ἐντός). However, this is not the only way to read the

---

[99] I quote the Greek of W. D. Ross's edition again:

οὐ γὰρ ἐπὶ ἐσχάτου τοῦ ὄμματος ἡ ψυχὴ ἢ τῆς ψυχῆς τὸ αἰσθητικόν ἐστιν, ἀλλὰ δῆλον ὅτι ἐντός· διόπερ ἀνάγκη διαφανὲς εἶναι καὶ δεκτικὸν φωτὸς τὸ ἐντὸς τοῦ ὄμματος. καὶ τοῦτο καὶ ἐπὶ τῶν συμβαινόντων δῆλον· ἤδη γάρ τισι πληγεῖσιν ἐν πολέμῳ παρὰ τὸν κρόταφον οὕτως ὥστ' ἀποτμηθῆναι τοὺς πόρους τοῦ ὄμματος ἔδοξε γενέσθαι σκότος ὥσπερ λύχνου ἀποσβεσθέντος, διὰ τὸ οἷον λαμπτῆρά τινα ἀποτμηθῆναι τὸ διαφανές, τὴν καλουμένην κόρην.

text. Aristotle can simply be saying that the perceptible soul is inside the perceiver and that is why the inside of the eye must be transparent and receptive of light. In other words, the passage states two claims: (1) 'the perceptive part or the soul is not at the surface of the eye but clearly inside' (438b8–10: οὐ γὰρ ... ἐντός) and (2) 'therefore it is necessary that the eye be transparent, that is that the inside of the eye be receptive of light' (438b10–11: διόπερ ... ὄμματος). To understand how (2) follows from (1) we need not identify the seeing part of the soul with the inside of the eye. It is open to us to say that the inside of the eye must be transparent because otherwise the seeing part of the soul further inside cannot see.[100]

This suggests again that the role of the transparent inside the eye is not to perceive the sense-quality but rather to mediate the sense-quality to the seeing part further inside the perceiver. This suggestion should be understood in relation to the preceding lines, 438b6–7, where Aristotle says that just as there is no vision if there is no light outside, so there is no vision if there is no light inside the eye. If the inside of the eye is not actually transparent, then that has the same effect as switching off the light outside you. The light outside is necessary as a medium. So saying that there is no vision if there is no light inside the eye, just as there is no vision if there is no light outside, suggests that the light inside the eye is also required as a medium. Both when the light outside goes out and when the light inside the eye goes out the problem is that the medium is not working. Just as actual transparency is a necessary medium outside the perceiver, so it is inside the perceiver. The reason why the inside of the eye has to be actually transparent is, then, that there must be light inside the perceiver to mediate the sense-quality, just as there must be light outside. If so, the role of the transparent inside the eye is to mediate the sense-quality to a perceiving part further inside the perceiver.

---

[100] Cf. *De an.* II.11 423b22–3: ἦ καὶ δῆλον ὅτι ἐντὸς τὸ τοῦ ἁπτοῦ αἰσθητικόν. Though Aristotle here, as at *Sens.* 2 438b10, does not make it explicit what he means by ἐντός, it is clear that he must be referring to the area around the heart.

Lloyd's interpretation, then, stands strengthened by the attack, for if the transparent inside the eye serves as an internal medium of the sense-quality then the sense-quality will not be perceived simply by being transmitted to the inside of the eye. The sense-quality will have to be transmitted in turn from the inside of the eye to the perceiving part further inside the perceiver. Connectives called *poroi* might be required for this transmission to take place. If so, vision will be interrupted when these *poroi* are severed.

But is this conclusion compatible with the example of the wounded soldiers? Aristotle said that when 'the *poroi* of their eyes are cut off,[101] it appears dark just as when a light has been extinguished because the transparent, the eye jelly, which is a sort of lamp, has been cut off' (438b13–16). The metaphor suggests that when the *poroi* are cut off the eye jelly is cut off from what provides it with light. As G. R. T. Ross argued, it therefore suggests that the *poroi* transmit light from the source of light outside the eye to the inside of the eye. To do this the *poroi* would have to be in between the outside and the inside of the eye, for surely the light is not provided through the *poroi* to the eye jelly from further within the perceiver? If the *poroi* do not just mediate the sense-quality to the perceiving part but also provide the inside of the eye with light, then surely the *poroi* have to connect the inside of the eye to the outside of the eye?

In response to this objection, let us start by noticing that there is something curious about the idea that *poroi* should be required to transmit light from the surface to the inside of the eye as what is needed for the light to shine through to the inside of the eye is simply that the eye be transparent at its surface. *De Generatione Animalium* v.1 780a27–36 first suggests that what is required for the change from the sense-quality to go straight through to the *korē* is for skin at the

---

[101] Or, 'cut out', if we read ἐκτμηθῆναι with some manuscripts rather than ἀποτμηθῆναι; cf. W. D. Ross (1955) critical apparatus *ad* 438b13. There is reason, however, to prefer ἀποτμηθῆναι, for in Aristotle ἐκτέμνειν usually either means very specifically to castrate or it has a mathematical sense. ἀποτέμνειν, on the other hand, is used in general for cutting off hair or parts of the body; cf. Bonitz (1870) *s.v.* with examples.

surface of the eye to be transparent. There is no suggestion that *poroi* are required for the colour to go through to the *korē*. Aristotle next compares the eye with a lantern (780a35). He says that the skin of the eye has to be transparent for the colour to pass through to the *korē* just as the skin of a lantern has to be transparent for the light to shine through the lantern. The question for G. R. T. Ross to answer is then: why should there be *poroi* for the light to pass through to the *korē*, when *poroi* are not required for colours to pass through and when Aristotle's analogy with the lantern strongly suggests that what is required both for light and colours to pass through is simply transparency?

Second, there is a problem with understanding what to be 'cut off' [ἀποτμηθῆναι, *Sens.* 2 438b15; cf. ἀποτμηθῆναι, 438b13] means in this passage. When Aristotle says that the *poroi* are 'cut off' it is no more problematic than if he were to say that any other part of the body was cut off. The *poroi* are physically severed. But what does it mean for a lantern 'to be severed' or 'cut off'? G. R. T. Ross suggested that the lantern 'is cut off' when its wick is cut off and the light inside is extinguished. In other words, the lantern is cut off just insofar as its wick is cut off. Hett, in contrast, translates λαμπτῆρά at *De Sensu* 2 438b15 as 'lamp screen', thereby implying that the lantern is severed when its screens are cut off.[102] Hett's translation may be influenced by Empedocles' use of the lantern metaphor, for Empedocles said that the lantern was fitted with screens to protect the light inside from the winds outside. So if the light inside was extinguished one might think that it was because the protection of the screens had gone. The lantern is cut off, then, on Hett's interpretation insofar as its screens are cut off. Neither Hett nor G. R. T. Ross, however, gives any specific sense to what it means for the whole lantern 'to be cut off'. For both scholars a lantern is cut off only in the extended sense of one of its parts being cut off: the lantern is cut off insofar as either its wick (G. R. T. Ross) or its screens (Hett) are cut off. Can we do better?

---

[102] Hett (1957).

I suggest that we can. The answer lies again in observing the way in which Aristotle appropriates the lantern metaphor at 438b15–16. Aristotle appropriates the lantern metaphor from Empedocles, but he uses it to sum up both Empedocles' theory of vision and Plato's in the *Timaeus*. This is because Aristotle takes Empedocles' and Plato's theory to be the same.[103] We need to keep this point in mind, for I want to argue that the *Timaeus* contains the clue to our problem. Timaeus explained why we do not see at night as follows. At night there is no light outside the eye, so when the ray tries to exit the eye it meets with no kindred fire. Timaeus says:

> when the kindred fire disappears into the night, it [sc. the fire trying to exit the eye] is cut off [ἀποτέτμηται]. For being no longer akin to the surrounding air, inasmuch as the air no longer has fire, it [the fire from within] when going out to something dissimilar is changed and extinguished [κατασβέννυται]. (*Ti.* 45d3–6)

When this happens there is no vision, we feel tired and close our eyes. Our eyelids shut up (καθείργνυσι, *Ti.* 45e1) the power of the fire within, which makes us calm (*Ti.* 45d6–e3).

What is meant by saying that the fire is extinguished when it meets with darkness is not that the fire inside the eye is extinguished, for the fire inside the eye continues to exist inside the eye, shut up and, as Timaeus says, protected by the eyelids. Being cut off means, rather, that the fire inside the eye has been shut off from the kindred fire outside the eye in such a way that the fire inside the eye cannot leave the eye. Darkness has come between the eye's fire and its kindred outside. It is therefore no longer possible for the two to merge and form the single, continuous body of fire that is required for vision. The eye's fire is extinguished when trying to leave the eye because it meets with what is opposite, darkness. But the fire is preserved inside the eye. This is what it means to say that the fire is cut off (ἀποτέτμηται). When the fire is cut off in this sense a visual ray cannot be formed and there can be no

---

[103] Cf. *Sens.* 2 437b10–14: ἐπεὶ εἴ γε πῦρ ἦν [sc. ὁ ὀφθαλμός], καθάπερ Ἐμπεδοκλῆς φησὶ καὶ ἐν τῷ Τιμαίῳ γέγραπται, καὶ συνέβαινε τὸ ὁρᾶν ἐξιόντος ὥσπερ ἐκ λαμπτῆρος τοῦ φωτός, διὰ τί οὐ καὶ ἐν τῷ σκότει ἑώρα ἂν ἡ ὄψις;

vision. If we again compare the eye to the lantern, the lantern is cut off in that it is prevented from shining. It no longer illuminates its surroundings. So we can no longer see.

If we keep in mind this sense of 'to be cut off' in the *Timaeus and* the changes that Aristotle makes to the lantern metaphor, we can deduce what Aristotle means by saying that the lantern is cut off in *De Sensu* 2. The lantern in Aristotle is the transparent *korē*. Aristotle compares the *korē* to a lantern because it enables us to see by having light in it. To that extent his use of the lantern metaphor is similar to that of Empedocles. But for Aristotle the *korē* does not enable us to see by illuminating its surroundings. It enables us to see because light is actually transparent and it is only what is actually transparent that can be changed by colour. We have also seen that for Aristotle light is a state and not a body that travels through space. For Aristotle cutting off the *korē* at *De Sensu* 2 438b15–16 can therefore no longer mean preventing fire inside the eye from travelling outside the eye, as it did in the *Timaeus*. Instead, what it must mean is preventing the *korē* from being actually transparent, for this is the state that for Aristotle qualifies the *korē* to be compared with a lantern. Being actually transparent corresponds, in Aristotle's use of the metaphor, with illuminating the surroundings, in the Empedocles/Timaeus account.

Now on the interpretation I wish to defend, the *korē* must be transparent not just for itself to be changed by the sense-quality but also, in turn, to relay this change to the seat of perception located in the area of the heart. For when our *korē* is changed by the sense-quality then that does not in itself make us perceive colour. No vision will take place until the change has been received by the seat of perception. The role of the *korē*, then, is not just to be changed by the colour. It is more specifically to be changed by the colour and convey the change to the seat of perception. To do so, the *korē* must be transparent in exactly the same way as the external medium, for the external medium too is transparent in order not only that it may be changed by the colour but also that it may mediate the colour to the eye. The medium and the *korē* have the function of mediating colour and are both transparent for that reason.

If we keep the point in mind that the *korē* is actually transparent so as to mediate the sense-impression, we can understand the way in which the *korē* is said to be cut off when the *poroi* are severed. Cutting off the transparent means destroying its actual transparency insofar as it prevents you from seeing through it. Compare the case of a telescope. If the lenses at both ends are uncovered, you can see through a telescope but if you put a cap on the eyepiece you can no longer look through the telescope. By putting the cap on, you do not prevent the light from entering the telescope at the other end: light can still enter, as you find out if you look into the telescope at the uncovered end. However, you do ensure that there is no light, that is no actual transparency, *all the way* through the telescope. Because there is no longer continuous light or actual transparency all the way through the telescope, it ceases to be useful as a medium through which you can see other objects.

Similarly, when you cut off the *poroi* from the transparent *korē*, you need not prevent the light from entering the *korē* from the outside. However, you are disrupting the required continuity of transparency from the external medium to the central seat of perception through the *korē*, thereby preventing the perceiver from seeing through it. I suggest that this is the way the lantern metaphor should be taken at *De Sensu* 2 438b15–16. The *korē* is compared to a lantern insofar as it is actually transparent, as Aristotle's theory of vision understands this phrase. There may still be light in the *korē* if you cut it off from the *poroi*, but it no longer amounts to continuous actual transparency all the way to the central seat of perception.

To sum up the argument so far. Aristotle, like Empedocles, compares the *korē* with a lantern because he thinks that the *korē* has to have light in it for vision to take place. However, Aristotle and Empedocles/Timaeus have different ways of construing the claim that the *korē* must contain light. For

Empedocles/Timaeus the *korē* must have light in it because the light illuminates the surroundings of the eye. In contrast, Aristotle says that the *korē* must have light in it because actual transparency implies light. It must be actually transparent in order to mediate the colour to the perceiving part further inside. In the *Timaeus*, cutting off the light meant preventing it from illuminating its surroundings. For Aristotle, since illumination was not the reason why the *korē* had to have light in it, cutting off the light had to mean something else. I suggested that it meant preventing the *korē* from being transparent, the quality that makes Aristotle compare the *korē* with a lantern, by cutting it off from the *poroi* that connect it to the seat of perception, for the *korē* has to mediate the sense-quality to the seat of perception through the *poroi* before you can see the sense-quality.

The difference between Aristotle's and Timaeus' ways of construing the notion of cutting off the *korē* relates to the different directions of causation in Empedocles/Timaeus' and Aristotle's theories of vision. In the previous section I argued that the views of Empedocles/Timaeus and of Aristotle on the function of the eye's membrane reflected how Aristotle saw the causal direction of perception as different from that of Empedocles. For Empedocles, vision happened when sight, that is the visual ray, affected the sense-objects. For Aristotle, vision happened when the sense-object affected sight, that is the sense-faculty, in a certain way. Correspondingly, the membrane in Empedocles let the visual ray out of the eye, whereas the membrane in Aristotle let the change from the sense-object into the eye. We can usefully see the difference between the notion of cutting off the visual ray in Empedocles/ Timaeus and Aristotle in the same terms. Because the direction of causation in Empedocles/Timaeus goes from eye to sense-object the visual ray has to be cut off in the direction of the sense-object, namely, at the surface of the *korē*. However, because the direction of causation in Aristotle goes from sense-object to the inner sense-faculty, which as I have argued we should at *De Sensu* 2 438b8–10 take to be the central sense-faculty, the cut-off point for the *korē* lies in the direction of the central sense-faculty. That is to say, the cut-off point lies behind the *korē*.

One final disambiguation is required to understand the passage. Aristotle says that when the transparent is cut off it is as if a light has been extinguished. However, it is important to notice that Aristotle makes two different comparisons when he says first that 'it seems to have become dark to those whose *poroi* have been severed' (438b14–15) and then that this is because the transparent, the so-called *korē*, like a lantern has been cut off (438b15–16). We should be careful not to run the two comparisons together. The first comparison illustrates how the soldiers experience having their *poroi* severed. They experience darkness just as if the lights had been extinguished in a room. The second comparison shows how, through the severing of the *poroi*, the transparent has been cut off. It implies, I have argued, that the transparent has been cut off from the *poroi* that it has to be in contact with if it is to establish the continuity of transparency between the external medium and the central sense-faculty required for vision.

G. R. T. Ross runs the two comparisons together, for he says that the light in the *korē* is extinguished when the *poroi* are cut off. But, as the analogy with the telescope showed, to say that the *korē* has been cut off does not mean that the light in it has been extinguished. This is clear also from the *Timaeus* where it is made clear that when the fire is extinguished it is extinguished outside the eye while the fire inside the eye is preserved. Similarly, there is no need to say that the light in the *korē* is extinguished when it is cut off. What we should say is that the *korē* is prevented from doing what in Aristotle's theory corresponds to lighting up the outside, that is, mediating the sense-quality to the perceiving part further inside the perceiver. This is what happens when the *poroi* are severed, which is why the soldiers experience darkness *as if* a light had been extinguished.[104]

---

[104] Cf. Alexander, *in de Sensu* 36.7–37.5. Alexander starts by interpreting the part that Aristotle says is not at the surface of the eye as the part that perceives the

The answer to the puzzle of the *poroi* is therefore not as G. R. T. Ross argues to posit *poroi* in between the surface and the inside of the eye. Instead, the answer is to take the *poroi* in *De Sensu* 2 to be features that mediate the sense-quality from the transparent *korē* to the heart. Aristotle's discussion of *poroi* in *De Generatione et Corruptione* I.8 shows that *poroi* should, if at all, be spoken of as features especially likely to be affected by a quality. Such features make good media of perception, for mediation is a case of being affected by a quality, namely, the sense-quality, and in turn affecting something else with that quality. Given this understanding of the *poroi* as good media of sense-qualities, all that is required for Aristotle is to establish that the *korē* is continuous with the seat of perception in the heart. He does so at at *De Generatione Animalium* II.6 743b35–744a5:

The reason[105] is that the sense-organ of the eyes is, just as the other sense-organs,[106] set upon *poroi:* but the organ of touch and taste is simply the body or some part of the animal's body. Smell and hearing are *poroi* connecting with the outer air and full of connate *pneuma*, and ending in the veins [φλέβια] from the heart that extend around the brain.

This passage may suggest that *pneuma* is the content of all the *poroi* that extend from the sense-organs and that it is in

proper objects of all the sense-faculties (*Sens.* 2 438b8). He then (36.22–37.5) argues that the reason why the soldiers experience darkness when their *poroi* have been severed is that

> the *korē* has been cut off from the transparent behind the *korē*, the *korē* being like a lantern that spreads light, through which all of what is inside up to the faculty of vision is lit up by the light outside. The blow separates the continuity of light and prevents it [sc. the inside all the way to the visual principle] from being lit up just as if the light in it had been extinguished. But if we do not see with the extremity of the eye it is also necessary that the inside is transparent all the way to the perceiving soul.

Alexander's interpretation agrees with mine on two points: (a) it takes the *korē* as part of a continuous medium extending to the seat of all perception; and (b) it makes the point that the *korē* is a lantern insofar as it establishes transparency in the direction of the seat of perception rather than in the direction of what lies outside the perceiver.

[105] Aristotle is explaining why the eyes are large at the beginning of the animal's formation but then shrink. The reason why the *poroi* explain this phenomenon is that the *poroi* are a key element in the process that explains the formation of the eyes, as we are about to be told at *GA* II.6 744a8–b11; cf. above pp. 75–6.

[106] Platt finds ὥσπερ καὶ τὰ ἄλλα αἰσθητήρια suspect; cf. Peck (1953) 224.

virtue of containing *pneuma* that the *poroi* are able to mediate sense-qualities to the heart. The subject of *pneuma* is a highly complex one. It can, if at all, only be tackled through an analysis of its role in Aristotle's physiology as a whole. I shall not attempt such an analysis.[107] There is, however, a potential challenger to *pneuma*, for a passage in *De Insomniis* says that the blood plays a role in mediating sense-impressions from the sense-organs to the central sense-faculty *in dreams*.[108] This passage might be taken to suggest that it is generally the blood in the blood vessels (φλέβες, φλέβια) that mediates in perception between the sense-organs and the central sense-faculty. However, the concern in *De Insomniis* is with how the movement in the blood may *distort* the sense-images. There is no need to assume on that basis that the blood, or movements in it, play a role in the mediation of normal perception. On the contrary, Aristotle's claims that the blood has no perceptive power and that it is no part of the animal body seem to rule out any role for the blood in perception proper.[109]

There is thus no *clear* statement in Aristotle as to the contents of the passages that mediate in perception. However, we can see how he might think that he need not commit himself as to the exact contents of the *poroi* if he (a) takes the function of *poroi* in perception to be one of being especially affected by the sense-qualities and therefore an appropriate medium of the sense-quality and (b) finds sufficient evidence for there being *poroi* with this function of mediating between the sense-organs and the heart from the fact that he observes features that connect the sense-organs with the heart.[110] To

---

[107] Cf. Peck (1953), 'Appendix B', 578–93. For the (possible) role of *pneuma* in perception as a medium between the sense-organs and the seat of perception in the heart, cf. Beare (1906) 334; Solmsen (1961) 172–8; Verbeke (1978) 197–9; Lloyd (1978) 222–3; Freudenthal (1995) 130–4.

[108] Cf. *DI* 3 461b11–30.

[109] Cf. *PA* II.10 656a21–2, b19–22; III.4 666a17–18. (Contrast the way in which the flesh mediates tangible qualities; cf. *PA* II.3 650b2–8.)

[110] *GC* I.9 326b34–327a1 quoted above (p. 73) said that, 'in this way, one might rather speak of *poroi*, just as continuous veins [φλέβες] of what is specially liable to be affected extend in ore'. The illustration of *poroi* with continuous veins (φλέβες) that are specially liable to be affected suggests that there need be no functional

establish that sense-qualities are mediated in perception from the sense-organs to the heart, it is enough for him to establish that there are features that connect the sense-organs with the heart and to identify these features as having the function of *poroi* as he understands it. So once features connecting the sense-organs to the heart have been identified as *poroi*, there is no need to inquire further into their exact contents in order to show that the sense-qualities can be mediated by them to the heart, for he understands a *poros* as something that has mediating qualities. The point is again that Aristotle's functional interest in the sense-organs motivates an inquiry into the material composition only to the extent that it shows the necessary material conditions of perception to obtain but no further.

On this interpretation of *poroi*, Aristotle finds his place in a tradition of thinking about *poroi* and veins as mediating in perception between the sense-organs and the seat of perception. Alcmaeon's *poroi* went from the eyes to the brain, which he took to be the seat of perception. Alcmaeon seems also to have held that our perception is at least impaired if the *poroi* are blocked. This suggests that the *poroi* for him had the function of mediating between the senses and the brain in perception. Similarly, in Diogenes of Apollonia, according to Solmsen, 'the transmission of perception from the nostrils and the ears to the brain materialises by way of the veins, and there is room for the impression that veins in the eye had a similar function'.[111] But as we have seen, Aristotle's *poroi* are also importantly different from this tradition. For Aristotle, the seat of perception is the heart and not the brain, so the *poroi* have their destination not in the brain but in the heart, and perception involves qualitative change and no spatial change. So the *poroi* do not function as conduits that allow particles to travel from the sense-organs to the seat of perception. They function instead as a continuous medium be-

---

distinction between the *poroi* that connect the eyes with the brain and the veins (φλέβια) just because the ones are called '*poroi*' and the others 'veins'.

[111] Solmsen (1961) 540.

tween the sense-organs and the seat of perception that allows the sense-quality that affects the sense-organ also to affect the seat of perception.

As Lloyd argues, the precise identity and location of the *poroi* in *De Sensu* 2 must remain vague. The *poroi* could be any of the *poroi* mentioned in connection with the eye in the biological works. Lloyd argues that the vagueness of the reference to the *poroi* is significant because it shows that Aristotle does not specify his physiological evidence beyond what is required to make a particular point: 'once he has given evidence, or what he believes to be evidence, for his immediate point – that the faculty of sensation cannot be located at the outer extremity of the eye – we hear no more of the πόροι'.[112]

However, we can now see Aristotle's vagueness about the *poroi* as more philosophically pointed. The vagueness shows that his interest in the *poroi* is restricted to pointing to the need for a mediating feature between the *korē* and the seat of perception around the heart. The severing of the *poroi* provides evidence of the need for mediating features and it therefore furthers the argument that the *korē* must, in Aristotle's sense, be actually transparent. To the extent that the identity of the *poroi* is determinable, it is so only within Aristotle's theories of vision and causation. The *poroi*, like the terms that we have so far seen him use to describe the eye, have been fixed by ascribing a function to them within his theory of vision. They have not been fixed by pointing to a specific part that we can clearly identify by observation, whether or not we share that theory.

We have seen how Aristotle establishes the reference of these terms within his own theory of vision at the same time as he criticises the theories of vision of his predecessors, particularly those of Democritus, Empedocles and Plato. He appropriates his predecessors' descriptions of the eye by redefining them within his own theory of vision. As we saw, Aristotle receives from Democritus the view that the eye is composed of water. But he was less interested in the fact that the eye is

---

[112] Lloyd (1978) 220.

composed of water than in the question of what attribute of water it was that makes water useful for vision. His answer is that the attribute is transparency and he therefore insists against Democritus that we should refer to the matter of the eye as water *qua* transparent. The superficial agreement between Democritus and Aristotle on the watery composition of the eye is thus dwarfed by the disagreement on the function of this water. It is this disagreement that is really important to Aristotle because his own interest in the matter of the eye is functional. Similarly, his discussion of Empedocles and Plato allowed Aristotle not only to appropriate the *korē* and the membranes by redefining their function in vision within his own theory but also to refute the emission theory of vision. When Aristotle has ascribed a different function to the parts of the eye from that of his opponents, he feels free to use the same physiological description of the eye as his opponents without implying that he has the same theory of the eye. This is as we would expect if Aristotle's theory of the sense-organs is functional or formal all the way down. For Aristotle, then, there is no point at which different theories of the sense-organs meet up at the level of material description *once* different functions have been ascribed to the sense-organs. Therefore the appropriation of terms that Democritus, Empedocles and Plato used to describe the eye requires no further justification for Aristotle and he gives none.

11. Eye colour

I conclude the discussion of the eye by considering eye colour. Besides those mentioned, the eye has two further features: what is called 'the black' or 'the dark' (τὸ μέλαν), corresponding to what we would call the iris, and the white, that is the white surrounding the iris.[113] The white is fat and oily in sanguineous animals. It serves the purpose of preventing the transparent liquid in the eye from freezing.[114]

---

[113] *Sens.* 2 437b1; *HA* 1.9 491b21; cf. Lloyd (1978) 218 and 231, n. 13.
[114] *Sens.* 2 438a20–3.

By τὸ μέλαν we are probably to understand the dark rather than simply the black. For in *Historia Animalium* I.10 492a2–3, Aristotle says that τὸ μέλαν, so called, in some animals indeed is μέλαν, whereas in other animals, most notably man, it can also be blue, grey or yellow/green.[115] If brown eyes are not to be excluded here, the contrast must be between dark-eyed animals, whose eyes may be brown or black, and light-eyed animals, whose eyes are blue, grey or yellow/green.

Historia Animalium I.10 makes it clear that when Aristotle talks about eye colour he, like us, means the colour of the iris, for he says that the iris has different colours in different species of animal, whereas it is only in human beings that eye colour differs from individual to individual. The colour of the eye is here identified with the colour of the iris.

Now water is transparent, a quality which Aristotle in *De Anima* II.7 418b28 says is colourless. So how can the eye be coloured? If the transparent is colourless, and the whole point about the eye is that it should be made of water because water is transparent, should the eyes not be colourless too?

To answer the question we need to turn to Aristotle's general account of colour in *De Sensu* 3 where he says that water has a colour. As evidence, he points to the sheen (αὐγή) that both water and air have. He says that the sheen is a quality like colour (439b1–3). The colour of the water appears at its surface. The colour, indeed, of all bodies, both those that by nature have a limit of their own and those, such as water, that do not, appears only on the body's surface. Aristotle defines colour as a *limit*. He says that colour is 'the limit (πέρας) of the transparent in a body when the body is limited (ὡρισμένῳ) (439b11–12). Since the surface is the limit of the body, this definition explains why colour appears only at the surface of bodies.

However, there is a difference between the colour of those bodies that by nature have their own limit and the colour of

---

[115] Literally, 'goat-eyed', αἰγωπόν. Peck (1965), vol. I, 41, n. (c), suggests 'greenish' as an alternative translation; cf. also *GA* v.1 779a27–b1.

those bodies which have no such limit by nature, that is those
bodies which, when they are limited, have their limit imposed
on them by another body. The difference is that the colour of
the naturally unlimited bodies is changeable, whereas the colour of the limited bodies is fixed. Aristotle contrasts the limited with the unlimited bodies by saying that 'unless what
surrounds the [limited] bodies causes some sort of change, the
appearance of their colour is *also* limited (ὥρισται)', that is
their colour as well as their bodies is limited (439b5–6). As
Alexander comments, 'just as the unlimited bodies get their
limit from another body, since they do not have a determined
limit of their own, so indeed they also get their colours'.[116] In
other words, if a body has its own fixed limits, then it has its
own fixed colour too. But if its limits are changeable, so are its
colours.

Neither water nor air has a natural limit. Both elements
have to be limited by something else. Now the eyes consist of
water because water is transparent. But the reason why the
eyes consist of water rather than air, which is also transparent,
is that water is *more easily limited* than air.[117] This suggests
that though water as such has no limit it is given a limit when
confined in the eye. What it is about the eye that limits the
water we are not told. Perhaps it is the skin around the eye
that I discussed in the previous section. However this may be,
the point that the water gains a limit in the eye also explains
why the water in the eye appears to have a colour. If the water
in the eye had simply been unlimited water, it would not have
a colour, for Aristotle says that the same conditions that create colour in a limited body create light and darkness in an
unlimited body (439b16–18). So if the eye consisted of unlimited water it would not be brown or blue but just light or
dark. The eyes, then, have colour because they consist of a
transparent body, which insofar as it is limited has a colour at
its surface. This answers the question posed above: how was it

---

[116] *in de Sensu* 45.18–20.
[117] *Sens.* 2 438a15–16; cf. *PA* II.10 656b2.

that Aristotle could, on the one hand, say that the eyes are transparent and that the transparent is colourless and, on the other hand, say that eyes have colour? The answer is that the eyes insofar as they are made of transparent water are colourless. However, insofar as the transparent water they are made of *is limited* the eyes have a colour which appears at the limit or surface of the water in the eyes. It is this coloured surface of the eye's liquid that constitutes the *iris*.

It is important to notice that this means that the colour appears *only* at the surface of the eyes and not also inside the eye (*Sens.* 3 439a31–b1). It is important to notice this because it explains why what we see is not coloured by the colour of our own eyes. A brown-eyed person does not see the world tinted by brown. The colour that appears at the surface of the eye to us looking at the eye from the outside does not appear to the perceiver from the inside, for Aristotle says that there is no colour inside a transparent body.

I have tried to explain why our eyes have a colour. But why do eyes have different colours, some brown, others green, and others again blue? Aristotle introduces his account of eye colour by saying that he will assume the reason why the eyes are composed of water was the one given in *De Anima* and *De Sensu* (*GA* v.1 779b21–6). In other words, he assumes that the eyes are made of water because water is transparent. As before, a reference to transparency as what determines the composition of the eye serves to rule out rival explanations. Empedocles said that eyes that have more fire in them were blue while eyes that have more water in them than fire are dark (*GA* v.1 779b16–21). This explanation has to be wrong. If the eyes have to be transparent in order to receive colour, then the eyes cannot have a fiery composition, for fire is not transparent. If the eyes have no fire in them, then, *a fortiori*, the colour of lighter eyes cannot be explained by saying that they have *more* fire in them than darker eyes.

Against Empedocles, Aristotle then says that the explanation given in *De Anima* and *De Sensu* of why the eyes are made of water also explains why eyes have different colours

(*GA* v.1 779b21–6).[118] The point, in other words, is that transparency is also what explains variation in eye colour:

> Some eyes contain more water, some less, than the fitting [συμμέτρου] change, others have a fitting amount. Those eyes which contain much water are dark. For you cannot easily see through large amounts of water. Those which contain a little are blue, just as it appears also in the case of the sea. For the seawater that is easy to see through appears blue, the less easy to see through appears pallid and water of unfathomable depth appears black or dark blue. Eyes intermediate between these eyes differ only by degree. (*GA* v.1 779b26–34)

Eye colour is explained by the fact that different volumes of water have different colours. Large volumes of water are less transparent. Smaller volumes of water are more transparent. The key to understanding how these different degrees of transparency are expressed in different shades of colour lies again in the idea that colour is how the transparent appears at its limit. There is no difficulty in understanding how a larger body of transparent water may appear darker, that is less transparent, than a smaller body of water. The difficult point is to understand how this degree of transparency translates into different coloured eyes, that is eyes of different hue. It is well known that Greek colour terms generally tend not to distinguish between hue and luminosity. As G. E. L. Owen and others have pointed out, this bit of information is crucial

---

[118] Platt's translation in Barnes (1984) and Peck's Loeb translation in Peck (1953) of *GA* v.1 779b26 are both unsatisfactory. The passage in full (779b21–6) goes: ἀλλ' εἴπερ ἐστὶν ὥσπερ ἐλέχθη πρότερον ἐν τοῖς περὶ τὰς αἰσθήσεις καὶ τούτων ἔτι πρότερον ἐν τοῖς περὶ ψυχῆς διωρισμένοις, καὶ ὅτι ὕδατος, καὶ δι' ἣν αἰτίαν ὕδατος ἀλλ' οὐκ ἀέρος ἢ πυρὸς τὸ αἰσθητήριον τοῦτ' ἐστί, ταύτην αἰτίαν ὑποληπτέον εἶναι τῶν εἰρημένων. Platt translates the last line 'then we must assume *the water* to be the cause of the colours mentioned' (my italics). But ταύτην naturally refers back to δι' ἣν αἰτίαν, not ὕδατος. So Aristotle is saying that the reason why the eye is composed of water, namely, that water is transparent, is also the reason why the eye can have different colours. In other words, eye colour is to be explained with reference to the fact that the eyes are transparent rather than simply with reference to the fact that they are composed of water. Peck translates, 'then we should take it that *the following* is the cause responsible for the phenomena just described' (my italics). It is no doubt possible to take ταύτην as referring forward. However, this translation makes it vague what it is in the following that explains the things said. It seems better, therefore, to avoid Peck's translation when a clear reference for ταύτην is available in the immediately preceding context.

in order to make sense of Aristotle's view that the other colours can be produced by a mixture of τὸ μέλαν and τὸ λευκόν.[119] By τὸ μέλαν we should, as we saw, understand dark colours, not just black, and by τὸ λευκόν light or bright colours, and not just white. The point that Aristotle uses colour terms to refer also to degrees of luminosity seems to fit well with his view that both colour and light are states of transparency, colour being the appearance of transparency at the surface of a limited body and light the actuality of transparency in an unlimited body. It may be because Aristotle sees both colour and light as states of transparency that he can see degrees of hue and saturation to correspond with degrees of luminosity. The less transparent a body is the darker its hue; whereas if the body is more transparent, its surface will appear a darker colour. Though Aristotle makes no explicit statement to this effect, this interpretation would make sense of why having more or less transparent eyes translates into having a colour of a particular hue such as blue or brown at their surface.[120]

We may, of course, still wonder why eyes seem to have colours that we hardly ever, if at all, observe in other bodies of water, such as the sea. When, for example, was the last time you saw the sea as yellow-green?[121] However, the difficulty of determining with any precision the semantic ranges of colour terms such as 'goat-eyed' (αἰγωπόν) makes it difficult for us to say whether Aristotle applies colour terms to the eye that we would not apply to other bodies of water, whether for example he would be willing to call the colour of the sea 'goat-eyed' as well.[122] We may tend to use colour terms such as 'yellow'

---

[119] Cf. *Sens.* 3 439b19–440b25, 4 442a12–13; Owen (1965) 253.

[120] It seems to me obvious that one can make this point without being committed to any position in the debate about the defectiveness or otherwise of Greek thinking about colours; cf. Maxwell-Stuart (1981) 1–5.

[121] I ignore here the sense in which the sea appears yellow when you see yellow sand through the water, for in this case the sea becomes coloured by taking on the sand's colour as a medium of vision. It is not therefore the sea itself that appears yellow.

[122] Notice that the pseudo-Aristotelian *Physiognomica* 6 812b6 describes the eyes of goats as οἰνωποί. This might be taken to support Aristotle's analogy between the

to the exclusion of other colours which may be within the semantic range of the nearest equivalent Greek term.

Aristotle's introduction to *De Generatione Animalium* v.1 shows that the account of eye colour has a different explanatory status from the accounts of the other features of the eye that we have met so far. Aristotle says that we must now study the 'affections by which the parts of animals differ' (778a16–17). By 'affections' (παθήματα), he explains that he means conditions such as blue or dark eye colour or different colours of hair. He then (778a20–2) says that in some species of animal all the members of the species have the same affection. In other species, notably in man, different members of the species have different affections, for example in some species all the animals have the same colour of hair whereas different human beings have different hair colour (778a26–7).

By this distinction Aristotle wants to draw our attention to an important difference in the way that we explain these affections. If all the members of a species have the same affection, say, if all lions have the same colour of coat, then we can explain the affection by reference to the nature of the animal. We can say that the animal has the affection because it is the kind of animal that it is. For if all the members of the kind have the affection, then it follows from being a member of that kind that the animal has the affection.[123] In other words, we can refer to the animal's nature, what makes it an animal

---

colours of the eye and the sea *even in the case of the colour 'goat-eyed'*. οἶνοψ (as in Homer's οἴνοπα πόντον) is, of course, famously applied to the sea (cf. Maxwell-Stuart (1981) 6–11 for other examples and a discussion of the considerable literature). Maxwell-Stuart (197, n. 24) further notes, in support of his own view that οἶνοψ means a deep reddish-brown, that 'the eyes of most goats are amber or dark reddish-brown'. If so, perhaps we have to complicate matters further by adding amber and reddish-brown to the semantic range of αἰγωπόν. In any event, these comments should illustrate the difficulty of determining the precise range of meanings of Aristotle's colour terms.

[123] Cf. *GA* v. 1 778a30–2 where the affections that the animal has by virtue of being the kind of animal it is include both its essential attributes and its 'properties' (τὰ ἴδια). 'Property' is defined at *Top*. 1.5 102a18–22 as

something which does not indicate the essence of a thing, but yet belongs to that thing alone and is predicated convertibly of it. Thus it is a property of man to be capable of learning grammar; for if he is a man, then he is capable of learning grammar, and if he is capable of learning grammar, he is a man.

of a certain kind, as the cause of the animal's having that affection. However, if the affection differs in different animals of the same kind, then we cannot say that the animal has the affection because it is the kind of animal that it is, for other animals of the same kind do not have the affection and they are still animals of that kind.

Eye colour may fall into either category of affection. In some species of animal there is no variation in eye colour between individual members of the species. In these species, Aristotle says, 'it is not natural for the animal to have more than one eye colour' (*GA* v.1 779b2–3). However, in other animals, such as the horse and especially man, individual members of the same species display a wide variety of eye colours. In this case, we cannot put the affection down to the nature of the animal. Where the eye colour is not even a property of the animal (cf. 778a30–4), we should look for the cause of the eye colour in 'the matter and the moving principle' (778a35–b1).

The contrast is here one between looking for the cause in 'the matter and the moving principle' or looking for it in the animal's form and final cause. It is the form and the final cause that tell us what kind of animal an animal is. That is why in cases where all the members of the species have the same affection we can explain the affection by the form and the final cause, for we say that the animal has the affection because it is the kind of animal that it is. (If it did not, then it would be accidental that all the animals of the kind had the affection and there would be no reason why a particular member of the species should not have a different affection.) And the reason why the animal is the kind of animal it is we said was the form and final cause. Hence we can explain the affections that all members of the species share by their form and final cause.

Earlier in this chapter, we saw in connection with *Physica* II.9 that a particular notion of necessity accompanied the notion that the parts of the body should be explained by reference to their form and final cause. This was the notion of *hypothetical* necessity. For example, *if* the form and goal of the eye was to be realised, *then*, necessarily, the eye had to be composed of a certain sort of matter. The matter was only necessary in relation to the realisation of a certain form. By contrast to the notion of hypothetical necessity there was also the notion 'material necessity'. Here the conditional went in the other direction. We said that if certain materials with such-and-such attributes were present, then necessarily something with this form and function would be realised.

Now Aristotle says that eye colour is necessary in the sense of material necessity.[124] But it is important to notice that this only applies to eye colour in those species where it varies from animal to animal. We cannot, therefore, say generally without qualification that eye colour is to be explained by material necessity, for in species where all the animals have the same eye colour the eye colour can be explained by the form and final cause of the animal. In these species, therefore, eye colour can be explained by hypothetical necessity. Thus if all lions have grey eyes, then that can be explained by reference to hypothetical necessity, but if I as a human being have grey eyes, then that is to be explained by material necessity since it is a fact that cannot be put down to my membership of my species.

We saw that it was necessary for the eyes to have a colour because they were made of a limited transparent body. What is transparent on the inside appears coloured at its limit. Colour simply is the limit of the transparent that we observe from the outside. So colour is what we call the transparent at its limit. Since the matter of the eye, by hypothetical necessity, is a transparent body, the limit of that transparent body will be a colour. In this way, the fact that the eye appears coloured on the outside is a necessary consequence of the fact that the eye is transparent. But here we need to be careful, for though it is hypothetically necessary to have transparent eyes and it is a necessary consequence of having transparent eyes that one's eyes are coloured, the hypothetical necessity does not carry over to the fact that one's eyes are coloured. Eye colour is

---

[124] *GA* v.1 778a35, b16–19.

merely consequential on having transparent eyes. It is not it-self the result of hypothetical necessity, for eye colour is not for the sake of anything as it is simply a necessary result of transparency which is for the sake of vision. As Aristotle says, 'though the eye is for the sake of something its blueness is not, unless this affection is proper to the species' (GA v.i 778a33-4).

There is a connection between an affection's not being for the sake of anything and its varying within the species. We can explain the connection as follows. The fact that my eye colour is different from that of other human beings ensures that I cannot have this eye colour in order to execute any of the functions that are essential to my species. More particu-larly, it ensures that it cannot be in order to see that I have blue eyes, for, if so, why do I have blue eyes when other of my fellow human beings do not? Since the fact that I have blue eyes, unlike the fact that I have eyes, cannot be put down to my nature as a human being, my eye colour cannot be ex-plained hypothetically with reference to my human nature. It remains for it to be explained by material necessity.

The explanation by material necessity is the following. *If* I have eyes that are made of water of a certain volume, *then* it is necessary for my eyes to have a certain colour. The specific eye colour is here an attribute of water *qua* having *a specific* volume. Contrast again this explanation with the explanation that the eye is made of water. It is hypothetically necessary for us to be able to see that there is water in the eye, but that the water has *this specific* volume and *this specific* colour is not hypothetically necessary.

Aristotle's comparison with the sea brings out the point further that eye colour is not to be explained by reference to the form and final cause of the eye. He compares the water in the sea with the water in the eyes. If you find water in this volume in the sea it is blue and so is the water in eyes. The water in the sea and the water in eyes are both blue for the same reason, namely, that the water is present in a certain volume. This shows that the reason why the water in the eyes is blue is nothing to do with the fact that the water is the water of *eyes*. In other words, the fact that the water in my eyes is blue is not explained by the fact that the water is the matter of my eyes for, given its volume, the water in my eyes would be blue wherever it was located.

We explained the matter of the eye as hypothetically necessary by showing that this matter was necessary if the eye was to be serviceable as a sense-organ of vision. As we saw, it was the ability to serve as a sense-organ of vision that defined the eye *as an eye*. Take away the eye's ability to see, we said, and what you are left with is an eye only homonymously. Since the eye would no longer have sight, it would no longer have the attribute by which we define an eye. So, it could no longer be called an eye by reference to the definition of an eye.

The explanation of eye colour in this way contrasts with the explanations of the other features of the eye that we have looked at. Most notably, the explanation contrasts with the explanation of the *korē*. We said that the *korē* was made of water because water was transparent and transparency was required if we were going to be able to see. So this was an instance of explaining the matter by reference to the form and function, that is, an instance of hypothetical necessity. Similarly, the membranes, the *poroi* and the white were all necessary in order either to protect the eye's transparency or to transmit the *kinēsis* from the sense-object to the transparent *korē*.

However, with the explanation of eye colour in species of animals in which it varies, we have passed from explanation by hypothetical necessity to explanation by material necessity. It is important to mention Aristotle's explanation of eye colour because it shows that not all features of the eye are always to be explained by means of hypothetical necessity. Similarly, Aristotle reminds us in *PA* IV.2 677a15–19 that we should not try to find a final cause for all the features of the body. Sometimes features are simply due to (material) necessity.

But does that mean that eye colour is of no interest to somebody who is interested in the features of the eye only insofar as they are hypothetically necessary for vision? And if eye colour is of no interest to such a person, why should Aristotle bother with it? Does not Aristotle's interest here show that he is not just interested in the eye's potentiality as an organ of vision?

Notice first that in the quotation above from *De Generatione Animalium* v.1 779b26–34 the specific eye colour was not simply said to depend on whether there is more or less water in the eyes. It depends on whether there is an amount which is in the right proportion to the change. The change in question, as 780a1–3 makes clear, is the change from the sense-object. To contain too little water is understood as being so transparent that even the smallest impulse from a sense-object changes the eyes. Next, Aristotle says that:

> We should suppose that there is the same cause of the fact that blue eyes do not see accurately by day and that dark eyes do not see accurately at night. For blue eyes are changed, *qua* liquid and *qua* transparent [ἧ ὑγρὸν καὶ ἧ διαφανές], more easily by the light and the sense-objects because there is little water in them. Dark eyes are changed less easily because there is much water in them, for nocturnal light is weak. Add to this the fact that water in general becomes difficult to change at night. It is necessary therefore that the liquid *qua* transparent [ἧ διαφανές] neither does not change nor changes too much. (779b34–780a8)

This, at first, suggests that the eye undergoes both a material change (*qua* liquid) and a formal change (*qua* transparent). In 'ἧ ὑγρὸν καὶ ἧ διαφανές', however, καὶ is to be understood as corrective.[125] This is clear from the next line, which says that 'seeing is the change of this part *qua* transparent *but not qua* liquid'. The right translation is therefore '*qua* liquid *or rather qua* transparent'. This is further confirmed by the final sentence of the quotation where Aristotle has dropped the qualification ἧ ὑγρὸν καὶ ἧ διαφανές in favour simply of ἧ διαφανές.

The change, then, is a change that affects the eye insofar as the eye is transparent, not insofar as it is liquid. Another way of putting this point is to say that vision takes place insofar as the eye's form, its transparency, is changed and not insofar as

---

[125] For this use of καί, cf. Smyth (1920) §2870; Denniston (1953) 292, *s.v.* καί, I(8).

the eye's matter is changed. This, of course, does not exclude that the eye in vision is also affected in terms of its matter. It simply says that whether or not there is an affection of the eye *qua* matter, it is not in terms of such an affection that vision should be explained.

What decides, therefore, whether the eyes have the right amount of water is whether that amount of water gives the eyes the right degree of transparency. In other words, it is not the amount of water as such that determines whether the eyes will see well in certain circumstances but the degree of transparency that the eyes have. Thus it is not the fact that blue eyes contain a smaller amount of water than brown eyes that explains why blue-eyed people see better at night than do those with brown eyes. Rather, it is the fact that blue eyes are more transparent than brown eyes that explains why they see better at night. For it is properly speaking the eyes *qua* transparent that are changed in vision. Blue eyes are more easily changed because they are more transparent and not because they contain less water.

One might think that being more easily changed always means being able to see better, for if to see an object is to be changed by it, then being changed easily by an object suggests being able to see it without difficulty, or, in other words, being able to see it well. So having blue eyes should always make you able to see better. But things are not that simple. Eyes do not simply get better the more transparent they are. This was the point of saying that there should be the right amount of water in the eyes in proportion to the change by the sense-object, for if the change coming from the sense-object is very strong, it will be better for the eyes to be less transparent because if the eyes are very transparent, the change in them will be too intense. For example, the change that bright light sets up in dark eyes might be moderate since dark eyes insofar as they are less transparent are less easy to change, but the same change will be much more intense in blue eyes because they, insofar as they are more transparent, are easier to change. This, indeed, explains why blue-eyed people see worse than brown-eyed people by day. Blue eyes are too sensitive to light.

They are so easily changed by the daylight that there is no scope for any other sense-objects to affect them when they are already affected by daylight. As Aristotle says, the stronger change knocks out the weaker (*GA* v.1 780a8–9). He compares it to the experience of going out of a dark room into the sun. You are blinded because the change brought about in your eyes by the sunlight is so strong that no other changes from sense-objects can affect you. Similarly, if you have blue eyes, the change that the daylight constantly brings about in your eyes is so strong that it excludes the eyes' ability to react to other objects.

The best state for your eyes, then, is not to be too transparent. In contrast, the eyes should not have too little transparency either, for then the danger is that they will not react at all to the weaker changes. This is what may happen to dark-eyed people at night. Because their eyes are less transparent they fail to react to the changes at night which are weaker because there is less light. Dark-eyed people are therefore prone to night-blindness. By contrast, it takes only a little impulse to set up a perceptual change in eyes that are more transparent. The changes at night are much weaker because there is less light at night. (Remember that the change from the sense-object requires an actually transparent medium, that is light, in order to affect the sense-faculty. Since the transparency of the medium is less actualised at night, that is there is less light, the change from the sense-object is less able to affect the sense-faculty.) Eyes that are more transparent will be better able to pick up weaker changes. So more transparent, that is blue, eyes will see better at night. By contrast, the changes are much stronger by day, for then the medium is more transparent and therefore mediates the change from the sense-object better. However, here the change may well be too strong for the more transparent eyes which are over-stimulated by the stronger changes. Less transparent, that is darker, eyes come into their own in these circumstances since, because they are less transparent, they are less easily changed and therefore less affected by the stronger changes coming from outside.

In general, the best state for the eyes to be in is somewhere in between the very transparent and the less transparent. 'The best eyes [ὄψις]', Aristotle says at *De Generatione Animalium* v.1 780a23–5, 'have a medium amount of liquid. For such eyes neither interfere with the change from the colours by being disturbed, as when there is little liquid, nor are they difficult to change because there is too much liquid.' There is the right amount of liquid in the eyes in proportion to the sense-object when the change set up in the eyes by the sense-object is neither too strong nor too weak but in between these two extremes. The eyes should be in a condition such that we are neither unaffected by colours nor completely dazzled by them.

We can use the comparison of the mean in action to clarify the notion of a mean degree of transparency.[126] If you are a champion wrestler like Milo you should eat much more than if you are a sedentary office worker. The mean in eating for a wrestler is different from that for the office worker. What is just right for the one is too much for the other, what is just right for the other is too little for the first. The mean in relation to office work is different from the mean in relation to wrestling. So the important point is that the mean is relative to an activity and not an absolute mean.

Similarly, the mean degree of transparency in the eye is not determined absolutely. It is determined relative to an activity, namely, the sort of change that the sense-object sets up in the eye. The mean condition of the sense-organ is not a mean condition that can be determined apart from this change. To be in the mean condition is to be in a condition such that the change set up by the sense-object will neither fail to take place nor take place too violently. The mean is in other words not an absolute condition of the sense-organ that can be determined simply by looking at the sense-organ. It is a mean determined in relation to the activity that the sense-object sets up in it. What is, to use Aristotle's example at *De Generatione Animalium* v.1 780a10–11, an appropriate degree of transparency for us in relation to the stronger changes that sunlight

---

[126] Cf. *EN* II.6 1106a28–b7.

sets up in the eyes is not an appropriate degree of transparency when we enter into a dark room. Like brown-eyed people at night, we may temporarily be struck by blindness until the changes in us from the sunlight have subsided.

In *Historia Animalium* I.10 492a2–3, Aristotle said that eyes could be dark, blue, grey or yellow/green. He says that yellow/green is 'a sign [σημεῖον] of the best character [ἤθους] and best in relation to accuracy of sight' (492a3–4).[127] There are two different means in play in this passage: one is a moral mean, the other is what one could call a 'perceptual' mean, that is to say a mean that will enable us to perceive as well as possible. The moral mean may or may not coincide with the perceptual mean. In the case of eye colour the moral mean and the perceptual mean do coincide. For having green eyes is both the best in relation to accuracy of vision and a sign of the best character. In other cases, the two means may not coincide. For example, with regard to accuracy of vision deep-set eyes are the best, whereas eyes in between deep-set and protruding are 'a sign of the best character' (492a10).

Let us focus on the perceptual mean. What does having yellow/green eyes have to do with having sharp eyesight? *De Generatione Animalium* v.1 suggested an answer. For if an eye has a colour in between dark and blue, then that would, on the account in *De Generatione Animalium* v.1, indicate that the eye contained an intermediate degree of liquid. The eye would therefore also have an intermediate degree of transparency. This was the degree that was recommended as the best because it made the eye neither too easily changed by colours nor too difficult for colours to change. What makes eyes able to see accurately is having the right degree of trans-

---

[127] It is clear that καί cannot be explanatory here. The context makes it clear that having a good character is not the same as having accurate eyesight. Aristotle goes on to say that people's eyes may blink a lot or not at all or with intermediate frequency. The people who blink with intermediate frequency have the best character, whereas those who blink a lot are shameless and those who do not blink are shifty (ἀβέβαιος, 492a14). So, by 'character', Aristotle here means ethical character. In other words, when Aristotle talks about the sense-organs being a sign of a good or bad character (ἤθος), he is making what we would call a physiognomical point.

parency, that is having neither too much nor too little transparency. Eye colour indicates the amount of water in the eye, which in turn determines the degree of transparency in the eyes. Yellow/green eyes are the best, then, because they indicate the intermediate degree of transparency which is overall best for vision.[128]

Now it is important to distinguish this point about the desirability of having a mean eye colour from another point that Aristotle sometimes makes. Aristotle on occasion says that the sense-faculty is a mean.[129] By this, he has in mind that the sense-faculty is a mean between the extremes of the sort of sense-object that is able to exert change upon it, for example the sense of sight is in between the very dark and the very light colours. But Aristotle makes it clear that we should not take this to imply that the sense-faculty has a colour in between the very dark and the very light, for it is only a potentiality to be coloured. In other words, the sense-faculty *qua* potentiality is only potentially coloured and not actually coloured.

An analogy may clarify the point. Think of a car whose gearbox has five gears and a neutral position. First position is the lowest gear, fifth the highest. The numerical mean is third. Now when Aristotle says that the sense-faculty is a mean he is not saying that the sense-faculty is in third position. He is saying that the sense-faculty is in neutral position. The sense-faculty's being a mean corresponds, not to being in a middle

---

[128] Notice that it is only overall that yellow/green eyes are the best, for we can still say that it is better to have blue eyes at night and brown eyes by day. By having yellow/green eyes, you avoid the disadvantage of being too easily blinded which blue-eyed people experience by day and the disadvantage of being night-blind which brown-eyed people experience at night. But you also miss the corresponding advantages of these eye colours. The perceptual mean seems to be determined as what avoids the disadvantages of either extreme rather than as what combines the advantages of either extreme.

[129] Cf. *De an.* II.11 424a4–7. These lines are directly about touch (cf. *De an.* III.13 435a21) and we may be concerned about the extent to which we can here generalise from touch to all perception. However, insofar as Aristotle says that the mean is discerning (κριτικόν) and we know from elsewhere (cf. *De an.* III.2 426b8–13) that all perception for him is a form of discernment (κρίνειν), the lines suggest that the sense-faculties in general can be understood as a sort of mean. Notice also that in the following lines Aristotle goes on to make the point about the sense-faculty's being only potentially the same as its objects quite generally.

gear, but to being in *no* gear, for neutral is the position from which you can *change* into all gears, including third. Similarly, the sense-faculty is transparent, and therefore colourless, because this is the position from which you can *change* into all the colours.

It is important not to confuse Aristotle's statement that the sense-faculty is a mean with his point that it is best for the eye to have a mean colour. For Aristotle does not believe that eye colour *as such* is relevant to how we see. Blue eyes do not see well at night *qua* blue. They see well at night *qua* highly transparent. The sense of sight is a mean insofar as it is able to be changed by colours, and it is able to be changed by colours insofar as it is transparent. Having a certain degree of transparency enhances your ability to be changed by colours. Also, having a mean colour, that is being yellow/green, coincides with having this favourable degree of transparency.

We see, therefore, that for Aristotle eye colour is highly revealing of the eye's ability to function as a sense-organ of sight. The discussion of eye colour is cast in terms of degrees of transparency because transparency rather than eye colour as such is the feature of the eye that is relevant to its ability to see. So even here, where Aristotle, exceptionally, refers us to material necessity to explain a feature of the eye, his interest in function and form shines through.

There is one further point to be made about eye colour, for Aristotle said more than what I have focussed on so far. He said not just that eye colour is to be explained by reference to the matter of the eye. He said that eye colour was to be 'led back to the matter *and the moving principle*. We have seen how it may be led back to the matter, for we have seen how the variation in eye colour within the same species is to be explained by the necessity of the matter.

But how is it also to be led back to the moving principle? By the moving principle, or efficient cause, Aristotle seems to have in mind the process by which the eyes are formed that was described at *De Generatione Animalium* II.6 743b33–744b11. The main result of the concoction that produces both the brain and the eyes is that the amount of fluid is reduced.

In the beginning of the process, the brain is very big (relative to the rest of the body, presumably), which also makes the head of the foetus very big. Later, the brain is smaller (again, I presume, relative to the rest of the body), for by then its fluid has become more concocted. For the same reason, the eyes are larger in the early stages of their formation and smaller later on (744a18–21).[130] Aristotle says that the process of concoction continues in the baby's brain even after it has been born (744a26). Since the concoction of the eyes is said to be completed after that of the brain (744b2–3), it seems reasonable to suppose also that the concoction of the eyes continues after birth.

Aristotle says that it is by necessity that the eyes are concocted (744a13–14). Whether we can relate this necessity to the necessity which in *De Generatione Animalium* v.1 is said to explain why the eyes have a particular colour is doubtful. It might seem relevant to the discussion of eye colour that the account of the formation of the eyes includes reference to a process (concoction) by which it is possible that some eyes contain more fluid than others because the concoction may have progressed further in some people than in others. There does not seem to be any simple correlation between the degree of concoction in the eyes and eye colour, however, for if the more concocted eyes contained less fluid of the sort that determines eye colour, then we would expect new-born babies, with their less-concocted eyes, to have darker eyes, for their eyes would contain more fluid. In fact we are told at *De Generatione Animalium* v.1 779b10–11 that young animals have blue eyes, which would indicate that they had less fluid in their eyes than older members of the species, in other words, that their eyes had been more concocted. All we can say, then, is that Aristotle thinks the process by which the eyes are produced can explain their final colour. But how exactly this explanation would go is unclear.

What general conclusions can we draw from the discussion of eye colour as to Aristotle's method of explanation? At the

---

[130] Cf. *HA* vi.3 561a18–b1 on the details of this process in bird embryos.

start of his discussion of eye colour in *De Generatione Animalium* v.1 779b22–3 Aristotle referred us back to *De Sensu* 2 and *De Anima*, assuming that the eye is composed of water for the reason given in these works, that is because water is transparent and transparency is what enables the eye to serve as an organ of sight. The reference was required in *De Generatione Animalium* v.1 since it was only if we kept in mind the reason why the eyes have transparency that we could understand why blue eyes see better at night and brown eyes worse. The eyes were transparent so that they could be changed by colours and it was this susceptibility to change by colours that defined vision. Hence different degrees of transparency would show different degrees of ability to see. The discussion in *De Generatione Animalium* v.1, just as the discussion in *De Sensu* 2, therefore continues the focus in *De Anima* on the eyes as organs of sight insofar as it too focuses on transparency. The point, however, is not simply, as in *De Sensu* 2, that transparency gives the eye the ability to see. The point is, more specifically, that different degrees of transparency make you able to see better or worse in different circumstances.

12. Conclusion

The eye, both as a whole and in respect of its individual parts, is identified and explained in terms of the contribution those parts make to its transparency. Transparency is the attribute that gives the eye the potentiality to see, the attribute that gives the eye the potentiality to be changed by colour, the potentiality that in *De Anima* II.7 defines the faculty of sight. Showing how the different parts of the eye contribute to transparency is therefore showing that the eye provides the matter necessary for the potentiality that defines sight. It is difficult to identify both the location and the composition of many of the parts with any degree of precision. The empirical data that lie behind the physiology of the eye are, as Lloyd argues, vague. This may of course be because the research behind the data is incomplete[131] or because Aristotle's presentation of the data is incomplete. But his vagueness about the precise structure of the eye becomes philosophically pointed when we take into account his explanatory procedure. Aristotle is interested in showing how animals have the parts required for perception. The eye is therefore approached from this point of view as the matter that gives the animal the potentiality to see. Aristotle is therefore interested in the physiology of the eye to the extent that he can identify the parts that are required to fulfil this potentiality. Firstly, there is the transparent *korē*; secondly there are such features as are required for the transparent to be transparent all the way to the seat of perception in the heart, hence the *poroi*; and finally, there are such features as are needed to preserve and protect the transparent eye jelly – hence the membranes and the white. In short, Aristotle draws a functional map of the eye in terms of his notion of transparency and then identifies features of this functional map with its material parts. Once this is done, he shows no further interest in the composition of the eye.

---

[131] *PA* II.10 656a9–10 might suggest that Aristotle thinks more research is needed on the external sense-organs of animals other than man.

2

THE MEDIUM

1. Introduction

In this chapter I want to explain how, according to Aristotle, the medium of perception works. The discussion focuses on the medium of vision, that is, the transparent. In chapter 1 we saw how the transparent dominates Aristotle's account of the sense-organ of vision. Aristotle said that the inside of the eye had to be actually transparent (light) just as the medium in between the sense-object and the eye had to be actually transparent. I argued that this meant that the inside of the eye had to be transparent in order to be able to receive the sense-quality and mediate it to the seat of perception around the heart. The role of the transparent both outside the eye and inside the eye was to mediate the sense-quality.

In this chapter I shall inquire into the role of the transparent as a medium. This inquiry follows on the argument of chapter 1. For if I was right in chapter 1, this inquiry will not only affect the way we understand the transparent medium in between the eye and the sense-object as working but also the way in which we understand the transparent inside the eye as working for, according to chapter 1, the role of the transparent inside the eye was the same as the transparent outside the eye.

I shall have more to say specifically about the mediation of hearing and smell in the relevant chapters on hearing and smell (chapters 3 and 5). However, the discussion in this chapter aims to be generalizable to the media of hearing and smell, for it focuses on two aspects of the medium of vision that ought to be aspects of any medium of perception: (1) the medium as a causal link between sense-object and perceiver and (2) the medium as that through which the sense-object appears to a perceiver. My aim, then, is to give an account of the basic causal role of the medium in perception.

2. What the medium has to be like if we are going to see the sense-object and not the medium

The 'transparent' is literally that through which something can appear. So if I wave a red flag in front of you and what is in between you and the flag is all transparent, then the flag will appear to you. In contrast, if I hold up the same flag in front of you but something has been put in between you and the flag that is not transparent, say a dark screen, then the flag will not appear to you. What you will see instead is the screen – provided again that what is in between you and the screen remains all transparent.

The presence of something transparent in between you and an object allows you to see that object through it, for the transparent will not introduce anything else in between you and the object so that you will see *it* rather than the object. Aristotle considers the proper object of sight colour. So when you see the red flag it is the redness of the flag that affects your sense of sight as such. Now it is clear that if what is in between you and the red flag in your line of vision also has a colour, then that will be the colour that affects your sense of sight, rather than the redness of the flag.

Another possibility is that the redness of the flag will merge with the colour of what is in between you and the flag. A blue dress in yellow light, for instance, might appear green, for when you mix blue and yellow you get green. But even so, it is clear that you will not properly speaking be seeing the colour of the *dress*. Rather you will be seeing another colour, green, one of whose ingredients is the colour of the dress, blue.

So one problem that the transparent medium seems to solve is this: how can we ever see something at a distance in its own right without having to see something else because of the interference of what is between us and the object? Or, in other words, how can our perceptions at a distance ever be representative of how things are, if what we perceive is influenced and changed by what is in between us and the things we would like our perceptions to represent?[1] If I am trying to find out what colour the flag is by looking at it, then it is no good if I am able to see only the colour of what is in between me and the flag or a mixture of the medium's and the flag's colour. If the medium is transparent, however, and does not have its own colour, then this problem does not arise.

3. What the medium has to be like if there is no perception by direct contact

This line of thought is connected with a second problem about what the medium has to be like given that there is no vision, hearing, or smell by *direct contact* between the sense-organ and the sense-object. As Aristotle says, in *De Anima* II.7 419a12–13, 'if one places something that has colour upon the eye itself, it will not be seen'. And he says the same about sound and smell at 419a25–30. So the object will only be perceived if it first affects the medium and the medium then affects the sense-faculty. That was also why Democritus was wrong to say that we would see an ant in the sky clearly if there was nothing in between us and the ant (419a15), for if there was nothing in between, then there would be no medium that the ant could affect first and that in turn could affect our sense of vision.

So we need a medium in vision. But it follows immediately from what Aristotle says that if the medium itself had a colour, then we would be unable to see it for the medium stretches all the way up to the eye and we cannot see something that is put directly upon the eye. The medium cannot then be coloured. If it were, then that colour could not be seen. It is the role of the medium to be continuous all the way up to the sense-organ. Therefore the medium will be in direct contact with the sense-organ. But if so, its colour will not be

---

[1] Aristotle's claim that we become one with the sense-object in form when we perceive it suggests that our perceptions are representative of the sense-object; cf. *De an.* II.12 424a17–26, III.4 429a14–18; *Int.* 1 16a4–9.

visible to the eye, for nothing that directly touches the sense-organ can be perceived by it.

This argument affects any interpretation of Aristotle which would have him say that the medium mediates by itself becoming coloured and that what sight perceives directly is the colour of the medium and only indirectly the colour of the sense-object. In fact, saying that what is perceived directly is the colour of the medium is a natural corollary of saying that the medium becomes coloured, for, as we saw above, if the medium becomes coloured, then it will no longer be transparent in such a way that something else can be seen *through* it. The medium would itself become an object of vision. But if so, it would no longer be a medium.

The same conclusion applies to the other mediated senses. We cannot say that the air becomes noisy when it mediates sound, for just as putting a noisy object directly up against the ear produces no hearing, so also putting a noisy medium up against the ear will produce no hearing.[2] And, again, because smelling does not happen by direct contact with a smelly object, being in direct contact with a smelly medium will not affect the sense-organ perceptively either.[3]

So this brings us back to the point that the medium itself has to be without any of the sensible qualities that it mediates in perception. This applies to the medium both before and during the mediation. If the medium had any of the sensible qualities before perception, then it would not be able to receive the sensible quality. The medium would already have this quality. So there would be no alteration. But if, during perception, the medium received any of these qualities when mediating the sensible quality, it would lose its purpose. Its purpose was to establish an indirect contact between the sense-object, the red flag, and the sense-organ, the eye. If there

---

[2] Aristotle, if presented with a Walkman, might say that though you hear the music on a Walkman through ear plugs inserted in the ear, the ear plugs are still not in direct contact with the *proper* sense-organ of hearing since this is set further inside the ear. More on the proper sense-organ of hearing in ch. 3.

[3] Cf. *De an.* II.7 419a25–b3. For the idea that smell occupies a middle position between the distance and the contact senses, cf. *Sens.* 5 445a4–13 and ch. 5, sec. 4.

is a problem about seeing an object that is laid directly upon the eye, then there is equally a problem about perceiving a medium that is in direct contact with the eye. Of course we do not want to say that it is the medium we perceive. But if the idea is that the medium mediates by itself taking on the sensible quality and, as it were, laying it before the eye, then the implication *is* that the medium is required because the sensible quality cannot be perceived at a distance as it is not directly in touch with the sense-organ. This is obviously a wrong notion of how the medium works, for if the sense-quality directly touched upon the sense-organ it could not be perceived.

4. The medium as what sense-objects appear through and the medium as a causal link

The problem that I now want to raise is this. If the medium is not affected by the sense-object by itself becoming coloured and if the medium does not affect the sense-organ by passing on its own colour to the sense-organ, what exactly is the causal role of the medium? Let me start out afresh by setting up two approaches to the medium. The question will then be how the two are to be reconciled. The first approach is the one I started out with. It says that the medium makes the colour accessible to the sense-organ by allowing it to appear through it. The medium mediates exactly by being free of any of the sensible qualities that the sense-object has because having any of those qualities would make it, the medium, the sense-object, for example it is the sense-object, the flag, that is red and it is *its* redness that is seen, not some redness in the medium caused by it. Let me call this a 'phenomenal' approach because it focuses just on the role of the medium in allowing the sense-object to *appear* to a perceiver unhindered and undistorted through it.

Another approach to how the medium makes the sensible quality accessible to the sense-organ starts out from asserting that the medium bridges a 'causal gap' that the distance introduces between the sense-object and the sense-organ. Because the two are not in direct contact, we need a medium in between them. The medium is at one end in direct contact with the sense-object and at the other end in direct contact with the sense-organ and thereby establishes an indirect contact between the sense-object and the sense-organ. This is how Aristotle describes the causal connection between the sense-object and the perceiver in *Physica* VII.2 245a2–11:

So when what is being altered is altered by sensible objects certainly in all such cases it is clear that the last thing that alters is together with the first thing that is being altered. For the air is continuous with the first and the body is continuous with the air. But again the colour is continuous with the light, and the light with sight [τῆ ὄψει]. And in the same way also with hearing and smelling. For what changes first with relation to what is being changed is the air. And that equally applies to taste. For the flavour is together with the sense of taste. But the same holds also for soulless things and things which cannot be perceived. Thus there will be nothing in between what is being altered and that which does the altering.

Aristotle thinks perception is a case in favour of his general thesis that there can be nothing in between the agent and the patient in alteration. To get to this conclusion, however, we first have to realise that by agent and patient Aristotle understands the *immediate* agent and patient. So the agent and the patient are the *last* agent and the *first* patient in the causal chain. They are, as it were, the neighbouring links in the chain. Now perception might at first seem a counter-example to Aristotle's general thesis, for we do see a ship at a distance or hear a train approaching from afar and we say that it is the ship or the train which, though distant, causes us to perceive it. But this is where the medium comes in, for even though the sense-object and the perceiver may be apart from each other – they are not 'together' in the way that a flavour and the tongue are together – the sense-object and the medium are together and so in turn are the medium and the perceiver. So in perception the medium ensures that there is an unbroken chain of agents and patients which are in direct contact with one another. That is why perception serves as inductive evidence for the general thesis that there is no alteration at a distance.[4]

It is this causal role ascribed to the medium in *Physica* that we are reminded of in *De Anima* II.7. Here Aristotle explains his statement that there is no perception of an object that touches (ἁπτόμενον, 419a26) the sense-organ by saying that the intervening medium, on the one hand, has to be changed by the colour or the sound, and the sense-organ, on the other hand, has to be changed by the medium. I recall here that Aristotle's word in *Physica* for there being nothing in between the mover and the moved is 'ἁπτόμενον'.[5] When Aristotle in *De Anima* II.7 points out that there is no perception by direct contact with the sense-object, he means only that there is no perception if the sense-organ directly touches the sense-object, not that there is no perception if the sense-object touches something that in turn touches the sense-organ. For the point in *Physica* VII.2 is that there is no alteration, including perception, unless there is at least indirect contact between agent and patient, that is unless they are both continuous with something that touches upon the other. So by pointing to the medium and the fact that mediation is necessary to alteration in respect of the senses, Aristotle in extension of the *Physica* passage also points to what establishes the necessary causal contact between the sense-object and the perceiver.[6] This is the reason for saying that the medium bridges a causal gap between the sense-object and the perceiver.

Now to explain how the medium is first affected by the

---

[4] Cf. *Phys.* VII.2 244b3: τοῦτο δὲ δῆλον ἐξ ἐπαγωγῆς.

[5] Cf. *Phys.* VII.2 244b1.

[6] Cf. *Sens.* 3 440a16–20:

> But to say, as the old philosophers also did, that the colours are effluences and that they are seen for such a reason is absurd, for it is necessary for them anyway to account for perception through contact. So they had better straightaway say that perception is brought about by the perceptible through the medium of perception, that is by means of contact and not by means of effluences.

The 'old philosophers' thought that the contact between the sense-object and the sense-organ had to be a *direct* contact. That is why they stipulated effluences emitted by the sense-object and impinging directly on the sense-organ. Aristotle shows that the contact between sense-object and sense-organ not only is but must be indirect.

sense-object and then affects the sense-organ Aristotle uses as his analogy local movement. He talks about pushing, for instance, in *De Anima* III.12 434b29–435a5:

For that which produces movement in respect of place produces a change up to a point, and that which has pushed something else brings it about that the latter pushes, and the change takes place through something intervening. The first thing that produces change pushes without being pushed, and the last thing alone is pushed without pushing, while that which intervenes does both, there being many intervening things. So it is too with alteration, except that things are altered while remaining in the same place. *For instance, if something were dipped in wax, the wax would be changed as far as the object was dipped, whereas a stone is not changed at all, while water is changed to a great distance. And air is changed to the greatest extent and acts and is affected as long as it remains and is one.*

The causal mediation in perception is similar to a case of transmitting motion from one body to another through an intermediary body that is moved by the one body and in turn moves the other body. The intermediary body thereby both moves and is moved.[7] We are supposed to understand mediation in perception as similar to this but without the change of place. Nothing changes place when the medium mediates in perception.

But what is left then of the comparison with local movement? What at least must be left is the claim that the first agent, the sense-object, brings about a change in the medium and that the medium then brings about a change in the patient, the perceiver. So there remains the idea of what I shall call a 'causal sequence' or 'chain'. But it is not clear why a local movement should be a better illustration of a causal sequence than an alteration, if it is not simply for the general reason that when we think of change or causation we think first of local movement.[8] So it would be to local movement that we first turned to understand other kinds of change.

However, in addition to the idea of a causal chain, there is the idea that in such a chain the first link changes its sequent without itself becoming changed, the last link in the chain is

---

[7] Cf. also *Phys.* VIII.10 266b25–267a20.
[8] Cf. *Phys.* IV.1 208a31–2, VII.2 243a10–11.

changed without changing anything itself (it is of course the *last* link, so it has no sequent) and the intermediary links are both changed by their antecedent and change their sequent.

5. Teleological and 'mechanical' explanations

Now the question I want to ask is: If our notion of the causal role of the medium in perception involves a causal gap and this causal gap is bridged by a medium that both changes and is changed, how does this notion fit in with the other approach to the medium, what I called the phenomenal approach, according to which the medium operates by letting the sense-object appear through it to a perceiver?

There seems to be at least one difficulty here. For what happens when the medium is moved in local movement is that there is an effect on the medium that can be described independently of the movement that the medium in turn brings about in the object that it moves. For instance, if I move my hand, which in turn moves the pencil, then it is possible to describe the movement of my hand without referring also to the further movement that it brings about in the pencil. But the case of the sense-object appearing through the medium is different for, on the phenomenal approach, there seems to be no description of the change in the medium apart from referring to the effect that this change has or would have on a perceiver at the end of the causal chain, namely the sense-object's becoming apparent to a perceiver in perception. The medium changes only insofar as the sense-object becomes apparent to a perceiver through it, and this too is just how we would describe the change in the perceiver. Both the medium and the perceiver change insofar as the sense-object appears to the perceiver.

Now the notion of 'descriptive independence' is relative to what we are trying to explain. Thus if I am trying to explain *why* I am moving my hand, in the sense of what I am trying to achieve by doing so, the answer may be because I am writing a letter. So I move my hand in order to move the pencil that my hand holds; and I move the pencil in order to write on the paper; and thereby I write the letter, which was my goal. Here is a causal chain in which we understand each link as necessary for bringing about the next link and all links as jointly sufficient for achieving the goal. So if I am trying to explain why I am moving my hand with a view to the goal of this movement, then the movement of my hand cannot be described independently of what happens next, for insofar as the movement is considered as a means to an end, letter-writing, it cannot be described independently of the end to which it is a means. Let me call this kind of explanation of my movements 'teleological' insofar as it explains them in terms of their τέλος or goal.

But if I am trying to explain *how* I am moving my hand, the answer may well be independent of what happens next. The answer I give may be that I move my hand in this way by moving my wrist in this way and my lower arm in such and such a way, etc. None of this need make reference to the further fact that I am also holding a pencil in my hand and that my hand's movement brings about a certain movement in the pencil and that the pencil's movement produces letters on the paper.[9] So from the point of view of the way in which the movement occurs, the 'how', the movement seems to be descriptively independent of what happens further down the causal chain. Let me call this a 'mechanical' explanation of the movement, since it explains the mechanism by which or the way in which (Gr. μηχανή) a movement happens. A 'mechanical explanation' is an explanation of a causal sequence that says what moves what and how the movement occurs. Thus my wrist moves my hand and my hand moves the pencil by moving its fingers, etc.

However, the point about the phenomenal approach to the medium of perception seems to be that it is not just a teleological approach to a causal sequence that could also be explained mechanically. If this were so, we could say that there are such and such changes happening in the medium when a sensible quality affects it and these changes in turn give rise to

---

[9] Cf. Frede (1992) 101.

such and such changes in the sense-organ. So far the mechanical explanation. We could then add a teleological explanation. This would say that the reason why these changes occur is in order for the sense-quality to appear to a perceiver. And when all the changes in the medium and the sense-organ happen, then the sensible quality appears to the perceiver.

The problem is rather that if we give a purely phenomenal account of the medium, then we seem to be excluding a causal sequence that could also be explained mechanically. This is because of the way in which transparency is understood. A teleological account of the movement of my hand when writing a letter explains why I move my hand the way I do. But it supports rather than excludes a mechanical account, for given the mechanical account we can then say why the causal chain proceeds in the way it does. But the phenomenal account of the medium denies that the medium undergoes any other change in perception than letting the sensible quality appear through it. And this is not the kind of change in the medium that can support a mechanical explanation, for it is not based on there being any causal sequence that we could recognise as having a mechanical explanation.

If we look at an ordinary case of alteration the point may become clearer. I light a gas ring and put on the kettle. The heat of the gas heats up the kettle, which in turn heats up the water in the kettle. The kettle thereby mediates the heat from the fire to the water in the kettle. But it does so by itself becoming hot. So the effect that the fire has on the kettle is the same as the effect that the kettle has on the water. Both the kettle and the water become hot.[10]

Now the medium of perception cannot work just like the kettle for, if it did, the problems that I described earlier would

---

[10] At *DI* 2 459a28–b5 Aristotle himself uses the analogy of one body heating up the next as an analogy for perceptual mediation. The analogy applies because both change of temperature and perception are alterations, that is changes in quality. Notice also, however, that Aristotle can be seen as immediately qualifying the analogy in line with *De an.* II.5: the actuality of perception is only *a sort of* alteration (ἀλλοίωσίς τις); cf. 459b4.

arise since it would be possible to perceive the sense-object without a medium. It would be possible to perceive a sense-object which was put directly upon the sense-organ just as it is possible to heat up something without a medium. Thus it is possible for the fire to heat up the kettle without any mediation. But, as I tried to argue above, what we would perceive would not strictly speaking be the sense-object but the medium.

It was to avoid these consequences that the medium had to be free of the sense-qualities it mediated. Being free of the sense-qualities was a reason for saying that the medium in vision had to be the transparent, for the transparent is colourless (*De an.* II.7 418b28). But if it is free of the sense-qualities it mediates in actual perception, then it is very difficult to see what it receives from the sense-object and what it imparts to the sense-faculty. If this is difficult, how are we to understand the notion of a causal sequence in perception? How can the medium both affect (ποιεῖν) and be affected (πάσχειν) in mediating, as *De Anima* III.12 435a4–5 says the air does when it mediates; πάσχειν insofar as the sense-object affects it and ποιεῖν insofar as it affects the sense-faculty, for the medium is not affected by taking on the sense-quality from the sense-object and it does not affect by passing the sense-quality on to the sense-faculty?

So if the only change in the medium that happens in perception is the phenomenal change of letting something appear through it to a perceiver, then the mediation of sensible quality to a perceiver is quite different from the mediation of heat because, in the mediation of heat, we can say something about the change that the medium undergoes apart from the change that the medium in turn brings about in another object. Similarly, we could describe the movement of the hand without describing the movement of the pencil. But we cannot describe the change in the medium of perception without also describing the change in a perceiver, namely, that the sense-object becomes apparent to him. So here there seems to be a fundamental difference between the medium of perception and the medium in other causal sequences.

6. Can sensible qualities have non-perceptual effects?
An argument by Sarah Broadie

My argument is connected with a wider issue pointed out by Sarah Broadie.[11] She argues that even if Aristotle does allow of mediating 'physical' events in the medium or in the sense-organ or in both, the way in which these mediating events have to be understood is radically different from how modern philosophers understand the role of physical events in mental acts. As a consequence, it is impossible to assimilate Aristotle's theory of perception to any post-seventeenth-century philosophy of mind. The radical difference lies in the causal role of sensible qualities in Aristotle's theory. Aristotle thinks that sensible qualities are real features of physical objects in the world. They are there even when we are not perceiving them. Indeed if they were not there before our perception of them, there would be no way that they could cause us to perceive them for, according to Aristotle, the cause has to be prior in actuality to its effect. That might be taken as an Aristotelian way of saying that the sensible qualities are real: they exist in actuality before the perception of them. The sense-qualities' only causal effect on the world is to be perceived.[12] We would agree with Aristotle that a colour as such has only the effect of being seen. If we put a coloured thing

---

[11] Cf. Broadie (1993).

[12] Smell as such can also act on the air so as to make it smelly. But even in this case, as Broadie points out, the effect of the smell is to be understood with reference to perception. For the air becomes smelly insofar as it can act on the sense of smell so as to be smelt. It might be argued, however, that if the causal efficacy of sense-qualities is restricted in a way that includes being able to make other things perceptible, then the causal efficacy is not so very restricted after all, unless we want to say that the only effect that sense-qualities have on those things that they make *perceptible* is to make them just that, perceptible. But it is much more doubtful whether Aristotle would hold this than whether he would hold that there are no 'physical' intermediary changes in actual perceiving. For example, I heat up the air in a balloon. I thereby make it perceptible, able to cause a perception of heat. But Aristotle would accept that heating the air causes also an expansion of the air's volume (cf. the way in which the parts of animals expand because of heat and contract because of coldness, *MA* 701b13–16). So heat has both the effect of making the air hot and the effect of making it expand. One is an effect that is properly described as making the air perceptible, the other is not. For further discussion of this point, cf. ch. 6, sec. 6 below.

next to anything other than a perceiver, *qua* coloured it will have no effect on that thing. But when we, unlike Aristotle, think of colours as having this kind of restricted causal efficacy on the world, then that is based on our understanding of colours as secondary qualities. There are primary qualities, such as extension, which things have as such. For us it is the primary qualities that are the real features of things, not the secondary qualities because the secondary qualities exist only insofar as they appear to us in perception.

Because we think of only the primary qualities as being the real features of objects, we also ascribe the causal efficacy in perception to the primary qualities rather than to the secondary qualities. Thus what ultimately explains the power of an object's colour to cause perception is that the object's primary qualities have the power to act on us. So the reason why we see red is not that the phenomenal quality of red as such causes us to see it. The reason is that the phenomenal quality of red is based on some primary qualities in the sense-object, for instance, those features of the object's surface that reflect light with a certain wave-length. These primary qualities act on us not as perceivers as such. They act on us insofar as we are also physical objects with certain primary qualities. For instance, we have sense-organs and a nervous system that behave in such and such a way given such and such electro-chemical impulses. So our belief in the causal efficacy of colours in perception is not based on the phenomenal qualities of colour as such, how red appears to us in perception. It is based on the primary qualities that underpin these phenomenal qualities.

Let me quote at length how Broadie contrasts Aristotle with the 'modern' idea that the causal efficacy of sense-qualities rests with primary qualities:

... since [Aristotle] thinks of the so called secondary qualities as literally qualifying the physical objects perceived in terms of them, and since he thinks of the objects *qua* thus qualified as causing the corresponding perceptions, he should positively avoid any theory that seeks to bridge some presumed gap between awareness and the external stimulus by means of a series of micro-changes in respect of primary qualities. For this would damage his causal account of perception, not only because it involves the strange notion that, say, a colored object as such gives rise to primary quality events, but also because it threatens to make color causally redundant. If the perception of color can be directly caused by those primary quality changes, then why suppose that the color is what indirectly causes the former rather than anything else that can trigger the latter? For if a color can do this, having so little affinity with its immediate effect, there is no limit to what else it might be able to do, no less normally and naturally. We can neaten the situation theoretically by supposing that the mediating changes are caused not by the color as such, nor by just any other quality happening to have those effects, but by the primary quality configuration of the object's surface. But now the color itself does no work at all, and it is absurd to continue to believe that colors, etc., are genuine qualities of objects. This is absurd because it ascribes colors, etc., to physical things while at the same time implying that the colors are incapable of making themselves known to percipients – percipients who are meanwhile experiencing colors as a result of quite other causes! A color that is real but incapable of being seen is more repugnant to the intellect than a color (considered as an external quality) that gets itself seen without mediation by special physiological events.[13]

So a theory of perception that requires there to be other features of the sense-object to explain the causal efficacy of colour in perception is also a theory that undermines the causal efficacy of colour as a phenomenal quality. But Aristotle says that the phenomenal qualities are real features of objects. That commits him to saying also that they have causal efficacy in their own right. They are able to bring about a perception in a perceiver in suitable circumstances. The colour that I perceive is the colour that the object has and it is because the object has this colour that it causes me to see it. There is no further 'primary' quality of the object in terms of which the colour's ability to make me see it has to be explained. If there were such a 'primary' quality, then there would be little point in saying that the colour was a real feature of the object, for if the colour did not in its own right have at least this causal power, to bring about perception of itself in a suitably disposed perceiver, then it is very difficult indeed to see what other causal power it would have. But

---

[13] Broadie (1993) 144–5.

something without any causal power at all is no candidate for being a real feature of an object.[14]

So far Broadie's argument. I should like now to bring this argument to bear on the question I asked earlier. The question was: how are we to understand the medium's role in a causal sequence if the medium does not change in perception in any other way than by letting the sensible quality appear through it to a perceiver? The difficulty was that the only change that the medium undergoes is the change that the perceiver undergoes: the sense-quality appears to him through the medium. There is no change we can say that the medium first undergoes and that the medium in turn imparts to the perceiver apart from what happens to the perceiver.

Now if, as Broadie says, the causal efficacy of sensible qualities is restricted to causing a perception in a suitable perceiver, then that would also seem to be a good reason for saying that the sensible quality cannot cause any change in the medium apart from just this, that it actualises its potentiality to be seen through by a perceiver. But the medium actualises this potentiality only when the perceiver perceives the sensible quality. So this does not seem to be an actuality which we can use to explain the medium as a mediating cause in a causal sequence, for if the actuality of the medium is to cause the actuality in the perceiver, then the actuality of the medium has in some sense to be prior to the actuality in the perceiver.[15] When the fire heats the water in the kettle, then the fire actualises the kettle's potentiality to become hot and the kettle's heat then in turn actualises the water's potentiality to become hot. There is no significant difference here between the effect that the heat of the fire has on the kettle and the effect that the heat of the kettle has on the water.

But in the case of the medium of perception, there is no effect on the medium apart from the effect that the medium has

---

[14] As Plato's Eleatic Stranger might agree; cf. his definition of τὸ ὄν as what has the power either to change something else or to be changed (even by the most insignificant thing and even if only once), *Soph.* 247d–e; cf. also Geach (1969) 65–6.

[15] Prior, but not necessarily chronologically prior; cf. *Sens.* 6 446a20–447a11 and sec. 9 below.

on the perceiver, namely, that the perceiver comes to perceive through the medium. This is as it should be if the sensible quality has no other efficacy than making itself perceived. That is why it is so difficult to understand the medium's role in terms of a causal sequence similar to the one we see when the fire heats the water in the kettle.

But if this is correct, then the consequence of understanding the causal efficacy of the sensible quality as restricted to causing perception in a suitable perceiver is not only as Broadie shows. It is not just that referring to other causal mechanisms in order to bridge the 'causal gap' between the sensible quality and the perceiver undermines the power of the sensible quality as such to cause a perception in the perceiver. The problem is also that this power is undermined by any reference to a causal intermediary in perception that is affected by the sensible quality but does not perceive it and that in turn may affect the perceiver so that he perceives it.

Any reference to a further causal sequence involving inter-mediary causes that are not affected perceptively by the sense-object suggests one of two possibilities. *Either* there are then changes in the medium that might occur even if no perception was brought about at the end of it. Thus the fire can heat the kettle even when there is no water in the kettle. The effect that the heat has on the kettle is in this respect independent of whether the hot kettle brings about any further changes in something. Similarly, I can move my hand even when I am not holding a pencil and writing. If this is the case also in perception, then the causal efficacy of the sensible quality is not restricted to causing perception. For it can cause changes in the medium irrespective of whether the changes in the medium cause further changes. *Or* perception involves changes in the medium that are not sufficiently explained by the efficacy of the sensible quality as a phenomenal quality. It is not the redness that appears to us that causes the changes in the medium. For this redness has only the power to appear in perception, not to cause other changes in a medium that does not perceive. So it has to be some other aspect of the redness. But if so, we seem to have gone back to assuming that there is another feature of the sense-object than its phenomenal qualities that brings about the causal changes in perception. We have returned to assuming causal powers other than the phenomenal quality of red in explaining perception. But this sort of assumption was part of the modern approach from which Broadie extricated Aristotle.

7. A solution

Now it seems to me that in order to get out of this difficulty one need give up neither the idea that the causal efficacy of a sensible quality is restricted to causing perception nor the idea that the sensible quality as such is a sufficient cause of perception. Rather one needs to have a much clearer idea of what it means to say that there is a 'causal gap' between the sense-quality and the perceiver and a much clearer idea of how 'transparency' is supposed to bridge that gap.

What I have said up till now suggests that perception introduces a causal gap of cause and effect. The suggestion is that we need *more* causes and effects in the medium in order to fill in a causal chain in which the sense-object and the perceiver occur as the first cause and the last effect only at either end. It is as if we needed intermediary causes and effects in the medium different from the sense-object and the perceiver in order to bring us from the first effect that the sense-object has on the medium to the last effect that the medium has on the sense-organ.

But in fact the gap seems much rather to be a gap in *continuity* between the sense-object and the perceiver. The 'causal gap' is the gap that has to be bridged because the sense-object and the sense-organ will be discontinuous if there is nothing between them that they are both continuous with. But there has to be continuity between the sensible quality and the sense-organ in order for the sensible quality to act upon the sense-organ. This was the point of the passage in *Physica* VII.2. The point was not to introduce further causes and effects in between the sense-object and the perceiver. It was to show that they were continuous in such a way that the one could act upon the other; to show, in other words, that the sense-object could be the cause of the perception, not that the sense-object could be the cause of *something else* which could be the cause of perception.

Once this continuity has been established we do not need further causes than the sensible quality, for it is the sensible quality that holds the causal agency all the way through the medium. It is the *kinēsis* of the sense-quality that continues all the way through the medium because the medium is continuous. Aristotle says, in *De Sensu* 2 438b4–5, 'whether the medium between what is seen and the eye is light or air, it is the change through this which causes seeing'. But the medium does not have its own *kinēsis* just as the transparent does not have its own colour and just as the wax does not have its own seal. The change in the medium is the change *of* the sense-object in the sense that it is the sense-object that continues causing the change throughout the medium. Similarly, it is the seal of the signet ring that in the image of *De Anima* III.12 continues all the way through the wax to its other end. When Aristotle says that the change in the medium is the change of the sense-object he means that the sense-object is the cause of the change.

This is a notion of the sense-object causing a change through the medium that we can well make sense of on the 'phenomenal approach', for we say that the colour appears all the way through the transparent. There is no other causal agency than that of the sense-quality at any stage in this mediation. If we were to say at any stage of the mediation what the immediate cause of the change in the medium was, we would say that it was the sensible quality, for the medium has changed just insofar as the sensible quality is apparent up to that point in the medium. The change is a change in the medium but it is a change by the sensible quality. Aristotle says of colour that it is its nature to be able to change what is transparent in actuality (*De an.* II.7 418a31–b2). Perhaps one can see more clearly now why this power of colour to change the transparent is an important corollary of its power to cause vision. The two powers are not distinct as it is impossible to actualise the one without actualising the other. The colour will not be seen unless it changes the transparent. But nor will the transparent be changed by the colour unless the colour is seen, for the transparent is changed only when the colour appears all the way through it, and here appearing implies appearing to a perceiver. It is only insofar as the colour appears to a perceiver that it appears through the medium at all. So the transparent could not be changed by the colour unless there was a perceiver at the other end of it to whom the colour appeared through the transparent.

So the phenomenal approach is consistent with the idea that the medium bridges a causal 'gap' between an object and the sense-faculty if we understand this idea correctly, that is, if we understand that the gap is not to be bridged by introducing intermediary causes other than the object's sense-quality but simply by establishing a continuum between the object and the sense-faculty through which the sense-quality can act on the sense-faculty.

What are we to say on this account about the effect of the sense-quality on the medium? The medium is said to be affected by the sense-quality and in turn affect the sense-faculty. If I am right, this means that the medium is affected by the sense-quality all the way up to the sense-faculty. The medium does not itself become the sense-object, for the medium is in direct contact with the sense-organ and nothing that is in direct contact with the sense-organ can be perceived.

The way in which the transparent medium receives colour therefore has to be rather different from the way in which an ordinary object receives the colour. For example the way in which the transparent medium takes on the red colour when I see a red pillar box has to be rather different from the way in which the transparent water goes red if you mix it with red dye. The transparent medium does not literally go red the way the water does. This is borne out also by everyday experience. If you look at a red pillar box and I look at the air in between you and the pillar box I do not see the air as red. But when I mix water with red dye everybody can see the water as red. Nevertheless there is a sense in which we can say that the transparent in between the pillar box and me goes red, for in my line of vision the transparent is red.[16] This is not a redness that the medium has in itself, for if you take away the pillar box the transparent is no longer red in my line of vision. The medium goes red insofar as the area of my visual field that the transparent occupies goes red. It is clear that the medium goes red only in a perceptual way. This is shown also by the fact that the redness does not appear to somebody who is not looking at the pillar box but at the air in between me and the pillar box. If the medium went red in any other way, how could it be that the medium only appears red in the perceiver's line of vision? Since there is no redness in the area of his visual field that the transparent occupies whereas there is redness in the area of my visual field that the transparent occupies the difference between the two cases must be that I am perceiving a red pillar box through the transparent whereas he is not. So the transparent goes red only in the sense that it mediates redness in vision.

The medium, then, goes red only insofar as redness appears in the part of the transparent that occupies the eye line in between the perceiver and the sense-object. The medium is red only insofar as the redness of the object acts on the perceiver through the medium. This is a notion of the medium's being coloured that nicely matches Aristotle's claim that the transparent is 'what is visible not in itself but because of the colour of another object'.[17] You do not ever see the transparent as such. You see it insofar as you see another object's colour through it.

8. Mediation and 'Cambridge' change

It might look as if my account of mediation makes the change in the medium into what has been called a mere 'Cambridge' change. Let me explain. Peter Geach defined a 'Cambridge'

---

[16] Cf. Burnyeat (1993) 425. For a similar suggestion for Plotinus, cf. Emilsson (1988) 85–93.

[17] *De an.* II.7 418b4–6.

change as follows: something has undergone a Cambridge change if a predicate that was true of it at one time is false of it at another time.[18] To use the example Geach took from Plato: if Theaetetus has grown to be taller than Socrates, then Socrates has changed, according to the Cambridge criterion, even though his height has remained the same throughout, for it is true that Socrates was taller than Theaetetus before and that he is not taller than Theaetetus now. That is sufficient, on the Cambridge criterion, for Socrates to have changed, for one of the predicates previously true of Socrates, namely, 'taller than Theaetetus', is now false of him.

Socrates has 'changed' insofar as his relation to Theaetetus has changed. And his relation to Theaetetus has changed only because Theaetetus has undergone a real change. Another way of describing Socrates' 'change' in becoming smaller than Theaetetus is therefore to say that he has undergone only a relational change, for he has changed insofar as his relation to Theaetetus has changed: before, he was taller than Theaetetus, now he is smaller. Socrates has not changed in relation to what Socrates was before. By contrast, Theaetetus has changed in himself. He is not just different now in relation to something else. He is different from what he himself was before the change. The same cannot be said for Socrates, whose change is therefore a *mere* Cambridge change.

Now it might seem that on my interpretation mediation is a mere 'Cambridge' or relational change. I argued that the medium is changed by the sense-object insofar as the sense-object appears to the perceiver through it. Unlike the kettle which itself had to become hot to mediate the heat to the water, the medium only became coloured insofar as the colour appeared through the medium to a perceiver. In other words, the medium only took on the colour insofar as the colour acted on the sense-faculty through the medium. It seems therefore that the medium only changes insofar as its relation to something that really does change changes. For the medium only

---

[18] Geach (1969) 71–2. As Geach notes (72), all real changes are also Cambridge changes, but not all Cambridge changes are real changes.

changes insofar as it comes to be in between that which causes a change and that which is changed. The only thing that really changes is the perceiver. The medium changes only insofar as its relation to the perceiver has been changed by the perceiver undergoing the real change of perceiving the object.

To use an analogy, 'mediates' is a relation like 'is in between'. If I travel to Britain from Africa I can say that France is now in between me and Italy, which it was not when I was in Africa. The 'change' that France has undergone is of course a mere relational change. I am the only one in the equation who has really changed position. All the countries are where they were before. Could we not similarly say when I am seeing an object that a certain stretch of transparent air or water is now in between me and the object? The fact that I see the object through the transparent involves no more of a change in the transparent than the fact that France is now in between me and Italy, which it was not before, involves a change in France. Both the medium and France have only changed insofar as their relation to something that really has changed has changed.

For various reasons we should resist this account of mediation. First of all, Aristotle has no truck with the notion of relational change. He denies that we can talk about change in the category of relation.[19] Second, in *De Sensu* 6 he denies that the relationship between sense-object and sense-faculty in perception is merely a relation like being equal:

it is certainly not the case that the one thing is seen and the other sees because they are related to each other in a certain way, just as equals are [equals because they are related to each other in a certain way]; for then there would be no need for either of them to be in a certain place: for the things that become equal it does not matter whether they are close to or far away from each other. (446b10–13)

The sense-object is not perceived by the sense-faculty simply by standing in a certain relation to the sense-faculty. An object is not perceived by a sense-faculty the way an object is equal to another simply insofar as there is a certain relation

---

[19] Cf. *Phys.* v.2 225b11–13, vii.3 246b11–12; Williams (1989) 43.

between them, for if the sense-object being perceived by the sense-faculty was like an object being equal to another object, then there would be no reason why vision should not take place even if the sense-object was very far away from the sense-faculty. I could be in Europe perceiving a panda in China, just as I can be in Europe being equal in height to the panda.

'Being perceived by' is not just a relation like 'being equal to' for the reason that perception happens when the sense-faculty is *acted on* by the sense-object. The sense-object makes the sense-faculty like itself. It is only if the sense-faculty is not too far from the sense-object that the sense-object can act on the sense-faculty. The colours, for example, of the panda make me see them; but only if I am within a certain distance from the animal. By contrast, the size of the panda does not cause me to be equal in height to the panda any more than my height causes the panda to be equal in height to me. There are independent causes of why the panda and I have the heights we have. Our heights only happen to be equal.

The fact that perception is not just a relation like equality imposes constraints on the medium. As we have seen, there must be a medium in between the sense-object and the sense-organ. For only then is the sense-object in contact with the sense-organ in the way required for the one to act on the other. For the same reason, the medium must be continuous. In the case of the medium of vision, for example, the medium must be transparent in the line of vision all the way from the sense-object to the perceiver's eyes. Asked why we do not see around corners, Aristotle could answer 'because the corners are non-transparent obstacles'.

The necessity of a continuous medium is relevant, then, to the question why we perceive objects only when we are in a certain spatial relationship to them. The continuity of the medium is relevant also to the question why it takes time for some sense-objects to be perceived. Aristotle says that there is a delay between the emission of the sound or smell and its reception by the perceiver (cf. *Sens.* 6 446b5–6). The delay is explained by the fact that the medium, though continuous, is divided. 'It is reasonable', Aristotle says, 'that this [sc. the delay] happens both in the case of sound and smell: for like air and water they are continuous though their change is nevertheless divided into parts' (*Sens.* 6 446b13–15). Aristotle's reasoning seems to be this. The medium is divided into continuous parts (*Sens.* 6 446b14). The change from the sense-object 'travels'[20] through the medium. Because the medium has parts the change must arrive at one part before it can arrive at the adjacent part (446b13–15). The change through the medium can be said to have parts insofar as the change arrives at successive parts of the medium (cf. 447a4–5). There is therefore a part of the medium which the change arrives at before it has 'travelled' through all of the medium. Let us imagine that I am standing at a certain location L^1 perceiving an object located at L^2. For me to perceive the sense-object the change from the sense-object has to 'travel' from L^2 to L^1. The change 'travels' through the medium in between those two locations. There will then be a part of the medium which the change arrives at before it arrives at L^1 for, as I said, there is a part of the medium which the change arrives at before it has 'travelled' through all of the medium. Let us call the location of this part L^3. Now if you stand at L^3 the change from the sense-object will reach you before it reaches me at L^1 since the change arrives at L^3 before it arrives at L^1. This is why people who stand closer to the source of a sound or a smell perceive the sound or smell before those who stand further away (446a24–5). For example, if you stand close to the

---

[20] *Sens.* 6 446a21–2 says that it is either the sense-object or the change from the sense-object that travels. But Aristotle's answer to the aporia at 446b17–20 (how can many people perceive the same object?) shows that his considered position is that it is the affection and form of the sense-object, without the matter of the object, that 'travels' through the medium rather than the sense-object itself; cf. 446b25–6. It is the sensible form rather than the form and the matter that is conveyed through the medium. That is why many people can perceive the same object. If the matter had to travel to different people, as suggested by the effluence theory, it is clear that different matter would reach different people and that they would therefore not perceive the same object. Burnyeat (1993) 429–30 argues, in line with his general interpretation, that the 'travelling' is only a quasi-travelling, not a literal motion through space. I flag the possibility of such an interpretation by using quotation marks around 'travelling'.

lightning you will hear the thunder before somebody who stands further away.

There will be a time, then, at which the change has 'travelled' through some parts of the medium but not through all of the medium. The time that it takes for the change to 'travel' through the medium to the perceiver can then be said to be divisible too (446a30–b1), for there is a time at which the change is 'travelling' through the medium which is different from the time at which the change has 'travelled' through the medium. The time it takes the change to reach L^3 from L^2 is not all of the time it takes the change to reach L^1 from L^2. So the time it takes the change to reach L^1 from L^2 must have parts.

For Aristotle to say that the change through the medium has temporal parts implies that it is what he would call 'a change' (*kinēsis*) as opposed to what he would call 'an actuality' (*energeia/entelecheia*). One of the ways in which he distinguishes *kinēsis* from *energeia* is by saying that in a *kinēsis* there is a time at which it is true to say that the *kinēsis* is happening but has not yet happened. Take for example the *kinēsis* of building a house. When you build a house there is a time at which it is true to say that you are building the house but false to say that you have built the house, for whilst you are building the house the house is not yet built. It is only when you have finished building the house that you can say that you have built the house. But when you have finished building the house you cannot say that you are building it. In other words, when you are building the house you have not (yet) built the house. But when you have built it you are not (still) building it. There is therefore no time, either during or after the *kinēsis,* at which you can say *both* that you are building a house and that you have built it.

By contrast with the *kinēsis*, it is always true to say of an *energeia* when it happens that it is both happening and has happened. In *Ethica Nicomachea* x.4 Aristotle seeks to show that pleasure is an *energeia* rather than a *kinēsis.* The test is whether we can always say when we are having pleasure that we have had pleasure. The answer is that we can, just as we can say whenever we are enjoying ourselves that we have (already) enjoyed ourselves. However, the interesting point for our purposes is that Aristotle in *Ethica Nicomachea* x.4 also uses perception as an example of an *energeia*. So whenever I am perceiving I have at the same time (already) perceived. Perception, then, is an *energeia* rather than a *kinēsis* on the criterion that whenever one is perceiving one has already perceived.

In contrast, it is clear that the mediation of sounds and smells takes time, for there is a time at which the change is 'travelling' through the medium but has not yet finished 'travelling'. This implies that the mediation is a *kinēsis* rather than an *energeia*. There is a time at which it is true to say that the change is being mediated but has not yet been mediated. Similarly, there was a time at which it was true to say that the house was being built but had not yet been built and that was what picked building a house out as a *kinēsis* rather than an *energeia*. We have the interesting situation, then, that whereas perception is an *energeia* the mediation of the change to the perceiver is a *kinēsis*. Let us explore.

At *De Sensu* 6 446b2–10 Aristotle distinguishes the point that perception is an *energeia* from the point that the mediation of the sense-quality is a *kinēsis*.

even if everything at the same time hears [or 'is hearing'] and has heard, and in general perceives [or 'is perceiving'] and has perceived, and if there is no coming to be of them [sc. hearing and perceiving], but they are without coming into being, nonetheless [ὅμως οὐδὲν ἧττον] just as the sound when a blow has just happened is not yet at the organs [τῇ ἀκοῇ] – that this happens is clear also from the transformation of the letters since the motion [φορᾶς] is happening in the medium: for people clearly have not heard what was said because the air is transformed whilst being moved – are the colour and the light also like that?[21]

He makes it clear that he does not want to repeat the point made in *Ethica Nicomachea* x.4 that it may not take time for

---

[21] Aristotle does not use the word '*energeia*' itself here. However, he seems to assume that his audience are familiar with the distinction between an activity that has taken place already whenever it is taking place and an activity that when it is taking place has not yet taken place. The fact that in these lines he does not label this as a distinction between *energeia* and *kinēsis* is less important.

the perceiver to perceive once the sense-quality has acted on his sense-faculty. He wants to make a point about whether the mediation takes time, that is whether it takes time before the sense-object reaches the perceiver, and not whether the perception takes time once the sense-quality has reached the perceiver. In short, Aristotle wants to focus on the time the change in the medium takes rather than on the time the change in the perceiver does or does not take.

It is only some of the sense-qualities whose mediation takes time. Aristotle takes it to be clear from experience that the mediation of smells and sounds takes time. We can see this from the fact that people nearer the source of the smell or sound perceive the smell or sound sooner than people standing further away. It is also clear that the delay is put down to what happens in the medium rather than what happens in perception, for the change from the sound or smell 'travels' through the medium. There is evidence of this again from experience, for the reason why people mishear what has been said to them is that the sound whilst 'travelling' is transformed by the movement in the air.[22]

Vision, however, presents a special case, for whereas the mediation in sounds and smells takes time the mediation in vision is instantaneous. The difference is explained by the fact, as Aristotle sees it, that the change by sound and smell through the medium is a different sort of change (*kinēsis*) from the change by colour through the transparent. The change by sound and smell is a sort of locomotion (*phora*). The change by colour is a sort of alteration (*alloiōsis*). Locomotion takes time, for when the change from the sound 'travels' through the medium it has to arrive at one part of the medium before it can reach the next. Alteration, by contrast, can be instantaneous. To illustrate the point, Aristotle uses the example of a (small) lake that freezes over all at once. This shows how a qualitative change can affect every part of a body instantaneously. Similarly, when the colour acts on the transparent the transparent is affected all at once.

[22] On this passage, cf. Burnyeat (1993) 430.

Again we should think about the implications for the question whether mediation is a mere Cambridge change. Geach argues that it is a sign of real change that it takes time. The implication may therefore seem to be that if a change takes no time it is a mere Cambridge or relational change. Consider again the case of Socrates' becoming smaller than Theaetetus because Theaetetus has grown. It has taken time for Theaetetus to become taller than Socrates because Theaetetus had to grow for a while before he could become taller than Socrates. However, when Socrates became smaller than Theaetetus there had been no corresponding process in Socrates leading up to the event. He did not have to shrink but only to remain the same throughout the time during which Theaetetus was growing. After a while, when Theaetetus had grown sufficiently he reached a height at which he was taller than Socrates and when this happened Socrates *ipso facto* became smaller than Theaetetus. So no process took place in Socrates that led him at this time to become smaller than Theaetetus.

One could, perhaps, say that it took Socrates as long to become smaller than Theaetetus as it took Theaetetus to become taller than Socrates. But if we reflect that Theaetetus' becoming taller than Socrates was constituted by his growing taller than Socrates whereas there was no corresponding process in Socrates of shrinking, we can see why for Theaetetus becoming taller than Socrates had to take time whereas for Socrates becoming smaller than Theaetetus happened immediately when Theaetetus had reached a certain height. Theaetetus had to suffer growing pains for years before he could outgrow Socrates. Socrates could stay the same.[23] You *could* say that Theaetetus when he was growing was in the process of becoming taller than Socrates. But to say during that time

---

[23] Cf. Williams (1989) 43:

> Socrates' coming to be shorter than Theaetetus is no more or less instantaneous than Theaetetus' own growth. The most we can say is that it may be possible to set up a contrast between them in terms of the present continuous tense: we say 'Theaetetus is becoming taller than Socrates', but not 'Socrates is becoming shorter than Theaetetus'. This may reflect the fact that there has to be a relevant process going on in Theaetetus, but not in Socrates. Nevertheless, there are not two distinct events, one instantaneous and one which takes time.

that Socrates was also in the process of becoming smaller than Theaetetus would be to ignore the asymmetry between the two cases. The reason why we can say that Theaetetus is in the process of becoming taller than Socrates is that *Theaetetus* is in the process of growing. And there is no process corresponding to Socrates becoming smaller than Theaetetus. To say that it took Socrates as long to become smaller than Theaetetus as it took Theaetetus to become taller than Socrates is to suggest that there was a process in Socrates during that time that corresponded to Theaetetus growing taller. But there was no such process.

Because the mediation of colour is instantaneous it might look like a relational or mere Cambridge change such as Socrates becoming smaller than Theaetetus, for the mediation of colour is instantaneous, and Geach said that it was characteristic of mere Cambridge changes to be instantaneous. But Aristotle does not explain the fact that the mediation of colour is instantaneous by saying that it is because the mediation is not a 'real' change. As his analogy with the frozen lake shows, his point is not that the colour does not really affect the medium; the point is that it affects the medium *all at once*. The alteration in the medium is contrasted with locomotion not in terms of being less of a real change than locomotion but in terms of belonging to a different species of change, alteration, that can happen at once. The mediation of colour, *insofar as it is instantaneous* (that is not necessarily in other respects), is simply like the ordinary and unexceptional alteration of a lake freezing over all at once. So the operative contrast for Aristotle is between two different species of change, alteration, which can be instantaneous, and locomotion,which takes time. The contrast is not between a real change that always takes time and mere Cambridge change that is instantaneous.

9. Conclusion

Mediation for Aristotle, then, is not a mere Cambridge change. It is a 'real' change insofar as it falls into the species alteration and alteration is a species of the genus 'change' (*kinēsis*). The fact that some mediation is instantaneous is explained by saying that it is an alteration, not by saying that it is a relational change. However, just because we should describe mediation as a 'real' change by contrast to a mere Cambridge change it does not follow that we should think that mediation shares all the features of normal alteration and locomotion. The conspicuous feature about mediation is the way in which the medium undergoes a 'phenomenal' change. The medium takes on the quality of the sense-object only insofar as the quality appears to a perceiver. For example, the transparent becomes coloured only insofar as the colour appears to a viewer through it. I argued that we should make sense of this by imagining the colour of an object appearing in the transparent in the viewer's line of vision.

In chapter I I suggested that the role of the transparent inside the eye is to mediate the sense-quality to the seeing part further inside the perceiver. The sense-organ was an internal medium. This suggestion emerged from a reading of *De Sensu* 2 438b6–8. Here Aristotle said that just as there is no vision if there is no light outside, so there is no vision if there is no light inside the eye. The light outside is necessary as a medium of the sense-quality. Saying that there is no vision if there is no light inside the eye just as there is no vision if there is no light outside suggested that the light inside the eye was also required as a medium. Just as actual transparency was a necessary medium outside the perceiver, so it was a necessary medium inside the perceiver. If so, the role of the transparent inside the eye is to mediate the sense-quality to a perceiving part further inside the perceiver.

If the medium and the sense-organ are transparent for the same reason, namely, to mediate the colour, it suggests that what happens in the external medium when it mediates colour is also what happens in the sense-organ when it mediates the colour. Since there is no literal colouration but only a phenomenal change in the medium, this suggests that there is no literal colouration but only a perceptual colouration in the *korē* also. The colouration of the medium was not a normal colouration of the sort that, for example, happens when you pour dye in water. It was a colouration of the medium only in the sense that the colour appeared in the medium to a perceiver.

If the *korē* is a transparent medium there can be no literal colouration of it for the same reasons that there can be no literal colouration of the transparent. The change in the *korē* must then be that the colour of the object appears to the viewer through the *korē*. The colour that changes all the parts of the medium and the colour that changes the sense-organ remains squarely the colour *of the sense-object*, for neither the medium nor the sense-organ becomes coloured in the way that a sense-object is coloured. This is important for it means that we can say that it is the colour of the sense-object that we see rather than the colour of the medium or the sense-organ even though both the medium and the sense-organ in a way receive the colour in vision. The analogy, then, between the transparent medium and the transparent *korē* tells against a literalist interpretation of vision.[24]

---

[24] In ch. 3, sec. 3 and ch. 5, sec. 4, I argue against a literalist interpretation of the mediation of sound and smell.

3

HEARING

1. What is hearing?

The explanation of the faculty of hearing and its organ, the ear, follows the same pattern as the explanation of sight and the eye. We need to understand first of all what sound is, for sound as the proper object of hearing is the actuality that explains the potentiality of hearing. Once we know what the potentiality of hearing is we can explain the sense-organ as the matter required for the presence of this potentiality.

2. The production of sound

Sound is produced, Aristotle says at *De Anima* II.8 419b4–7, by objects that are solid and smooth, a gong, for instance. Such objects are said to 'have sound' and to have the potentiality to make a sound. Aristotle explains the potentiality of such objects as the ability 'to produce an actual sound *in between itself and the sense of hearing*'. So direct reference is made to the sense of hearing in this initial explanation of what a potentiality to make a sound is. The reference to the sense of hearing is obviously not just meant to locate the sound spatially, that is it is not just supposed to tell us that the sound occurs somewhere in between the sounding object and the sense of hearing. The reference implies rather that the sound is set up so as to reach a sense-faculty of hearing. 'In between' is the language of *perceptual mediation*. What is in between what has sound and the sense of hearing is what mediates the sound from the one to the other in a perception of the sound. So saying that what it is for something to have sound is an ability to produce actual sound in between itself and the sense of hearing is another way of saying that to have sound is to have the ability to produce something that can be heard. To produce a sound is to produce something that can be mediated to a perceiver in an act of hearing. This is as we would expect if Aristotle's interest in sound is in sound as an object of perception, as what is audible, just as his interest in colour was in what was essentially visible.

How does what has sound actualise its potentiality to make sound? First, what has sound must receive a blow from another solid body. It is the blow that produces the sound.[1] But you cannot produce a blow if you just have one thing. You need to have something that you hit it with. This is the thing in relation to which (πρός τι, *De an.* II.8 419b10) the sound arises. The blow is described as involving a φορά, that is, a locomotion or spatial movement.[2] When you strike something, you move one object against another. The second condition is that the blow should occur in something (ἔν τινι, 419b10). This condition relates specifically to the medium of hearing. The reason why the blow has to occur not just in something but more specifically in air or water is that sound is only audible in air or water. This is because air and water are the only elements that will mediate sound to a perceiver. So only if the blow occurs in air or water will it produce an audible sound.

When Aristotle picks up the 'ἔν τινι condition' at 419b18, it is to say that 'sound is heard in air and, albeit less so, in water'. Throughout the passage, this condition continues to be a condition of audibility. Sometimes this is not immediately apparent from Aristotle's discussion. But that is because the air in which the sound is mediated has to resound or resonate in order for sound to be audible. So some of Aristotle's discussion is taken up with the issue of under which condition the air will resound. But this discussion is required only because the air has to resound in order to mediate the sound from the thing that has sound to the sense of hearing. The discussion of

---

[1] *De an.* II.8 419b10.

[2] *De an.* II.8 419b11–13: διὸ καὶ ἀδύνατον ἑνὸς ὄντος γενέσθαι ψόφον· ἕτερον γὰρ τὸ τύπτον καὶ τὸ τυπτόμενον· ὥστε τὸ ψοφοῦν πρός τι ψοφεῖ· πληγὴ δ'οὐ γίνεται ἄνευ φορᾶς. Striking something against something else involves a spatial movement.

the conditions in which the air will resound is parallel to the discussion of the transparent medium of vision. The actuality of the transparent as such, that is, light, was the condition under which colour could be seen, the condition under which colour was visible. Similarly, resonance in the air is now the condition under which sound is audible.

There is a difference between having sound, like a gong, and having the ability to resonate. Resonance is the ability to be affected by something *else* that has sound. In this sense, air is resonant to the sound of the gong when you hit it. But the air is not, as Aristotle goes on to explain at 419b19, responsible (κύριος) for the sound. What is responsible for the sound is the blow of one solid object against another. For instance, it is the blow of the hammer against the gong that is responsible for the sound. But the blow also has to be against (πρός) the air for there to be a sound. In other words, the air itself has to be one of the things that are struck when a sound is produced. However, air is easily dispersible. So unlike the solid objects, objects that themselves have sound, air is not something one can naturally strike. It is only under special conditions that air can be struck. These special conditions obtain when the air, against its natural tendency, is prevented from escaping or dispersing. However, the air can only be momentarily prevented from dispersing. That is why the blow to the solid object has to be quick and hard so that by its speed and force the blow can also hit the air before the air disperses.

Perhaps Aristotle has something in mind like tapping one's finger against a table. If one lowers one's finger slowly and softly till it rests on the top of the table, it will make no sound. But if one beats one's finger quickly on the table, there will be a sound. The difference is then, as Aristotle sees it, that the air has no time to escape when one moves one's finger quickly. The movement, as he puts it, anticipates or outstrips (φθάσαι) the escape of air, just as if one were quickly to strike a heap of sand before it collapsed (419b23–5). So the speed with which the blow is made has to be greater than the speed with which the air naturally disperses in order for a sound to occur.

In order for the air to convey the sound to the sense of hearing the air has to resonate. The air resonates when it is struck. But in order for it to be struck its natural tendency to be dispersed has to be kept in check. The air has to be contained, in other words. As an indeterminate body, however, the air has no natural limits of its own. Therefore the air has to be bounded by something else which will keep it together. By this reasoning, then, Aristotle is led to specify the kind of object that will contain the air. He says that:

Void is said correctly to be responsible [κύριον] for hearing. For it seems that air is void, and this [sc. the air] is what produces hearing, whenever it is changed as a continuous unity. But because of its tendency to disperse [ψαθυρὸς] the air does not make a sound [γεγωνεῖ] unless the thing that is struck is smooth. For then the air at the same time becomes one because of the surface. For the surface of a smooth thing is one. (419b33–420a2)

So it takes a smooth object to unify the air, for the surface of a smooth object is a unity and the air borrows the unity from the smooth object that encloses it. The air is one when next to a smooth surface. But when the air is one, it will resonate and can produce hearing. So, for instance, a smooth table will contain the air as a unity and prevent it from dispersing. But a rough carpet, for instance, will not. This is why tapping my finger on the table will make a noise whereas doing so on the rough carpet will not.

It is worth noting here that Aristotle says that air is responsible for *hearing*. For we have just (419b19) been told that air is not responsible for *sound*. Again the point is that air itself does not have sound in the way that a gong may be said to 'have sound'. But air may resonate to the sound of something else that does have sound in such a way that the resonance reaches a perceiver. In that case, we could say that it was the thing struck or the blow on that thing that was responsible for the *sound*. We would say that we heard the bell ring because the bell was responsible for the sound. But it is the air that is responsible for the sound being *audible* to the perceiver because it resonates. The reason why I do not just say that the air is responsible for hearing, as Aristotle puts it, is that it is strictly speaking also because a suitably disposed perceiver is present that the sound is actually heard. The resonance of the air, though necessary, is not sufficient for actual hearing. Hearing only occurs when the resonant air affects a perceiver.

3. The mediation of sound

The next point to address, then, is how the resonance of the air reaches the sense of hearing. *De Anima* II.8 420a3–5 starts out by redefining the ability to make sound, taking into account the results of the intervening discussion. The discussion has established that whether something has sound depends on whether it can contain the air around it in such a way that the air will resonate and will be able to cause hearing. That was why it was smooth objects that we said had sound since they make the air around them one and continuous. This idea that the air will only resonate if it is one and continuous, determines the rest of what Aristotle says about the mediation of sound:

That then has the ability to produce sound [ψοφητικὸν] which is able to change the air, which is one and continuous as far as the sense-organ of hearing [ἀκοῆς] because the sense-organ of hearing is of the same nature as the air. Because the sense-organ of hearing is in the air, the air inside will change whenever the air outside changes. (420a3–5)

So the condition under which the air mediates the sound to the inside of the ear is the same as the condition under which the air will resonate, namely, when the air is one and continuous. This condition of unity and continuity we recognise from the medium of vision and all the other mediated senses.[3]

Resonance serves the same function in the mediation of sound that transparency serves in the mediation of colour. Resonance is the ability to take on the sound of something else which has sound, just as transparency is the ability to take on the colour of something else. This is a mediating function because the air does not make its own sound (it is not re-

---

[3] Cf. ch. 2, secs. 2–4.

sponsible for the sound) but *re*sounds to the sound of something else. So when the air resonates it is not the air's own sound that can be heard but the sound of the object that is responsible for the sound. Similarly, when I see a colour through the transparent the transparent takes on the colour of the object but it does not have its own colour. That is also why the transparent is *trans*parent. Something else appears through it. It is not itself that appears to the perceiver.

Aristotle lacks a term similar to 'the transparent' for that through which a sound is heard. The ancient commentators aptly provided the term 'transsonant'.[4] This suggests the essential function that the resonant serves. The resonant is that *through* which the sound of another thing can be heard.[5]

The resonant takes on the sound of something else and conveys it as long as it remains resonant. That is to say, the air continues to convey the sound as long as it remains in the condition it was in when it first received the sound, that is, when it resonated around the object struck. It is the same fundamental condition of continuous unity that applies both to the air's ability to be struck and resonate and to its ability to convey the sound to a perceiver.

The condition that the medium should be one and continuous is not only fundamental to the mediation of sound but, as *De Anima* III.12 makes clear, applies to all media of perception. Aristotle (*De an.* III.12 435a2–5) compares the medium with a wax block that conveys the impression stamped onto one side of it all the way through the block to the other side as long as the block remains continuous and one. We can imagine how the transmission of the imprint might fail if there was a hole in the wax in which the imprint was lost, or

---

[4] 'τὸ διηχές'; cf. Burnyeat (1993) 425, n. 14.
[5] The argument of ch. 2 was that the transparent medium would not be a medium if it literally took on the sense-quality as its own quality. The medium must remain colourless throughout the mediation and take on the colour only to the extent that it appears through the medium. We see now that the resonant is described as what is soundless but which can take on the sound of something else *just as* the transparent was described as what is what is colourless but which can take on the colour of something else. The parallel suggests that the medium's taking on the sound must also be understood in a non-literal way; cf. Burnyeat (1993) 429–31.

a foreign body blocked or intercepted the imprint. Just as the transmission of the imprint through the wax would fail if the wax ceased to be one and continuous, so also would the transmission (the *kinēsis*) of the sense-object through the air fail if the air ceased to be one and continuous.

4. The sense-organ of hearing

We saw in the case of the eye that the sense-organ recreates the conditions of the medium. Like the medium, the eye had to be composed of transparent matter, for it is the transparent that has the ability to take on colour from something else and taking on the colour of something is what defines vision in something that has perception.[6] The same applies *mutatis mutandis* to the sense-organ of hearing. Just as the seeing part of the eye consists of transparent water, so the hearing part of the ear consists of resonant air. The sense-organ of hearing is, as *De Anima* II.8 420a5 puts it, 'in air'. The description of the air in the ear repeats the description of the air around the object struck. The ear in fact is composed so as to recreate the conditions under which the air will resonate.

For this reason the animal does not hear with every part of it, nor does the air penetrate everywhere. For the part which will be changed and which has soul does not have air everywhere.[7] The air itself is soundless because it is easily dispersed. But whenever it is prevented from dispersing, the change in it is a sound. The air in the ears has been walled up so as to be unchangeable [ἀκίνητος] in order that it may perceive accurately all the differences of the change. (420a5–11)

---

[6] Cf. *Sens.* 2 438b2–12.

[7] διόπερ οὐ πάντῃ τὸ ζῷον ἀκούει, οὐδὲ πάντῃ διέρχεται ὁ ἀήρ· οὐ γὰρ πάντῃ ἔχει ἀέρα τὸ κινησόμενον μέρος καὶ ἔμψυχον. I read ἔμψυχον at a8 with the manuscripts rather than Torstrik's emendation ἔμψοφον. I do not agree with Ross that ἔμψυχον is pointless, for the reason why hearing will take place in the ear when the still air is moved by sound is exactly that this air, unlike any other air, is ensouled. But if there is this point to ἔμψυχον, it must count against Torstrik's ἔμψοφον that, as Ross (1961) observes *ad loc.*, it requires us to make further changes to the text. We must add a further future participle after ἔμψοφον, such as γενησόμενον (thus: τὸ δὲ κινησόμενον μέρος καὶ ἔμψοφον γενησόμενον), for Aristotle goes on to say that the air in the ear is soundless so that it may, in a certain way, *become* sounding in hearing. Note also that ἔμψοφον is found nowhere in Aristotle and that the only occurrence mentioned by LSJ is as late as the sixth century AD.

The statement 'The air itself is soundless because it is easily dispersed. But whenever it is prevented from dispersing, the change in it is a sound' mirrors the statement at 419b22–3 that a sound is produced 'when the air remains after being struck and is not dispersed. For this reason the air makes a sound if it is struck quickly and forcibly.' The air needs to remain confined and not dispersed if it is going to resound to the sound that has already been produced. It need not receive another blow in order to resonate in the ear, for the blow that produced the sound is also sufficient to make the air in the ear resonate if the air in the ear is continuous and one with the air in which the blow was produced. So we do not need an additional spatial movement or φορά apart from the movement of the blow on the thing struck. We do not need the production of another sound in the ear but the preservation of the sound already produced. The air in the ear must be in a condition where it will receive a sound. This is what Aristotle refers to when he says that the air is itself ἄψοφον but will have a sound if prevented from dispersing.

Aristotle goes on to say at 420a15–20 that it is a sign of 'hearing or not hearing that there is a sound in the ear just as in a horn'. It is clear that we should take this to mean that it is a sign of not hearing that there is a sound in the ear and a sign of hearing that there is no such sound, for Aristotle goes on to say that the air that moves in the ear (when there is sound such as the sound in horns) has a 'movement' (κίνησις) of its own whereas (ἀλλά) the sound, that is the sound that we normally hear, comes from another object and is not 'native to the ear', as Hicks translates 'ἴδιος'. If the ear has a sound of its own, then that exactly prevents the ear from receiving the sound from without. Hence it prevents us from hearing.[8] The point is exactly analogous to the point made about the eyes in chapter 1. The eyes should be transparent, that is have no colour of their own, so that the faculty of sight is able to be changed by the colour of an external object. Similarly, the ear

---

[8] Cf. Burnyeat (1993) 429 with note 28.

should have no sound of its own in order for the faculty of hearing to be able to be changed by external sound.

We are now in a position to approach the composition of the ear from the same point of view from which we approached the composition of the eye, for we can understand why the ear is composed as it is by referring to conditions of resonance just as we could understand the composition of the eye with reference to conditions of transparence. Both resonance and transparency are functional attributes. They designate the ability to receive a sense-object at a stage in the act of perception.

A sign that we are dealing with a functional attribute in hearing too is that different elements may mediate sound. We hear both in air and in water (*De an.* ii.8 419b18). This suggests that it is not *qua* air or *qua* water or *qua* such and such a body that these elements can mediate sound but *qua* having a certain attribute. As Aristotle says of the sense-organ of vision in *De Sensu* 2 438a12–15: 'It is true that the eye consists of water. However, seeing takes place in it not *qua* water but *qua* transparent, and this is something water has in common with air.' Similarly, we see through water just as we see through air because they are both transparent. By the same reasoning, we hear through water and through air because they have some common attribute by which they can receive and transmit sound. This is the same attribute that enables the sense-organ of hearing to receive the sound in hearing, the attribute I have identified as resonance.

5. The composition of the organ of hearing

The ear has air walled up inside it and this internal air is the part that receives the sound because it is continous, through *poroi*,[9] with the external air that carries the sound from the object struck. The connate *pneuma* said at *De Generatione Animalium* ii.6 743b36–744a5 to be the content of these *poroi*

---

[9] Cf. *GA* ii.6 743b36–744a5.

is probably the same as the internal air referred to in other passages.[10] Thus at *De Anima* II.8 420a12 Aristotle calls the air walled up inside the ear connate (συμφυής).[11] It is noteworthy that this is all that he has to say about the composition of the inner ear. The proper sense-organ of hearing is, as Burnyeat and Lloyd have emphasised,[12] without any inner structure. The inner air is confined and connate but otherwise it is (and importantly, as we have seen, should be) no different from the external air with which it is continuous.

The air is inside the ear in order to be protected from the dispersal which would otherwise destroy its resonance. One way in which the air can be dispersed is if another body enters the inner ear. However, the fact that the air is hidden inside the ear makes this difficult and Aristotle suggests that the external structure of the ear also serves to prevent dispersal, for instance, by water entering the ear (*De an.* II.8 420a11–13). He says that we can hear in water because water not only does not enter as far into the ear as the ear's own air, that is as far as the hearing part of the ear, but also does not even enter the external ear. This is because of the outer ear's convolutions (τὰς ἕλικας).

What Aristotle says here is that the water does not even enter εἰς τὸ οὖς διὰ τὰς ἕλικας. Since the contrast is with the air inside the ear, 'τὸ οὖς' seems to be referring to the *external* ear. This is confirmed by passages in the biological works where Aristotle ascribes hearing to animals that do not have an οὖς. One such passage is *Historia Animalium* I.11 492a16–29. Aristotle first says that the whole of the ear is composed of gristle and flesh. A part of this is called the lobe and another part does not have a name. He then says that the inside has a composition, a φύσις, like spiral-shells (οἱ στρόμβοι, 492a17)

---

[10] Cf. Peck (1953) 591, appendix B (29).

[11] In Aristotle's similar discussion of the connate *pneuma* by which insects smell, the connate *pneuma* is contrasted with the external air, thereby indicating that we should think of the connate *pneuma* as a sort of internal *air*; cf. ch. 5, sec. 7 below. Again, however, I must defer to the literature mentioned in ch. 1, n. 107 (p. 92) for a discussion of the complexities of Aristotelian *pneuma*.

[12] Burnyeat (1993) 422–3; Lloyd (1991) 227.

and that the innermost part of it is a bone similar to τὸ οὖς. It is here that the sound finally arrives 'just as in a vessel'. It is clear that in order for there to be a comparison between the composition of the inner part of the ear and τὸ οὖς the two have to be distinct. Τὸ οὖς seems therefore specifically to be the external ear.

Having determined the reference of 'οὖς' in this way, Aristotle goes on to discuss which animals have (external) ears and which do not. He says that some animals such as the animals with feathers or horny scales do not have ears though they have a clear passage (πόρος).[13] This must be the passage that leads from the outside into the inner ear that was mentioned in *De Generatione Animalium* II.6 743b36–744a5,[14] where Aristotle said that 'smell and hearing are *poroi* connecting with the outer air'. The seal is, accordingly, an example of an animal that has no external ear but obvious aural passages by means of which (ᾗ) it hears.

The seal is mentioned in another passage in *De Generatione Animalium* v.2 781b22–8, where its lack of (external) ears is said to have been reasonably devised by nature.[15] The reason why it is reasonable that the seal should have no external ear appears to be that it lives in water. The external ear is 'a part of the body which is added to the aural passages in order to preserve the change of the air from a distance and it is therefore of no use to the seal; indeed ears would be counterproductive since they would receive a large amount of water' (781b25–8).[16] Living in water, the seal hears in water and not in air. But the external ear serves to preserve the change only when it is air that mediates sound. It does not serve to preserve the change in water when it is water that mediates sound. That is why the seal does not have external ears. As *Historia Animalium* suggested, the seal can hear simply by means of passages with no added external ear. Nature does

---

[13] Cf. *HA* II.10 503a5–6, IV.8 533a21–2.

[14] Quoted in full in Ch. I, sec. 10 (p. 91).

[15] εὐλόγως δ' ἀπείργασται ἡ φύσις καὶ τὰ περὶ τὴν φώκην ...

[16] It is not clear that this sentence is consistent with the *De an.* passage which said that the convolutions of the outer ear prevent water from entering.

nothing in vain. So since the seal does not need external ears it does not have any.

In *De Anima* II.8 Aristotle ignored what happens when water mediates sound. Perhaps that was because the focus was on human hearing and humans hear less well in water than in air (419b18). It cannot have been because sounds as such are heard less well in water, for at *Historia Animalium* IV.8 533b4–9 Aristotle says not only that fish hear but also that they hear extremely well, a fact that is exploited by fishermen in their fishing techniques (533b9–534a11). Fish hear well despite having no visible ears or apparently even such *poroi* as those with which birds hear. Aristotle suggests that this is because they live in water. He says that 'though a sound is very slight in the open air, it has a loud and alarming resonance to creatures that live in water' (533b6–7).

We know from *De Sensu* 2 438a15–16 that water is more easily confined than air. That was the reason why the eye consisted of water rather than air. So it may be that the reason why sounds are better heard in water than in air is that water is less easily dispersed than air. It therefore preserves the changes from the sense-object better than air. Water is naturally more resonant than air. This would explain why fish have less-developed ears. Less is required to preserve sounds in water than in air. So they do not need an external ear to do this job.

There may be an analogy here between the way in which fish hear in water and the way in which human beings see by day. Recall that by day the transparent medium is more fully actualised than at night because there is more light, which is why we see better by day than by night, the change from the sense-object being much stronger than at night. However, for people who had very transparent eyes, that was to say, blue-eyed people, the change from the sense-object could be too strong by day. It was preferable to have less transparent eyes when the medium was in such a condition that the change from the sense-object was conveyed very strongly to the sense-organ.

It seems that the hearing of fish in water is rather like the sight of people by day. In both cases the medium transmits the change from the sense-object exceptionally well. And in both cases it is preferable not to have a sense-organ that further increases the intensity of the change from the sense-object. In the case of human beings, it is preferable not to have eyes that are too transparent as that makes the change from the colour even more intense than it already is because of the excellent mediation. In the case of fish, it is preferable not to have an outer ear that further increases the resonance in the ear, thereby making the change from the sound even stronger than it already is because of the excellent mediating qualities of water.

The outer ear seems to be the functional analogue to the continuous tube that Aristotle in *De Generatione Animalium* v.2 781a8–10 imagines to extend from the sense of sight to the sense-object. This tube would create the optimal conditions of vision because it would prevent the change from the visible object from being dissipated. That is why animals see better at a distance if they have eyes that to a greater extent are like such a tube. For instance, animals with sunken eyes see better than animals with protruding eyes because the recess acts like the tube. (Compare using a rolled up newspaper as a telescope!) The recess prevents the dissipation of the change from the object. Similarly, the Laconian hound *smells* better because it has long nostrils that prevent the dissipation of the change from the fragrant object.

Aristotle suggests that the same applies to the ears. Thus 'animals that have ears which are big and stick out like the cornice of a house *and* a long internal spiral (ἑλίκην) hear better at a distance because they grasp the change from afar and transmit it to the sense-organ' (781b13–16). The function of the external ear and the function of the inner spiral seem clearly to be the same, to preserve the sound. This explains their similar construction.

However, Aristotle suggests that there is an aspect of perceiving well other than being able to perceive well at a distance. This is the ability to perceive accurately, that is the ability to perceive the finer details and differences in objects.

In this respect, the membrane surrounding the air walled up inside the ear (corresponding with the skin over the eye) is more important than the projection. If an animal has a long projection over its eyes but does not have pure liquid in its eyes and a thin skin covering the eyes, it may be able to spot objects at a great distance, but it will not be able to see them accurately (*GA* v.1 780b22–9). (If having a long projection from the eyes is like having a camera with a zoom lens, then having a fine membrane is like having a clean lens with no scratches.)

Human beings see more accurately than other animals but less well than some at a distance, for they have the most delicate skin on their eyes. As *De Partibus Animalium* II.13 657a34 says, 'it is to ensure keenness of vision that the skin over the *korē* is fine and delicate'. Therefore animals with hard skin over their eyes see less accurately.[17] The same applies to the membrane covering the inner ear. At *De Generatione Animalium* v.2 781b17, he seems to generalise his point to cover at least all the distance senses. The exceptional thinness of the skin around the sense-organ in man ensures that human beings, at least for their size, have the greatest accuracy of perception of all the animals.

What conclusions can we draw concerning Aristotle's explanatory procedure from his account of the ear? First, both the external ear and the membrane covering the inside of the ear are determined with direct reference to the function they serve, which is to preserve the change from the sense-object, thereby ensuring that the sound of the object will resonate in the ear. The external ear prevents the change from the sounding object from being dispersed when it arrives from afar. The membrane preserves the accuracy of the change. The outer ear and the membrane inside the ear do for resonance what the projection over the eye in some animals and the skin of the eye do for transparency. Like the composition of the eye, the composition of the ear is explained from the point of view of the sense-organ's potentiality to be changed by the sense-object.

---

[17] Cf. ch. 1, sec. 9.

Second, the differences between the organs of hearing in different animals tell us that whether a certain aural part belongs to an animal or not depends on the purpose that the part will serve for the animal in hearing and whether or not the part improves the animal's ability to hear, for example animals living in water do not need an external ear in order to hear. So the organ of hearing in fish has no further features than the inner sense-organ. In their case, the sense-organ proper is more than sufficient for these animals to receive the sound from the outside, for fish hear even better than many animals with complex organs of hearing.

6. How the environment determines the sense-organs

We can put the last point as follows: Aristotle ascribes those parts to the sense-organ that are necessary for a given species of animal to realise the actuality of perception *given its natural environment.*

How are we to understand the role of the environment in the composition of the sense-organs? We should notice first that the environment plays an important role for Aristotle in the explanation of animals in general. In *Historia Animalium* VIII.2[18] he says that animals have been divided according to their places: 'for some animals are land animals (πεζά) and others are water animals (ἔνυδρα)' (589a10–11).

The animals have the sort of parts that are serviceable to their natural activities given their natural environment. Thus animals are said to have lungs because they live on land (*PA* III.6 668b33). The explanation is as follows (668b34–669a7). All blooded animals are likely to get very hot. They therefore need cooling from the outside. The cooling can come either from taking in air or from taking in water. If the animal is a land animal it lives in air. So air is the element that is available to the animal to take in for which it must have suitable organs. These organs are the lungs. If the animal is a water animal, however, it must take in water to cool itself. Just as

---

[18] Book VII according to Balme (1991).

lungs are suitable organs for taking in air, so gills are suitable organs for taking in water. Hence water animals have gills instead of lungs.

The reason why water animals and land animals have different sense-organs is exactly parallel to the reason why they have different refrigeratory organs. Fish, insofar as they are animals, need perception. But if you are an animal that lives in water, then water is the medium that is available for you to perceive through. Perceiving through water requires you to have certain organs of perception. The organ of hearing that you need when hearing in water should not include an outer ear, for the outer ear might harm your hearing either by letting water into the inner ear or by increasing the resonance to a level that makes you over-sensitive to sounds. If you are a land animal living in air, however, you do need the outer ear in order to increase the resonance of the air in your ear to compensate for the fact that the air outside you is less resonant than water.

The mediating abilities of air and water are reversed in the case of sight, for whereas water is more resonant than air it is less transparent than air. It is therefore also a worse medium of sight than air. Water animals consequently need to enhance transparency in their sense-organs. Their sense-organs must be more transparent to compensate for the poor transparency of the medium. A medium that is less receptive to the sense-object requires a sense-organ that is more receptive.

Consider, for example, Aristotle's explanation at *De Partibus Animalium* II.13 658a3–10 of why fish have fluid rather than hard eyes. Fish move about over long distances. They therefore need to see well at a distance. Fluid eyes are more transparent than hard eyes (seeing through hard eyes is a bit like trying to see through one's eyelids; compare *De Partibus Animalium* II.13 657b35–6), so fluid eyes enable them to see better.[19] There is a further difference between water animals and land animals, however, that is determined by their natural

---

[19] For the same reason birds that fly long distances have fluid eyes; cf. *PA* IV.11 691a24–7.

environments. Air contains many objects that can hit the eyes, thereby damaging them. Land animals that live in air therefore need protection for their eyes. Hard eyes in themselves provide protection by being hard, but fluid eyes need extra protection because they are soft, which is why animals with fluid eyes have eyelids.[20] Fish, however, are the exception. Because they live in water they can do without eyelids for there are far fewer objects in water that can hit the eyes than in air. Since 'nature does nothing in vain' (658a8–9), fish, then, have no eyelids.

This point also shows that it may be the environment, not on its own but in combination with the animal's characteristic life and activities, that determines features of the sense-organ. Fish have fluid eyes not just because they live in water but because they are very mobile. Quadrupeds normally have ears that are movable and which stand up well in the air. This allows them when they move about to pick up sounds from afar and from all directions. The fact that determines the composition of the quadruped's ears is not just that it hears in air but that it moves about on all fours. For this explains why quadrupeds that live in air as opposed to bipeds that also live in air have ears that stand up. The fact that the quadrupeds have ears that stand up is to be explained by the environment together with the quadrupeds' ways of life and their characteristic activities. Where the animal lives cannot be separated from its way of life and characteristic activities and it is these that define the animal as a certain species of animal. The animal's natural environment is therefore part of the definition of the animal.[21]

I started this section by stating that 'Aristotle ascribes those parts to the sense-organ that are necessary for a given species of animal to realise the actuality of perception *given its natural*

---

[20] Cf. Aristotle, *Protrepticus* B15; Düring (1961) 188.
[21] At *HA* I.1 487a10–488b11 Aristotle does distinguish the natural environment from the differences in animals' lives and activities (διαφοραὶ κατὰ τοὺς βίους καὶ τὰς πράξεις). However, the subsequent examples show how closely the two are related. You cannot, for example, separate the fact that fish swim from the fact that they live in water.

environment'. We can now see that the clause 'given its natural environment' is in a way redundant for the environment is part of the definition of the animal. So the animal's natural environment is already implied in our understanding of what the animal is.

7. How a 'mixed environment' determines the sense-organs

So far we have seen how animals have sense-organs that are suited to perceiving in either water or air. The situation, however, is complicated by the fact that there are different ways of being a land or a water animal. An animal can be said to be a water or land animal (1) because it takes in water or air (*HA* viii.2 589a11–13). (By taking in water or air Aristotle has in mind an animal's taking in water or air through its gills or lungs as a means of cooling itself down.) But (2) an animal can also be said to be a land or water animal because it lives and feeds in either air or water.[22] Because there are these two ways of talking about water and land animals it is possible to be a land animal in one way but not in another.[23] There are animals that spend most of their time in water and get their food from the water. So they would be water animals according to (2). However, they also take in air. So according to (1) they would be land animals (589a18–21). For example, the seal, the crocodile and the hippopotamus all live in water but die unless they can breathe air at regular intervals (589a26–30).[24]

The problem of identifying some animals as (exclusively) water *or* land animals makes it difficult to draw any clear

---

[22] *HA* viii.2 589a16–17. *HA* viii(vii).2 590a14–15 mentions a third way (3) of dividing animals, namely, according to their 'bodily blend'. Balme (1991), note *ad loc.*, argues that (3) must coincide with (2). Whether he is right or wrong does not affect the present argument. All that matters here is that there is more than one way of understanding water and land animals, not how many ways there are.

[23] Balme (1987) 86ff. argues that such animals that escape classification illustrate that the aim of *HA* is not to classify animals in a system of genera, species and subspecies, but rather to find the causes of the differences between animals. For a different view, cf. Lloyd (1992) 160 with n. 60.

[24] Cf. *HA* i.1 487a10–488b11.

distinctions between the sort of organs that a 'land animal'
must have and the sort of organs a 'water animal' must have.
In *De Partibus Animalium* IV.13 697b1–4 the seal 'tends towards both'[25] the water animals and the land animals. The
seal belongs either to both groups of animal or to neither
(697b4).[26] That is why even though the seal has feet, an attribute of land animals, its hind feet look like fins, an attribute
of water animals.[27]

The intermediary position of some animals affects the
composition also of their sense-organs (*PA* IV.11 690b17–23).
Aristotle observes here that the crocodile has no tongue,
though it has the space for a tongue. This is explained by the
fact that the crocodile lives in water but also spends some time
on land. Insofar as the crocodile is a water animal it has no
tongue. Insofar as it is also to a certain extent a land animal, it
has the space for a tongue.[28]

The Libyan ostrich is one of those animals that escape clear
classification (*PA* IV.13 697b13–26). Some of its parts are the
parts of a bird, others those of a quadruped. For example, it
has feathers like a bird but, unlike a bird, its feathers are
hairy. That seems to be why it cannot fly. Also, like a bird and
unlike a quadruped, it has two feet. But unlike a bird and like
a quadruped, it has cloven hoofs and not toes. The reason is
that the Libyan ostrich has the size of a large quadruped. It
does not have the size of a bird.[29] The ostrich is therefore
heavier than normal birds, so it needs the sort of feet that larger
quadrupeds have to support themselves with, namely, hoofs.

The ambiguous position of the Libyan ostrich determines
at least one feature of its sense-organs, namely its eyelashes
(697b17–21). The eyelashes exist for the protection of the

---

[25] Balme's recommended translation of ἐπαμφοτερίζειν; cf. Balme *ad HA* 589a21.
Peck (1965) lxxiii–lxxv, prefers 'dualize'.

[26] *PA* IV.13 697b3–4: διὰ τοῦτο ἀμφοτέρων τε μετέχουσι [sc. αἱ φῶκαι καὶ αἱ νυκτερ-
ίδες] καὶ οὐδετέρων. (Logic requires us to take τε ... καὶ to mean 'either ... or'; cf.
Smyth (1920) §2976.)

[27] Cf. *IA* 18 714a20–b2: the reason why fish have fins and land animals feet is again
to do with what parts are useful for an animal naturally living in water or air.

[28] For more on the crocodile's tongue, cf. ch. 4, sec. 10 below.

[29] Birds are generally smaller because it is difficult for a heavy body to fly.

eyes. They keep things out of the eye, like palisades put up in front of an enclosure (*PA* II.15 658b14–26). Generally, it is only animals that have a hairy body that have eyelashes. The reason seems to be that since eyelashes are made of hair it is only animals that otherwise have hair that can have eyelashes. Because birds have feathers instead of hair they are therefore excluded from having eyelashes. However, the Libyan ostrich, again, is the odd one out (*PA* II.14 658a14–15), because it is both like a quadruped and like a bird. Like a bird, its lower parts are covered in feathers. Like a quadruped, its upper parts are covered in hair (excluding, however, the top of the head and the upper neck, which are bald). Since the upper parts of the Libyan ostrich are hairy, it is possible for it to have eyelashes.

The example is much like that of the seal's feet. The seal had feet insofar as it was a land animal but its hind feet looked like fins insofar as it was also a water animal. The example of the Libyan ostrich, however, shows a further point. It shows how different ways of classifying animals can work together in explaining a feature of the sense-organs. On the one hand, there is the distinction between quadruped and biped animals. On the other, there is the distinction between birds and land animals. The ostrich cannot fly but spends its time on land. So it has some of the features of a land animal (such as cloven hoofs). However, it does not just have some features of a land animal. It has some features of a *quadruped* land animal, which is why it has only upper eyelashes rather than both upper and lower eyelashes like man, a biped land animal.

There are two different distinctions involved here: bird versus land animal and quadruped versus biped.[30] The two sorts of classification work together in a way that allows Aristotle to explain the peculiar features of the ostrich. It would have been even more difficult than it already is for Aristotle to explain the peculiarities of the ostrich had he not been able to

---

[30] The classes sound more different in English than in Greek since Aristotle's word for land animals is τὰ πεζά, literally, 'the footed'. On the meaning of 'πεζόν' and 'ἔνυδρον', cf. Peck (1965) lxxvii–lxxxix.

bring in a second sort of classification, if he had had to operate solely with the distinction between bird and land animal
and had not been able to combine it with the distinction between quadruped and biped.[31] For example, saying that the
ostrich is also like a land animal explains only why it can have
eyelashes. It does not yet explain why the ostrich only has
upper eyelashes and not also lower eyelashes. To explain this
we need to bring in the distinction between bipeds and quadrupeds. For whereas man, a biped, has both upper and lower
eyelashes the quadrupeds all only have the upper eyelashes. It
is then insofar as the Libyan ostrich is like a quadruped that it
has only upper eyelashes.[32] The ability to combine different
sorts of distinction thus makes Aristotle able to explain some
features of the parts of animals that he would not have been
able to explain had he insisted that all the features should be
explained according to one classificatory distinction such as
bird and land animal.

8. How functions other than perception may determine the sense-organs

We have seen how the ambivalent position of the seal, the
crocodile and the Libyan ostrich determines their peculiar

---

[31] *PA* I.3 argues that it is necessary that each species of animal have many *differentiae*
that cannot be captured by *one* line of division (what Aristotle calls 'dichotomy').
For example, if we defined animals first as 'winged or wingless', we cannot then
bring in 'tame or wild' as a subdivision of winged and wingless, except *per accidens*
(in which case tame and wild are not introduced as essential *differentiae* of
winged). To use 'tame' and 'wild' as essential *differentiae* we need to introduce
another division. So the animal must be defined by a number of different divisions
that cannot all be ordered under one division such as 'winged or wingless'; cf.
Balme (1987) 73–8. Balme argues that 'the genus – e.g. animal – must be differentiated straightaway by all the differentiae that are exhibited by the *definiendum*.
If it is a species of bird, then it is biped, winged, has beak, neck, tail, etc.; these are
its generic differentiae' (73). If the *definiendum* is differentiated straightway by all
the generic *differentiae*, it might help explain why Aristotle thinks he can move so
easily from one sort of division, e.g. bird/land animal, to another sort of division,
e.g. biped/quadruped, when explaining the parts of a particular species, e.g. the
ostrich's eyelashes.

[32] For a similar example, see the explanation of why the bat has no tail (*PA* IV.13
697b7–10). The bat does not have a quadruped's tail insofar as it is a winged animal, but nor does it have a bird's tail, for it is also a land animal. Cf. also *GA* III.1
749b17–25.

sense-organs. However, even when an animal is clearly either a land animal or a water animal we cannot always predict exactly what sort of sense-organ it will have. We do not always find that the animal has the sort of sense-organ we would expect it to have given its natural environment. The reason for this is that the need for the animal to be able to perceive well in its natural environment is just one of the *many* needs an animal has. Perception is indispensable to animals since it is this activity that defines them as animals. However, perception is not the only activity that animals engage in. Animals also move about, digest, reproduce, take in water or air to cool themselves, and so on. The whole animal body is suited to the range of different activities that the animal engages in. Since the sense-organs are a part of the whole animal body, they will often also serve the animal's other activities. If (*per impossibile*) the sense-organs had existed on their own, then perhaps they could have been determined by perception alone. As it is, the sense-organs are one part amongst others in the whole animal body that *cooperate* to fulfil all of its natural functions.

A favourite example of Aristotle's of how a sense-organ may serve different functions at the same time is the elephant's trunk.[33] The trunk is the elephant's organ of smell. But that does not explain its unique shape and enormous size. This is to be explained by the fact that the trunk doubles (1) as an organ of breathing and (2) as a hand.

(1) The elephant spends much of its time in the water but, unlike animals that live exclusively in water, it breathes air. Because of its enormous size the elephant cannot move quickly out of the water onto land every time it needs to breathe. So nature has devised a trunk for it in such a way that the elephant when it is submerged in water can hold the trunk out of the water and breathe through it. Aristotle compares the trunk to a diver's snorkel.

(2) The trunk also doubles as a hand, again because of the elephant's enormous size. In small four-footed animals the

---

[33] Cf. *PA* II.16 658b33–659a36, II.17 661a25–9.

feet have fingers. The feet can therefore serve as hands as well as support the animal. The elephant, however, is so heavy that no feet can both support it and have fingers. Presumably, Aristotle's point is that if the feet had fingers they would not be sturdy enough to carry the enormous weight of the elephant. So the elephant needs to have another part that can serve as hands. This is where the trunk comes in. It doubles as a hand.

If we put (1) and (2) together, we can understand why the elephant's trunk has its peculiar shape and size. The trunk is long so that the elephant can breathe through it even when the rest of the elephant is submerged in water. It is flexible so that the elephant can manipulate objects with it in the way other animals manipulate objects with their fingers. The elephant's trunk then is not composed simply to be useful for smelling but also to enable the elephant to breathe and manipulate objects, given its intermediary status as both a land and a water animal and given its extraordinary size.[34]

So sometimes the sense-organ has to provide for a number of functions. Its composition will then not be determined by the function of perception alone but by a combination of different functions. The elephant's trunk is from this point of view a success story for nature. Not just two but three different functions are well served by the trunk: smelling, breathing and manipulating objects. Sometimes, however, the different functions cannot all be so well accommodated by the sense-organ. In that case, what may happen is that the need to perceive well is overridden by an even more important function.

An example. We saw that land animals have external ears. We might therefore expect that birds too have external ears. Birds, admittedly, are both winged animals and land animals. Nevertheless, they live in air, and this was the reason why land animals had external ears. Birds, however, have no external ears because they have feathers instead of hair.[35] Be-

---

[34] As we shall see in ch. 5, animals that take in air smell by taking in air. So there is no way the elephant would be able to smell (at least when submerged in water) if it could not also breathe in water. The two functions are therefore not quite distinct.

[35] Feathers are the analogue of hair; cf. *GA* v.3 782a16–18.

cause they have feathers, Aristotle says, 'they do not have the sort of matter [τοιαύτην ὕλην] out of which they could form ears' (*PA* II.12 657a19–20). In this case it is not the demands imposed by the form and function of the sense-organ as such, that is, the ability to hear well, that explain the absence of the external ear. It is rather the restraints imposed by the matter (the feathers). However, this is not simply a point about material necessity. For the feathers are there because of *another* function (for example the birds have feathers in order to be able to fly). The birds might have had an external ear. But in that case the birds could not also have had feathers. So the birds would not have had the parts that, given the sort of animal that birds are, serve a more important function for them than hearing well, namely, the function of flying.

To see that this is not just a point about material necessity compare the case of a teapot. If you have some potter's clay you can make a teapot. If you make your teapot out of clay, the teapot will break if you drop it on the floor. That follows from the necessity of matter. Clay is breakable. So anything that is made of clay, teapots or whatever, is likely to break. However, the point that Aristotle is making in the present context is more like saying that if you use your clay to make a teapot you cannot also use the same clay to make a plate. Whatever implement serves the one function cannot also serve that other function.

The case is similar with the ears of birds. Aristotle says not just that there is no matter for ears in birds. He says that the sort of matter is not there out of which ears could be made. The sort of matter is here matter determined by the form and function. Given that the birds have the matter determined by the function of flying, there is no available matter that can also serve the function of preserving resonance, that is no matter available for an external ear. This is like saying that given that the clay has been made into a teapot there is no way that the same matter in that arrangement can also serve the function of a plate. The point then is that given the demands that the two functions impose on matter there *could* be no matter that simultaneously is the matter of both the function of preserving resonance and of the function of flying, because the two functions are mutually exclusive.

Compare also the case of the eyelids of oviparous quadrupeds, such as the lizard. The lizard is covered in horny scales, that is hard skin which serves to protect the animal.[36] Hard skin is not very flexible but eyelids must be flexible, which is why the lizard has no upper eyelid (lower down the skin is softer and so allows for a lower eyelid).[37] Just as the feathers of birds do not allow them to have external ears, so the hard scales of oviparous quadrupeds do not allow them to have upper eyelids. Since the lizard has no upper eyelids to protect its eyes the skin over its eyes must be harder to protect the eyes. But, as we have seen, if the skin over the eyes is harder vision will be less accurate. So the need for the lizard to protect itself leads to its having hard skin, which leads to its having hard skin over the eyes, which leads to its having less accurate vision.

So in both the birds and the lizard the demands of other functions than sense-perception (flying, protection) outweigh the demands of sense-perception (hearing and seeing accurately). Their sense-organs are therefore composed in a way that makes them less than ideal for perception, because the sense-organs are parts of the *whole* animal body. The sense-organs may therefore have features that serve other functions than sense-perception. In other words, not all the features of the sense-organs need be features of the sense-organs *qua* sense-organs.

9. How the available matter may determine the sense-organs

Sometimes the restraints that the matter imposes on the composition of the sense-organs come not, as in the case of the birds' ears, from the fact that the matter has to serve another function. Sometimes they come from the fact there is not *enough* matter to go around for all the parts that the animal

---

[36] Cf. *GA* II.6 743b14: τὴν τοῦ δέρματος σκέπην.
[37] Cf. *PA* II.13 657b11–15.

might have had. 'Nature', Aristotle says, 'gives something to one part of the body only after it has taken it away from another part' (*PA* II.14 658a35–6). So when we explain why a particular part is present or absent we should take into account the composition of the entire body. We should ask what matter was available for the formation of one part given that matter has to go into all the other parts that the animal requires. For example, there is only so much matter available for an animal's hair. If, then, an animal's torso is particularly hairy, there may not be enough matter to go around for the animal's tail. This is why the bear, for example, does not have a hairy tail (658a36–b2).[38]

The point affects the sense-organs too. At *De Generatione Animalium* II.6 744b16–26 Aristotle says that nature is like a good housekeeper. A good housekeeper gives the best food to the freemen first and then gives the servants the inferior leftovers. Similarly, nature first 'gives' the best materials to the most important parts of the body and then distributes the leftovers to the less important parts. Since perception is the most important part of an animal, that which defines it as an animal, the sense-organs (including the flesh) get the purest matter. The less important parts, such as the bones, hair and nails are made out of the residual matter from the formation of the sense-organs. In other words, these parts get the leftovers.

We would expect, therefore, that there would always be at least enough matter for the formation of all the necessary or useful features of the sense-organs. When nature doles out the available matter we would expect the sense-organs always to be at the front of the queue and not at the end, like the bear's tail. However, it seems that even here the fact that the sense-organs are part of the whole body means that matter may be diverted to other parts of the body that could have have been usefully spent on the sense-organs. For example, the quadrupeds could have had lower eyelashes if nature had not spent

---

[38] In the case of the eyelashes of the Lybian ostrich (mentioned above) it seems to work the other way around: the fact that the matter available for hair is not spent on covering the top of the ostrich's head and its upper neck seems to make matter available for the eyelashes to be extra hairy; cf. *PA* IV.13 697b17–20.

all the matter available for hair on covering their backs with hair. Since eyelashes protect the eyes, quadrupeds could have had greater protection for their eyes, but then they would have had less protection for their backs, for the matter now going towards hair on the back would have been diverted towards the eyelashes. Given that there was not enough matter for both, nature made a choice in favour of protecting the back rather than the eyes. So nature, like a good housekeeper, acted for the best *given the possible means*.[39]

10. Conclusion

The composition of the ear is primarily determined by its function as a sense-organ of hearing. Hearing is the actuality of a potentiality to be changed by sound. This potentiality is present only in matter that is resonant to sound. That is why we have a sense-organ of hearing composed of matter resonant to sound, namely, the air inside the ear. The sense-organ proper of hearing is simply this confined air. It contains no internal structure. For land animals the air inside the ear is continuous with the air outside through *poroi*.[40] In some animals an external ear is further needed to protect and promote the resonance of the inner sense-organ. By contrast, other animals, such as fish, have no features observable to us. So we assume that these animals have the inner sense-organ only. Exactly what further features, if any, are needed apart from the sense-organ proper depends on the conditions in which hearing takes place. That is why the ear of an animal that lives and hears in air is different from that of an animal that lives and hears in water. Quadrupeds normally have an external ear, but fish do not. However, some animals spend their time both in air and in water. These animals have sense-organs that

---

[39] Cf. *PA* II.14 658a23–4: ἀεὶ γὰρ ἐκ τῶν ἐνδεχομένων αἰτία τοῦ βελτίονός ἐστιν [sc. ἡ φύσις].

[40] These *poroi* are also connected with veins that lead to the heart, thereby ensuring the mediation of auditory impressions to the central sense-organ; cf. *GA* II.6 744a3–5 and ch. I, sec. 10 on the general function of *poroi*.

reflect their 'mixed' environment. For example, the crocodile has no tongue but nevertheless space for a tongue.

However, which features the sense-organ has does not just depend on its function as a sense-organ. The sense-organs are part of the whole animal body and may therefore serve other functions than just perceiving. For example, the elephant's extraordinary sense-organ of smell, its trunk, was explained by the animal's need also to be able to breathe and manipulate objects. (Here too the mixed environment of the elephant played a role.) We must always assume that the animal has organs that enable it to perceive, for without perception there is no animal. However, sometimes it seemed that other functions might be more important than the ability to perceive *accurately*. In that case, nature might divert matter from the sense-organ to make organs for functions other than perception. The missing ears of birds and the missing lower eyelids of lizards seemed to be examples of this. The fact that perceiving accurately is not always the first priority for an animal, given its particular nature, might explain why some animals perceive some sense-objects better than others. Sometimes there simply is not enough matter to go around. Just as there was not enough matter for hair on the bear's tail, so it seemed that there was not enough matter for lower eyelashes on quadrupeds. On all these points, we are reminded that nature does the best job possible given the available means.

What are the implications for the thesis of this study, that the sense-organs are composed as the matter necessary for the ability to perceive? The thesis only holds true if we qualify it by saying that the sense-organs *qua* sense-organs are composed in this way, for they may have functions other than perception. This qualification makes the thesis more plausible, however, for the qualification relieves the thesis of the impossible task of having to find perceptual functions for all the features of the sense-organs that Aristotle describes. This is important also for another reason, for if a feature of the sense-organ cannot be explained from the point of view of its usefulness to perception, then we might think that it had to be explained by material necessity. In this way, we saw in chapter

1 that when the particular colour of a human eye did not contribute to eyesight it meant that it had to be explained instead by the attributes of the matter as such. However, it now appears that when we cannot find a *perceptual* function for a feature of the sense-organ, we may be able to find another function for it. This shows that we do not need to resort to material necessity since the feature after all can be explained by hypothetical necessity. It is not a hypothetical necessity that says that the sense-organ must have that feature in order to be able to perceive. Rather it is a hypothetical necessity that says that the sense-organ must have the feature in order to do some other function.

For example, some animals such as the ant and the gadfly have a hard tongue.[41] This variation might seem difficult to explain from the point of view of the tongue as an organ for taste. After all, humans have a soft tongue which enables them to taste better than any other animal. Since a hard tongue does not contribute to better perception we might feel tempted to attribute the hardness of their tongue to the attributes of their matter as such. But that would be to ignore the secondary function that the tongue serves in these animals, namely, as a sting or a bore. Like the elephant's trunk (Aristotle explicitly makes the analogy, *PA* II.17 661a27), nature here employs the sense-organ for more than one function.

The sense-organs thus display the complexity and flexibility of Aristotle's teleology. It is correct to say that their primary function is to be organs of perception,[42] which is why we can explain *most* of their features from the point of view of their usefulness to perception. But if we proceed to explain the sense-organs exclusively *qua* sense-organs, then the picture we will have of them will to a certain extent be an abstraction because we need to consider the secondary or even tertiary functions that the sense-organs may serve in order to explain all their features. But not only that. We need also to consider the sort of matter and the amount of matter available for the formation

---

[41] Cf. *PA* II.17 661a12–30.
[42] Cf. *De an.* II.12 424a24–5.

of the sense-organs given that the matter might already have been formed to serve different functions (compare the lizard's eyelids and the bird's ears) or similar functions in other parts of the body (compare the quadrupeds' eyelashes).

At the end of chapter 1, I concluded that Aristotle drew a functional map of the eye. It appears now that this map is part of a larger functional map of the whole animal body, where all the functions of the animal combine. To understand all the features of the smaller map of the sense-organ we need to be able to read the larger map of the whole body.

4

THE CONTACT SENSES

1. Touch is the sense of direct contact

The verb 'to touch' can be used in two ways. We can say that a bottle touches the table. By this we may mean that the bottle is in direct contact with the table, that there is nothing in between the two. However, when I say that I touch the hardness of the table I may mean something different, namely, that I feel or perceive the hardness of the table. I touch the table in this way only when I am using my sense of touch. Similarly, we can say that the touch of your hand is cold. In that case too it is implied that I perceive your hand as cold by my sense of touch.

Perhaps it is more usual to use the verb 'to feel' rather than the verb 'to touch' as a verb of perception.[1] One would say 'I feel the hardness of the table' rather than 'I touch it' if one wants to say that I perceive the table rather than that I am simply leaning on it with some part of my body. That is perhaps also why it seems more natural to use the verb 'to touch' when the idea is just that there is contact between two things and no perception takes place. So one says, for instance, that the bottle touches the table, but the bottle does not and cannot feel the table for a bottle is not such a thing as to have perception. English has a verb 'to feel' which can be used instead of 'to touch' where perception is particularly referred to, and so 'to touch' will normally be taken to mean simply 'to be in contact with'.

'To touch' then has two uses in English, of which 'to be in contact with' is the most common. The situation is similar in

---

[1] As noted by Sorabji (1971) 85.

Greek. The verb 'ἅπτομαι' means primarily 'to fasten oneself onto' or 'to grasp', secondarily 'to grasp with one's senses'. The cognate noun 'ἁφή' correspondingly means 'grasp' and 'perception' but, in particular, 'perception by touch'.

These lexicographic observations are relevant to Aristotle's theory of touch, for he argues that touch is the sense of that with which one is in direct contact. For instance, when I feel the hardness of the table, there is a part of my body which touches the table. That, Aristotle says, is exactly why this sort of perception is called touch. Perceiving something by touch involves that one is in direct contact with the sense-object.[2]

2. Taste is a form of touch

The sense of taste, Aristotle believes, has this feature in common with touch, that we are in direct contact with the object that we taste. You taste something by putting it directly on the tongue. So you taste things by direct contact. That there is direct contact between object and perceiver in taste is in Aristotle's view enough for taste to qualify as a form of touch.

'Touch' therefore picks out not just the one sense-modality that we normally call 'touch', as when we talk about touching the softness of the hand. It picks out the group of all sense-modalities with which we perceive objects by direct contact.[3] This group, as we saw, includes touch in the narrow sense and taste. But we might imagine there to be other senses than taste and touch that operate by direct contact. In that case we should also call those senses 'touch'.

3. Two criteria of defining a sense-faculty

This claim seems to go against Aristotle's normal method of defining the senses, which is first to define the proper sense-

---

[2] De an. III.13 435a17–18: ἡ δ' ἁφὴ τῶν αὐτῶν ἅπτεσθαί ἐστιν, διὸ καὶ τοὔνομα τοῦτο ἔχει.

[3] Cf. De an. III.1 424b27–8: καὶ ὅσων μὲν αὐτῶν ἁπτόμενοι αἰσθανόμεθα, τῇ ἁφῇ αἰσθητά ἐστιν.

object of a sense-faculty and then to define the sense-faculty as that which has the potentiality to be changed by that sense-object as such.[4] Thus the proper sense-object of hearing is sound and the sense of hearing is that which has the potentiality to be changed by sound as such. The proper sense-object of vision is colour and the sense of vision is that which has the potentiality to be changed by colour as such. On this criterion two senses are the same if and only if they have the same proper object. I shall therefore call this criterion the 'object criterion'.

But the previous section suggested that there is another way of defining a sense-faculty than by its proper object. The suggestion was that one can define a given sense as the sense of touch if it operates by direct contact with its sense-object, whatever its sense-object might be. Thus if it had been the case, as it is not, that colours were perceived by direct contact instead of at a distance, then the sense that perceived colour would qualify as a form of touch.

In *De Anima* II.11 423a5–10 Aristotle imagines that the medium of the distance senses, air, was part of the body. In that case, he says, we would think that the three distance senses were the same because they operated by means of a single instrument. In this passage Aristotle is trying to distinguish the organ of touch from the medium of touch. He wants to establish that the organ of touch lies inside the body, whereas the flesh and skin are only the medium of touch. The difficulty in distinguishing the organ from the medium is caused by the fact that the organ is affected along with the medium. This is just the way in which the distance senses would be affected if the medium was part of the body.

I shall return to the notion that the flesh is the medium of touch in section 7. For now, the interesting point is that Aristotle imagines that the three distance senses would be thought of as one if they operated like the sense of touch. This is so irrespective of the fact that the three distance senses have

---

[4] Cf. *De an.* II.4 415a14–22.

already been separately defined by their different sense-objects. When Aristotle talks about touch he often focuses on the way in which something is perceived, that is by direct contact, rather than on what is perceived. In this passage the distance senses are, temporarily, being dragged into this way of thinking. On this criterion a sense is a sense of touch if and only if it operates by direct contact with its object. Let me call this criterion the 'contact criterion' of touch.[5]

The contact criterion is not only different from but also in potential conflict with the object criterion. For Aristotle sometimes uses the object criterion to define the sense of taste as the sense that has the ability to be changed by flavour, that is to say, the sweet and the bitter.[6] Again, he uses the object criterion to define touch as the sense that is changed by the hot, the cold, the wet and the dry. Touch has some other objects as well, namely, the hard and the soft, the fine and the coarse and the viscous and the brittle.[7] However, he thinks that the other tangible qualities can be 'reduced' (ἀνάγονται) to the hot and the cold and the wet and the dry.[8]

---

[5] Following Sorabji (1971) 86, who also mentions Aristotle's criticism of Democritus at *Sens.* 4 442a29–b26: Democritus reduces all the senses to touch because he says that all perception happens by direct contact between the body of the perceiver and the effluences from the object perceived. The criticism again reflects Aristotle's own preoccupation with the sense of touch as the sense-faculty that perceives by direct contact in that the criticism ignores what Democritus might have to say about different effluences giving rise to different sorts of perception.

[6] Cf. *De an.* II.6 418a13; II.10.

[7] Cf. *De an.* II.11 423b27–9; *GC* II.2.

[8] Cf. *De an.* II.11 422b25–7. A word on 'reduction': in *GC* II.2 330a25 Aristotle says that the other tangible differences can be 'reduced' (ἀνάγονται) to the dry, wet, hot and cold. But 'reducing' should not be taken to mean 'reducing away', in the sense that one often associates with reduction, viz. showing something to be nothing else than what it can be reduced to. The word 'ἀνάγω' is used in the *APr* for the way in which the other figures of a syllogism can be reduced to the first figure; cf. *APr* I.32 46b40. The reduction is here to be understood as 'leading back' the other figures to the one that is more clearly understandable and immediately persuasive. In other words, the leading back is explanatory. In *Ph.* II.3 194b22 'ἀνάγειν' is the word used of leading back a problem to the four causes. Aristotle's explanatory 'reduction' of the other tangibles to the primary four should be contrasted with the attempt to reduce them away as we find it in, for instance, Armstrong (1962). The point is worth making because the other tangibles cannot be reduced away if they are to be causally active as such. For instance, it is viscosity as such that causes a perception of viscosity.

As appears from this list, flavour is not among the proper objects of touch. Conversely, the hot, the cold, the wet and the dry are not among the proper objects of taste, for they are not flavours and the proper object of taste is just flavour. According to the object criterion, then, it seems that taste and touch have to be distinct sense-faculties, for they have distinct objects.

We call sight and hearing different senses because they have different objects. We do not call sight and hearing the same sense just because they both happen to operate through a medium. So given that taste and touch too have different objects, why should we call them the same sense just because they both operate by direct, rather than mediated, contact? What is so special about direct contact that should make us identify senses that we would otherwise, that is if these senses both operated by means of a medium, have said were different because of their different objects?

4. What is flavour?

The two questions, however, are based on a faulty premise. The last section suggested that the proper objects of taste and of touch were completely distinct, that they had no more in common than, say, sound and colour. It was important to make this suggestion to bring out the point that the contact senses are not defined in quite the same way as the distance senses. But the suggestion is wrong. For Aristotle insists on several occasions that flavours *are* a sort of tangible object. If he can show this, if he can show that the proper object of taste is somehow one of the proper objects of touch, then applying the object criterion to taste will give us the same result as applying the contact criterion. Both criteria will give us the result that taste is a form of touch. Since the objects of taste will also be objects of touch, taste will not be distinct from touch. As regards taste and touch the two criteria will be consistent in their results after all.

Let us consider then how Aristotle shows that flavour is a

tangible object. In his run-down of the senses in Book II of the *De Anima* Aristotle arrives at taste in chapter 10. He starts the chapter as follows:

> The object of taste is a form of the tangible which is why it is not perceptible through another intermediary body, for neither is touch. And the body in which the flavour, the tastable, resides, namely the wet, it resides in as in matter, but this is something tangible. (422a8–11).

In Greek:

τὸ δὲ γευστόν ἐστιν ἁπτόν τι· καὶ τοῦτ' αἴτιον τοῦ μὴ εἶναι αἰσθητὸν διὰ τοῦ μεταξὺ ἀλλοτρίου ὄντος σώματος· οὐδὲ γὰρ ἡ ἁφή.[9] καὶ τὸ σῶμα δὲ ἐν ᾧ ὁ χυμός, τὸ γευστόν, ἐν ὑγρῷ ὡς ὕλῃ· τοῦτο δ' ἁπτόν τι.

Notice that the claim 'καὶ τὸ σῶμα δὲ ἐν ᾧ ὁ χυμός' is linked to the previous sentence by a 'καὶ' rather than by an explanatory 'γάρ'. 'καὶ' may, but certainly need not, introduce an explanation. So one might argue that the fact that the tastable is in the wet is not presented as a reason for saying that the tastable is something tangible. The meaning of the passage would then be that it is also (καὶ) because the tastable is in a body that it is not mediated. So this would be a further reason not for saying that the tastable is a tangible, which at least here would be axiomatic, but for saying that the tastable is not mediated. In other words, it would be a reason for saying that the tastable is not perceived through another body rather than for saying that the tastable is a tangible; and it is of course the immediacy of taste that Aristotle goes on to argue for.

However, in 'τοῦτο δ' ἁπτόν τι', 'τοῦτο' must be taken to refer to 'τὸ σῶμα' rather than to 'τὸ γευστόν'. The wet body that the tastable has as its matter is something tangible. So this is a rather different claim from the initial claim that the tastable simply is something tangible. How are these two claims related? On the interpretation that I would like to argue

---

[9] I follow the reading of the MSS and take οὐδὲ γὰρ ἡ ἁφή to be Aristotelian short-hand for: 'For neither does touch perceive through the medium of another body.' Ross's emendation of ἡ ἁφή to τῇ ἁφῇ is thus unnecessary.

for, call it interpretation A, the argument of the passage runs as follows:

(1) the tastable is in a tangible body;
(2) the tastable is not in a tangible body in the way that a mediated sense-quality is in a medium;
(3) (axiomatic) the tangible is not mediated; therefore
(4) the tastable is a tangible quality.

On the alternative interpretation of the passage, interpretation B, the argument would be:

(i)   the tastable is a tangible quality;
(ii) the tastable is in a tangible body; therefore
(iii) the tastable is not mediated.

But this is a rather impoverished argument, for here it is not clear how (iii) follows from (i) and (ii) jointly.

I cannot exclude that interpretation B is correct. I can only show that interpretation A is both possible and more explanatory than B. In particular, interpretation A is more explanatory when it comes to understanding the crucial relationship between taste and touch. I call this relationship crucial because it determines how we are to understand the criteria by which Aristotle defines both taste and touch as forms of touch. Again, why is it that Aristotle can define two senses that apparently have different proper objects as both being the same sense? Why does Aristotle apparently deviate from his normal procedure of defining a sense-faculty exclusively by its proper object when it comes to these two senses?

On interpretation A the discussion that follows 422a11 about the role of the wet in taste is meant to establish, first, (2), that the tastable is not in a tangible body in the way that a mediated quality is in the medium, in order then to establish (4), that the tastable is a tangible quality. *De Anima* II.10 thereby starts out by making the claim that the tastable is something tangible in order to prove it by investigating what it is to be mediated on the assumption that if something is not mediated then it is perceived by touch. The discussion of taste thereby serves to emphasise this assumption, that touch is essentially unmediated perception.

The discussion of taste in *De Anima* II.10 therefore also leads naturally up to the discussion in II.11 of the question whether the flesh acts as a medium in touch. Here too the central problem is to understand whether there is a medium in touch. The conclusion is that flesh does in a way act as the medium of touch. But it does not act as a medium in the important sense that characterised the medium of the distance senses, namely, that it is another body through which the perception happens. Touch does not happen 'διὰ τοῦ μεταξὺ ἀλλοτρίου ὄντος σώματος' (*De an.* II.11 422a9). In touch the mediation happens in the perceiver's own body insofar as it is affected along with the sense-organ. Both II.10 and II.11 would then be concerned with the same basic question, What constitutes mediation? Aristotle would be concerned in both chapters to find out whether, and if so in what sense, taste and touch can be said to be mediated, because he starts out from the position that direct contact is what singles out taste and touch as a distinct group of senses.

What, then, does Aristotle mean by saying (1) that flavour is in a tangible body, the wet? At 422a17–19 he says that:

Nothing produces a perception of flavour without moisture, but (only) what has moisture actually or potentially, such as salt. For it is easily dissolved [εὔτηκτικόν] and acts as a solvent [συντηκτικόν] on the tongue.

Let us consider Aristotle's own example of a flavoured substance, salt. Salt is something soluble. Salt dissolves when immersed in liquid. That, presumably, is what Aristotle means by saying that salt 'potentially has moisture'. Salt has moisture in the sense that even when it is not actually dissolved, that is, actually in a liquid state, it will dissolve if immersed in liquid. In modern terminology, we would say that salt has a disposition to dissolve. Aristotle thinks that it is a characteristic of everything that has flavour that it is soluble.[10]

The reason why flavour has to be soluble is more clearly

---

[10] Aristotle's word for 'flavour' is 'χυμός'. But 'χυμός' can also be translated as 'juice' (as seems appropriate in *PA* IV.11 690b29). So the connection between flavour and moisture is already suggested by the term Aristotle uses for 'flavour'. 'χυμός' is cognate with the verb for dissolving or making something liquid (χέω).

explained in *De Sensu* 4 441a20–b15. So let us look at this text first. The reason Aristotle gives here is presented as a general point about the conditions of causal agency. That is to say, the reason why flavours have to be soluble is a point about what flavours have to be like in order to act in a certain way. Salt, Aristotle says, is naturally dry for it is a kind of earth. This is just what is meant by saying that it is something earthy, for dryness is the proper attribute of earth.[11] However, if the dry is going to act on anything then it has to be on what is wet.

There is a general causal reason for this claim which we are familiar with from *De Generatione et Corruptione*[12] and *De Anima* II. 4–5.[13] Aristotle reminds us of it again in *De Sensu*.[14] The reason is that before change the patient has to be potentially like, but actually unlike, the agent so that the patient in actual change can be changed by the agent from being potentially like it to being actually like it. Thus the cold is the opposite of the hot and it is able to be acted upon by the hot so as to become itself hot. This, in my earlier example,[15] is what happens when the cold water in the kettle is heated by the hot stove.

From these considerations about the conditions of causal agency it follows that there must be something wet, some moisture, if the dry is going to realise its ability to act. The dry and the wet form a causal pair, the dry as the agent, the wet as the patient. It is out of the action of the dry on the wet that what is tastable arises. Thus Aristotle defines flavour as an affection that is produced in the wet by the dry.[16] In the example of salt, salt is identified with the dry element. But in order, as it were, to bring out the flavour of the salt the salt

---

[11] Cf. *GC* II.3 331a1–6.

[12] *GC* I.7 and *passim*; cf. *Ph.* I.5 188a31–b10.

[13] *De an.* II.4 416b3–9, II.5 417a18–21, 417b2–3.

[14] *Sens.* 4 441b14–15: 'everything acts and suffers insofar as there is an opposition in each thing [sc. in the agent and patient]'.

[15] Cf. ch. 2, sec. 5 (p. 126).

[16] *Sens.* 4 441b19–20: καὶ ἔστι τοῦτο χυμός, τὸ γιγνόμενον ὑπό τοῦ εἰρημένου ξηροῦ πάθος ἐν τῷ ὑγρῷ . . .

has first to act on some moisture. Aristotle seems to imagine this action on the moisture as a form of percolation of the moisture through the salt.[17]

Perhaps we can update his idea by imagining the action of the dry on the wet along the lines of an espresso machine. An espresso machine works by letting hot steam pass through a funnel that contains coffee. In the funnel the steam, the wet, is acted upon by the coffee, the dry, in such a way that the flavour of the coffee is brought out in the steam, which is then condensed into liquid coffee. The wet is sent through the dry coffee and thereby acquires the taste of coffee.

The example is apposite also because Aristotle thinks that heat plays a special role in bringing out the flavour of the dry in the wet. He says that it is by the agency of heat that the wet is sent through the dry and earthy.[18] Similarly, the espresso machine heats up the water to the point where it evaporates and presses through the coffee in the funnel. Heat is in this way an efficient cause in giving the liquid flavour.

Flavour is primarily associated with the dry element, but it is only tastable in a liquid state. Similarly, we might associate the ground coffee with the flavour in the liquid coffee insofar as it is what *gives* flavour to the water. The water is in itself tasteless.[19] But Aristotle would say that the dry element needs to act first on the wet before it is in a state in which we can perceive the flavour. It is only 'the affection produced in the liquid by the dry' which is 'capable of altering potential into actual taste'. Since Aristotle is concerned with flavour as an object of taste, the flavour is primarily identified by him with the flavoured moisture, with χυμός as a juice, rather than in a dry state.

This is an important point for another reason, for it shows that Aristotle is concerned with explaining the process which makes flavour something tastable: the dry needs to act on the

---

[17] *Ibid.* 441b17–19.
[18] *Ibid.*
[19] Cf. *Sens.* 4 441a4.

wet in order to become tastable. Aristotle does not describe flavour as a quality independent of its potentiality to cause tasting. Flavour has to be in moisture because flavour can only be tasted in a liquefied state. We saw earlier that he describes the transparent medium in the context of colour because he wanted to explain the colour as what is visible and colour was only visible in the transparent medium. Similarly, he now describes the moisture as that which is necessary in order to make the flavour tastable. Though, as we shall see shortly, he denies that moisture is a medium of flavour, moisture is introduced because it is a necessary condition of tastability. So Aristotle's description of flavour, like his description of colour, is meant to explain flavour essentially as a potential object of perception. Flavour is essentially something that has the ability to cause perception. It is necessary that the flavoured dryness should act on the moisture first if it is going to be a potential object of perception.

The *De Sensu* story of how flavour comes about appears in one respect different from the story told in *De Anima* II.10. The example of salt in *De Anima* II.10 suggested that the dry agent was completely dissolved in the moisture, for there was a mixture of dry and wet, and in mixtures there is no residue. *De Sensu,* however, suggests instead that the heat extracts the flavour from the dry agent in the moisture, thereby leaving a residue. The image I used was the way the flavour is extracted from the coffee in the espresso machine leaving behind some dregs. Nevertheless, the important point seems clear: the dry needs to act on some moisture (be it by solution or percolation) in order for its flavour to be brought out. It is in this liquid state only that the affection is produced which, as Aristotle puts it, is able to alter the sense of taste from potentiality into actuality.[20]

---

[20] *Sens.* 4 441b19–22: καὶ ἔστι τοῦτο χυμός, τὸ γιγνόμενον ὑπὸ τοῦ εἰρημένου ξηροῦ πάθος ἐν τῷ ὑγρῷ τῆς γεύσεως τῆς κατὰ δύναμιν ἀλλοιωτικὸν [ὂν] εἰς ἐνέργειαν· ἄγει γὰρ τὸ αἰσθητικὸν εἰς τοῦτο δυνάμει προϋπάρχον ...

5. Why moisture is not a medium of taste

This, then, is the reason why Aristotle says that flavour is found in moisture. It is clear that moisture thereby assumes a different role from the role that, for instance, light plays in vision. Light is a condition of the visibility of colour but in a different way from the way in which moisture is a condition of flavour being tastable, for the dry acts on the moisture by being mixed with it.[21] For instance, salt dissolves in water and is mixed with the moisture, but colour does not become visible by being mixed with light.

In order for there to be mixture there has to be a mixture of matter. Thus when red wine and white wine are mixed to make a kind of rosé, both the colours of the two wines and their liquid blend into one. It is quite clear that Aristotle thinks that there is no such blending of matter when the colour acts on the transparent medium in vision. In *De Anima* III.12 435a2–3, he uses the image of a seal being impressed all the way through a block of wax to illustrate the way in which the sense-object acts on the medium. The image should be taken to mean that it is only the form of the sense-object, the seal, which acts on the wax, not also its matter, the iron or gold of which the seal is made. That this is the right interpretation of the image is confirmed by *De Anima* II.12 424a17–24, where Aristotle says of the sense-faculties that they receive the sensible form of the sense-object without its matter. He compares this reception with the way in which the wax receives the imprint of a ring *without the iron or gold of which the ring is made*. It is crucially only the form that is transmitted when the sense-object acts on the medium and the sense-faculty.

There is then no mixture of matter when the sense-object acts on the medium, but there is a mixture of matter when the

---

[21] *De an.* II.10 422a13–16: 'But the perception does not arise for us through a medium, but by the flavour's being mixed with moisture, just as in the case of a drink. But the colour is not seen thus by being mixed, nor by means of effluences. Therefore there is no medium [sc. in taste].'

dry acts on the moisture. So the moisture is not a medium of flavour in the way in which the transparent is a medium of colour. Aristotle in *De Anima* II.10 refers to an imaginary situation in which human beings lived in water rather than air. The point is that even if our natural habitat was water, water could not be said to be the medium of flavour. This strengthens the case for saying that moisture is not a medium of flavour, for Aristotle himself tends to identify the element in which we live with the medium through which we perceive.[22] Thus animals that live in air hear through air *qua* resonant, see through air *qua* transparent, and smell through air *qua* the air's ability to 'wash and clean a flavoured dryness'.[23] As I argued in chapter 2 it is because we live in air and not in water, that air (*qua* its different mediating qualities) and not water is the medium of our distance senses. The fact that in the case of all the senses recognised as mediated air alone is the medium would make us think that taste (i) does not have moisture as its medium and, more strongly, (ii) does not have a medium at all for those animals that live in air, for if taste had a medium it would be air. It is against this background that Aristotle says that 'even if we lived in water, we would perceive something sweet thrown into the water, but the perception would not arise for us through the medium, but because the sweet is mixed with the wet, just as in the case of a drink'.[24] This shows that it is not just a fact about human beings that moisture is not the medium of taste because we live in air rather than in water, for even if we lived in water moisture would still not be the medium of flavour.

Let us imagine, then, that I spent my life under water in a swimming-pool. If you threw a certain amount of sugar into the water of the pool, the sugar would gradually dissolve and mix with the water until all the water would be mixed with the sugar. Aristotle says that something is a mixture (μίξις/κρᾶσις)[25] as opposed to a mere 'composition' (σύνθεσις) when its in-

---

[22] Cf. *De an.* III.13 435b21–2.
[23] *Sens.* 5 443a1–2; on smell, cf. ch. 5.
[24] *De an.* II.10 422a11–14.
[25] Cf. *De an.* II.10 422a14: μειχθῆναι; 442a15: μίγνυσθαι.

gredients react to each other in such a way that the result is actually different from each of the ingredients.[26] So if we have a mixture of sugar and water in the pool, we do not have two separate substances in the pool, water with bits of sugar floating about, for this would be a mere composition of water and sugar. Instead we have a mixture which is a new and different substance from the sum of the two ingredients that went into it. We have sugary water, not water plus sugar. If so, it is clear that when the sugary water hits my tongue when I am in the water I do not perceive the sweetness of the sugar. I perceive the sweetness of the sugary water. That is why we cannot say that I perceive the sweetness of the sugar *through* the water. I am not perceiving the sweetness of the sugar that you threw into the pool but that of a different substance, the sugary water. It is clear that this is different from what happens when I see a coloured object, say a red flag, through the transparent air, for there it is not the redness of the intervening air that I see but the redness *of the flag* that I see through the air.

The difference between perceiving the sugary water and perceiving the red flag nicely illustrates the difference between perception by direct contact and perception through a medium. For when I taste the sugary water I perceive a substance with which I am in direct contact. I am not perceiving the sugar at a distance through the water the way I see the red flag through the transparent. What enables me to taste the sugary water is that water stretches all the way to my tongue. What enables me to see the red flag is that the transparent medium, not the flag, stretches all the way from the flag to my eyes. In other words, in vision the object that is in direct contact with the sense-organ, that is, the medium, is not perceived. But in tasting, it is the object that is in direct contact with the sense-organ that is perceived and only this object. There is no way you can perceive the sweetness at a distance. Lying in my pool there is no way that I can perceive the sweetness of the sugar that you throw into it. The sweetness has to be that of the

<hr>

[26] *GC* I.10 327b22–31.

mixture that I am directly in touch with, the sugary water, for me to be able to taste it.

There would be an analogy between the mixing of the sugar and the water and the transparent medium in vision if the redness of the flag made the transparent medium red and it was the redness of the medium which the eye saw. That this would be the relevant analogy is confirmed by a passage in *De Sensu* 4. At 441b15–19 Aristotle says that

just as those who wash colours and flavours out in the wet make the water have such a quality [sc. colour or flavour], so also nature washes out the dry and the earthy and by sending the water through the dry and earthy by the agency of the hot invests the wet with a certain quality.

If mediation of vision were like the dry acting upon moisture, then the colour would make the transparent coloured. When I see a red flag the transparent air would literally go red for the red flag would make the transparent air 'have such a quality',[27] that is it would make the transparent go red like itself. The medium would, as it were, be dyed red by the redness of the flag. It therefore becomes a reason in itself for saying that the medium of vision does not become coloured in vision, that if the medium did go red, then it would act like moisture in taste. But, as we have seen, moisture is no medium of taste. Similarly, if the medium of vision went red it would not be a medium either.

What the analysis of the role of moisture in flavour shows is that flavour is liquefied in moisture and that the flavoured moisture acts on the sense of taste not as a medium but by being in direct contact with the tongue. In other words, the analysis of the role of moisture shows that it is not a medium. But if the moisture is not a medium, then by implication it is a direct object of taste, for either it is a medium or it is a direct object, *tertium non datur*. So the moisture is a direct object of perception. But then the moisture, or more precisely, the flavoured moisture, is also a sort of tangible object, for any direct object of perception is a sort of tangible object. As we

---

[27] *Sens.* 4 441b16–17: τοιοῦτον ἔχειν ποιοῦσι τὸ ὕδωρ; 441b18–19: ποιόν τι τὸ ὑγρὸν παρασκευάζει.

saw at the beginning of this chapter, *this* was the crucial point about tangible objects, that they are perceived by direct contact. If flavour is a tangible, then on the object criterion, too, taste is a form of touch.

My argument for interpretation A (p. 184) in *De Anima* II.10 has come full circle. It has been shown what flavour is, how it is in the wet, how this is not a case of being in a medium, why taste is therefore not mediated perception, and why taste is therefore a form of touch.

6. The sense-organ of touch

The fact, as Aristotle sees it, that taste is a form of touch is reflected in the fact that both senses have the same sense-organ, the flesh. If, as has been argued, the sense-organ is determined by the sense-faculty's potentiality to be changed by the sense-object, it is to be expected that two senses that have the same sense-object also have sense-organs that are similar in composition. We shall see that in the case of both taste and touch the sense-organ is flesh, though it is only the flesh of the tongue with which we can taste. Let us first consider what the sense-organ of touch is. In *De Anima* III.12 Aristotle says:

But if a body has perception, it must be either simple or complex. And it cannot be simple, for then it could not have touch, which is indispensable. This is clear from what follows: An animal is a body with soul in it. Every body is tangible, that is, perceptible by touch. Hence necessarily, if an animal is to survive, its body must have touch. All the other senses, for example smell, sight, hearing, apprehend through media. But where there is immediate contact the animal, if it has no perception, will be unable to avoid some things and grasp others. So it will find it impossible to survive. That is why taste also is a sort of touch. It is relative to nourishment, which is a tangible body, whereas sound, colour and odour are not nutritious and bring about neither growth nor diminution. Therefore taste also must be a sort of touch, for it is the sense of what is tangible and nutritious. (*De an.* III.12 434b8–22)

The first point made in this passage is that since an animal has a body and every body is tangible, an animal is a tangible thing. The reason why every body is tangible has been given in *De Generatione et Corruptione* II.2, namely that the principles of body *qua* body are the tangible qualities, hot and cold, dry and wet. As a consequence of having a body an animal is then said to need the sense of touch. The point is that the animal body is going to get into contact with other bodies. If an animal has no way of detecting which other bodies will be harmful to its body and which will be beneficial, the animal will quickly come to grief.

The passage starts by making a claim about what the *body* must be like in order to have perception. The body is here understood as an organ of touch. The body cannot be simple for then it would be unable to perceive by touch. In *De Generatione Animalium* II.5 741a10–13 Aristotle says that

> it is impossible for any part of the body whatever (face, hand, flesh or any other part) to exist unless there is perceptible soul in it, be it in actuality or potentiality, and be it in some respect or *simpliciter*. For it will be like a corpse or a part of a corpse.

It is only the tongue, the eyes, the ears and the nose that have perception otherwise, that is, as the organ of taste, sight, hearing and smell respectively. The flesh of the body has the perceptible soul in it insofar as it is an organ (alternatively, medium)[28] of touch. The remaining parts of the body, bone, tissue, tendons, etc., are there in order to support the flesh. These parts can be seen as also belonging to the animal body because they are indirectly instrumental in touch, for without the support of these parts the flesh would not be there to enable us to perceive by touch.

In the passage quoted from *De Anima* III.12 Aristotle says that if the body is going to have touch, then it must be a complex body. He does not explain this other than by saying that if the human body is a tangible body amongst other tangible bodies then it needs touch to discern other tangible bodies in order to survive. Turning to *De Partibus Animalium* II.1, however, we can give a more precise reason why the body must be complex for us to be able to perceive by touch. In II.1 Aristotle explains the difference between homoiomerous parts and anhomoiomerous parts. Something is homoiomerous if you can divide it into any parts and find that each part is of the

---

[28] Cf. sec. 7.

same kind as the other parts. That is what 'homoiomerous' literally means, having similar parts. For instance, flesh is homoiomerous. Divide it in any way you like and all the bits will still be flesh. Anhomoiomerous are simply those parts which are not homoiomerous, say a face. If you cut off a bit of the face, the cut-off bit will not also be a face.

Aristotle wants to argue that an animal body is composed both of homoiomerous and anhomoiomerous parts. The instrumental parts, like a hand or the face, are generally all anhomoiomerous, but the instruments of perception, the sense-organs, are all homoiomerous. The reason why they are homoiomerous is that:

> Perception happens in all animals in the homoiomerous parts since each sense is concerned with one kind [of sense-object]. And the organ of each is receptive of the sense-objects. But what is potentially is acted on by what is actually, so that the two are of the same kind and if the second is simple so is the first. That is why none of the physiologists [φυσιολόγοι] tries to claim of a hand or a face or any other such part that one is earth, another water, or another fire. But they do link each of the sense-organs with one of the elements. (*PA* II.1 647a6–12)

The sense-organs are homoiomerous because they are made of a single element. If something is all made of water, it is clear that if you take some of it away what you get is more water. Similarly with the sense-organs when we say that each of them is made of a single element. The sense-organs too are homoiomerous.

We recognise of course the principle of assigning single elements to the sense-organs from *De Anima* III.1 and *De Sensu* 2. But here we are given the rationale behind the principle. The rationale is that what is to be changed by something must be like what will change it. The patient must be like the agent. That means that the patient of the change has to be the same in kind as the agent. Aristotle solved the question whether the agent must be like or unlike the patient in order to change it by saying that before the change the agent must be like the patient in genus but unlike it in species.[29] When the change

[29] *GC* I.7 324a1–8.

happens the agent acts on the patient so as to make it like itself in species. Aristotle's point here is that if the patient is going to be changed by an agent that is simple in kind, then the patient must be simple in kind too, for if it is not it will not become actually like the agent when changed by it. It will not become like the agent insofar as the agent is one in kind whereas the patient is not.

The argument still looks a bit weak. But it is strengthened when we recall that the sense-faculty is in potentiality just what the sense-object is in actuality, nothing more, nothing less. The faculty of sight is a faculty of sight just insofar as it is able to be changed by colour so as to become like the colour. So if the sense-object is one in kind, for the sense-faculty to be of more than that kind would mean that it had attributes that were extraneous to its ability to be changed by that sense-object.

The simplicity of the sense-faculty is inherited by *the sense-organ* on the principle that has been the basis of my explanation of the sense-organs up till now, the principle that the sense-organs provide the necessary matter for the potentiality to be changed by a certain sort of sense-object. For example, that which is potentially coloured is the transparent since the transparent is what has the ability to be changed by colour as such. So the sense-faculty is transparent. But transparency is present only in a certain sort of matter. So the sense-faculty must have a material side, which is the transparent water inside the eye, the *korē*. Transparency is here a simple potentiality. It is of one kind in the sense that it is a potentiality to be coloured and coloured only. The matter *qua* transparent is simple too, for one sort of matter, water, is sufficient for the simple potentiality of transparency. So the sense-organ inherits the simplicity of the sense-object. That is why the *korē* only consists of water. Aristotle continues:

Though the ability to perceive is present in the simple parts, it happens very reasonably that the faculty of touch is found in the least simple of the sense-organs, though it is still homoiomerous. For the faculty of touch seems to be most [of all the senses] of several genera, and what is perceptible under it seems to have many oppositions, hot and cold, dry and wet, and the sense-organ of these [sc. oppositions], the flesh and its analogue, is the most corporeal of all the sense-organs. (*PA* II.1 647a14–21)

The same argument that gave us the simple composition of the *korē* now gives us the more complex, though still homo-iomerous, composition of the sense-organ of touch. The organ of touch inherits the complexity of the objects of touch. The objects of touch belong to different genera. Heat and cold belong to one genus, wet and dry to another. We would ex-pect then that if the ability to be changed by the one genus is an attribute found in one kind of matter and the ability to be changed by the other genus is found only in another sort of matter, then the sense-faculty of touch by having both abilities must have a sense-organ composed of more than one sort of matter. This is in fact the case, as we see in *De Anima* III.13:

It is clear that the body of an animal cannot be simple. I mean it cannot be made of fire or air for without touch it is not possible for it to have any other sense for the entire ensouled body is able to perceive by touch, as was said. Now all the other elements, except earth, could become a sense-organ, but they all bring about perception through something else and through a medium. Touch, however, is by direct contact with the objects, which is why it has its name ... Consequently, none of these elements would be the body of an animal. Nor indeed can the body be made of earth, for touch is as it were a mean between all the tangibles and the sense-organ is receptive not only of the differentiae of earth but also of the hot and the cold and all the other tangibles ... The organ of touch is not of earth nor of any of the other elements. (435a11–b4)

By 'not of earth nor any of the other elements' Aristotle here means 'not of a single of any of the elements'. So the sense-organ of touch cannot be something simple. It has to be a complex body. The last part of the passage fits with the ex-planation in *De Partibus Animalium* of why the sense-organ of touch is less simple than that of the other senses. The expla-nation was that the proper object of touch was not a single contrast within one genus but several contrasts within several genera. Compare again the case of the *korē*. Sight is con-cerned with the contrasts between white and black that fall within one kind, colour. Sight needs only to be potentially one kind, coloured, so it needs only to be transparent. Transparency is present in one kind of matter, water. So the sense-organ of sight is simple.

In the case of touch, there are at least two contrasts, hot and cold, dry and wet, and so two different kinds. The sense needs to be potentially both contrasts. The potentiality to become hot and cold or dry and wet is, like transparency, something that you only find in a certain sort of body. That is why the sense-faculty needs a material side to it, a sense-organ. But there is no simple body, no element, which is both hot and cold and dry and wet. Instead we find that earth is cold and dry, water wet and cold, air wet and hot, and fire hot and dry.[30] So in order for touch to have all of these qualities, it needs a sense-organ that is a complex body, a body consisting of all the elements.

Somebody might ask, 'Why cannot the organ of touch simply be composed of fire and water, since these two elements would give the sense-faculty all the four tangible qualities potentially? It would get the hot and the dry from fire and the cold and the wet from water.' One answer is that if the organ of touch needs to be a mixture of those two elements, *qua* mixture, it cannot be a mixture of *just* those two and no other, for *De Generatione of Corruptione* II.8 tells us that all mixtures are mixtures of all four elements.

Flesh is a complex body. As Aristotle says at *De Anima* II.II 423a12–15:

It is impossible for the ensouled body to consist of water or air, for it is necessary that it be something solid. It remains that it is a mixture of earth and these elements, such as flesh and its analogue profess to be.

Flesh is a suitable sense-organ of touch because it consists of all the elements, with the possible exception of fire.[31] It is

---

[30] *GC* II.3 330b3–5.
[31] Fire plays a special role in the composition of all the sense-organs. It seems to be connected more with the natural heat than with the particular constitution of any of the sense-organs. Cf. *De an.* III.I 425a6.

suitable because all of the contrasts that the sense of touch need potentially to have are present in these elements taken together. Hence also the conclusion of the *De Partibus Animalium* passage that 'the organ that deals with these varied objects is of all the sense-organs the most corporeal, being either flesh or the substance which in some animals takes the place of flesh', in other words 'flesh and its analogue'.[32]

7. Flesh as the medium of touch

There is a complication, however, for Aristotle sometimes says that flesh is only the medium of touch and taste, whereas the proper sense-organ of these senses is in the heart or somewhere around the heart.[33] At *De Anima* II.11 423b7 he insists that we perceive all things through a medium, but the presence of a medium in touch and taste escapes our notice because the medium, the skin and flesh, is directly attached to our bodies. The mediation of the sense-objects of touch and taste occurs simultaneously with our perception of them. This is compared with the way in which the body of a soldier receives a shock when his shield is struck. The blow on the shield and the blow to the body occur simultaneously. Similarly, in perception by touch and taste the skin and flesh are affected simultaneously with the sense-organ.

Touch and taste then seem to be mediated after all. Aristotle concludes by saying that:

It seems in general that just as air and water are to sight, hearing and smell, so the flesh and the tongue are to their sense-organ as each of those is. And neither in the one case nor in the other would perception occur when contact is made with the sense-organ itself, for example if someone were to put a white body on the surface of the eye. From this it is clear that that which can perceive the object of touch is internal, for then the same thing would happen as in the other cases; for we do not perceive what is placed on the sense-organ, but we do perceive what is placed upon the flesh. Hence the flesh is the medium for that which can perceive by touch. (*De an.* II.11 423b17–26; transl. Hamlyn)

---

[32] Cf. *PA* II.8.   [33] *Sens.* 2 439a1–2.

The passage shows that the fact that we do not perceive what is directly placed on the sense-organ overrides the tendency to think that the sense-organ of touch is that which is in direct contact with the sense-object. We feel something hot when a hot object is placed directly on our flesh. But this should not make us think that flesh is the sense-organ of touch. It should only make us think that the affection of the flesh occurs simultaneously with the affection of the sense-organ around the heart. In a way this is inconsistent with what was said earlier, namely, that the contact senses are those senses that perceive by direct contact with their sense-objects, for this meant that touch and taste were singled out as having no medium. But now we are told that what is in direct contact with the sense-objects, the tongue and the flesh, is in fact not the part of the body in which the sense-faculties of touch and taste are located. The tongue and the flesh are only the medium of taste and touch.

In another way, however, what we are told now is not inconsistent with what was said earlier, for the contact senses do operate by direct contact, not in the sense that excludes a medium, but in the sense that when you put something tangible directly on the body then you perceive it instantaneously. The tangible does not have to act on a different body before it can act on the sense-organ in the sense that a colour has to act on air or water before it can act on the eye. The operative distinction between the contact senses and the distance senses here is not the distinction between the sense-object's acting indirectly on the sense-organ through a medium and its acting directly on the sense-organ. It is rather the distinction between the sense-object's acting indirectly on the sense-organ through a different body, as in vision, and the sense-object's acting indirectly on the sense-organ through the perceiver's own body, as in touch and taste. 'The medium' has been shown to be ambiguous, meaning, on the one hand, what is in between the sense-organ and the sense-object, and, on the other hand, what is in between the perceiver's body and the sense-object. In the first sense touch and taste do have a medium, in the second sense they do not.

In *De Partibus Animalium* II.8 Aristotle continues the discussion of the homoiomerous parts of the body initiated in II.1 (quoted above, p. 195):

Let us first of all consider flesh in those animals that have flesh, but the analogue in the other animals. For this is the origin [ἀρχή] and essential body of animals. And this is clear according to reason. For we define animal by its having perception, but first of all by having the first sort of perception. But this [sc. the first sort of perception] is touch and the organ of touch is such a part [sc. flesh] either as the first sense-organ of touch, just as the *korē* is the first sense-organ of sight or as the medium of touch taken together [sc. with the first organ of touch] just as if somebody were to add all of the transparent to the *korē*. (*PA* II.8 653b19–27)

I want to show that this passage is crucial to understanding the ambiguity in Aristotle's location of the organ of touch. The entire body insofar as it consists of flesh is first considered the organ of touch. But a distinction is then introduced between the primary sense-organ of touch, which Aristotle presumably also here would take to be the heart, and the flesh. It might be that the flesh rather than being the primary sense-organ of touch is the medium of touch. So far the story is familiar. But the story does not end there, for we can take the sense-organ of touch to be the flesh and the primary sense-organ taken together, just as if we were to take the *korē* and the transparent medium of sight together to be the sense-organ of sight.

I have already argued that the sense-organ of sight and the medium of sight are determined by the same functional requirement of transparency, that is the ability to be changed by colour. The eye jelly had to be transparent like the medium for the same reason.[34] The *korē* and the medium were therefore identical *qua* transparent. The functional identity of the eye jelly and the transparent medium would therefore give some licence to a person who wanted to add the medium of sight to the eye jelly and call the compound of these two the sense-organ of sight.

---

[34] *Sens.* 2 438b6–8. 'Just as nothing is seen outside without light so also inside nothing is seen without light. It is necessary then that the inside be transparent.'

However, there is an obstacle to calling the transparent medium part of the organ of sight for the medium of sight is not part of the body. It is only the body and its parts that can be said to be a sense-organ of the soul. There is no such stumbling block when it comes to the medium of touch, however, for the flesh is part of the body. If the soul uses the flesh in perception by touch, there is no reason why the flesh should be not be called the soul's organ in touch, though we would still want to reserve for the heart the role of *primary* sense-organ of touch. The heart is the primary organ of touch for it is when the tangibles are received by the heart that they are perceived, though this fact escapes our notice since the affection of the flesh coincides with the affection of the heart. Again, as in the case of sight, we have here a licence to take the flesh and the first sense-organ of touch together, for compare *De Partibus Animalium* II.1 647a24–33:

Since the ability to perceive and move the animal and the nutritive faculty are in the same part of the body, just as it was said earlier in other works, it is necessary that the primary part that possesses such principles, insofar as it is able to receive all the sense-objects, should consist of all the simple parts, but insofar as it able to initiate movement and action it should be made of anhomoiomerous parts. That is why the analogue [sc. of the heart] in bloodless animals and the heart in sanguineous animals is such a part, for the heart divides into homoiomerous parts just like the other viscera but owing to its shape of appearance it is anhomoiomerous.

In the same way as the flesh was said earlier in *De Partibus Animalium* II.1 to be composed of all the simple bodies in order to be able to receive all the various tangible objects, so the heart is said to consist of 'all the simple parts' in order to be able to receive all the sense-objects. So the same principle of composition is involved both in the case of the flesh and in the case of the heart. The parts are composed in such way that they are able to receive all the sense-objects that they are required to perceive insofar as they are organs of perception. In the case of the heart, the sense-objects include all the sense-objects of the special senses, not just those of touch, for the heart is the ultimate sense-organ of all the senses. But it is clear that insofar as the heart is also able to receive the sense-objects of touch in particular, it should be composed of all the elements that the flesh is composed of. The heart too therefore has to be fleshy, which is why it is said to be a homoiomerous composition of the simple parts. We see then that the heart *qua* organ of all perception is composed according to the same basic requirement as the flesh *qua* organ of touch. That is, the composition should contain all the elements that are required to perceive the sense-objects. However, in the case of the heart that means that it is not just composed by those elements required to perceive tangibles. It is also composed by those elements required to perceive colour, sound, etc. So again we are back at the procedure of explaining the composition of the sense-organ in terms of providing the necessary matter for the reception of the sense-objects. In vision, we saw that the necessary matter was water, in hearing air. In touch, we now see that the matter for the ability to receive all the tangibles is a homoiomerous mixture of the four elements. This is the mixture that the flesh and the heart both provide.

The argument shows that whether we consider the flesh or the heart or both taken together to be the sense-organ of touch is indeterminate if we approach the question solely from the point of view of the ability to receive the tangibles. For both the flesh and the heart are composed in such a way that they can do this. Similarly, both the medium of vision and the eye were composed in such a way that they could receive colour. Because the flesh and the heart *qua* having the ability to receive tangibles are functionally equivalent, we have a licence to take the heart and the flesh together as a sense-organ of touch. From the functional point of view, that is from the point of view of being able to be changed by the tangible qualities, it really does not matter too much which we say is the sense-organ of touch. We can take either of them or both of them together.

There are, however, other reasons for preferring the heart. These reasons emerge when we consider those contexts in which Aristotle mentions the heart or the head as the only possible locations for a sense-organ. We saw in chapter 1 how Aristotle made the point in *De Partibus Animalium* II.10 that the heart rather than the brain is the seat of all perception (pp. 78–81). He referred us back to *De Sensu* 2 for the view that touch and taste were clearly dependent on the heart (656a28–30). The relevant passage seems to be *De Sensu* 2 438b16–439a5, where he argued that the organs of touch and taste were situated in the heart whereas those of the vision, hearing and smell were placed in the head.

It is clear then that when Aristotle says that the heart is the seat of all perception then he thinks that this is consistent with also saying that the sense-organs of some of the senses are situated in the head, that is near the brain. So when we are saying that the heart is the organ of touch and taste we are saying something rather different from saying that the heart is the seat of all perception and therefore also of touch, since we say also about the other senses that the seat of perception is the heart at the same time as we say that their organs are in the head and therefore not in the heart.

However, it is also clear from Aristotle's argument in *De Partibus Animalium* II.10 that saying that the heart is the seat of all perception creates the expectation that the organ of a sense will be the heart unless we can find other reasons why there should be a separate organ for the sense in the head. For having pointed out that taste and touch clearly depend on the heart, he goes on, as we saw in chapter 1, section 10, to argue that there are specific reasons why the distance senses should have their sense-organs in the head, reasons which do not include saying that their organs are in the head because the brain is the seat of perception. The implication seems to be that unless one can find such specific reasons for why the sense-organ should be located in the head the natural location for the organ is in the heart since the heart is the seat of all perception.

The reference to *De Sensu* 2 438b16–439a5 is not particularly helpful because of the difficulty of this passage. But let us see what we can make of it. Aristotle starts by reminding us of the task set at the beginning of *De Sensu* 2 – to find a way in which five sense-organs could be assigned to four elements. The organ of sight is composed of water, the organ of hearing of air, the organ of smell of fire and the organ of touch and taste of earth, taste being a form of touch. By saying that the organ of smell is made of fire, he seems to mean no more than that the organ of smell is potentially hot in order to be made actually hot by smells. This also explains why the organ of smell is located near the brain which is cold and it is the cold that is potentially hot. The brain is not only cold, however, but also liquid, which explains why the eyes are near the brain, for the eyes are made out of the brain's liquid.[35] We see, then, that it is appropriate for sense-organs that need to be liquid and potentially hot to be situated near the brain.

Next, Aristotle says that the organ of touch and taste is earth and 'this is why their sense-organ is near the heart ... for the heart is opposed to the brain in that [καί] it is the hottest of the parts [of the body]' (439a1–4). Saying that the organ of touch is made of earth cannot be taken to mean that the organ of touch is composed solely of earth, for at *De Anima* III.13 435a11–b4 he says that no sense-organ is made of earth because nothing that is composed of earth has perception. As I suggested in chapter 1, section 5, saying that the organ of touch is made of earth should probably instead be taken to mean that it is solid as opposed to being either liquid (water) or gaseous (air). We have seen that the organ of touch is a complex body. Since, according to *De Anima* II.11 423a12–15, complex bodies are also solid, the organ of touch can be described as earthy in the sense of solid.

Rather paradoxically, however, the organ of touch now appears to be earthy insofar as it is composed of all the four elements. But the air of paradox disappears when we recall that none of the other organs contains earth, whereas they do contain either fire or air or water. The sense-organ of touch can therefore be said to be earthy both insofar as it is unique

---

[35] Cf. ch. 1, sec. 10, above; *PA* II.10 656a37–b2.

in containing earth as well as the other elements and insofar as it is therefore solid.

A second point to bear in mind has been made above: the organs that are near the brain are either wet (the organ of sight) or potentially hot (the organ of smell),[36] for the brain is wet and cold and the heart is opposed to the brain, for the heart is very hot.[37]

Now in *De Anima* III.13 435a22–4 Aristotle says that the sense-organ of touch is receptive not only of the qualities of earth but also of both the hot and the cold and all the other tangibles. This is as we would expect given the claim in *De Anima* II.11 that touch is a mean between all the various tangibles in order to be able to receive all the tangibles. However, the way Aristotle puts it in *De Anima* III.13 suggests that the sense-organ of touch *first and foremost* is receptive of the qualities of earth. *De Sensu* 2 too highlights the qualities of earth amongst the sense-qualities of touch. For Aristotle says that the tangible principle is of earth, but the tastable principle is a sort of touch; and this is why their sense-organ is next to the heart. Following on what he has said about the location of smell, the relevance of the point that the tangible principle is of earth to the question of the location of the sense-organ of touch seems to be this. It is right that the sense-organ of smell should be near the brain, for the brain is cold and therefore potentially hot. The sense of smell needs to be potentially hot as its proper object, odours, are actually hot. Being near the brain makes the sense-faculty of smell the temperature it should be to receive its proper object. Similarly, it is right that the organ of touch should be near the heart. The heart is hot and therefore potentially cold. Earthy qualities and particularly the cold are predominant amongst the tangible qual-

---

[36] No reason is given here for why the organ of hearing, being made of air, should be near the brain. However, in *PA* II.10 656b15–16 Aristotle explains this location by saying that there is a space in the head called 'the vacuum' (τὸ κενόν) which is full of air. So the airy organ of hearing is in the head because there is another airy part in the head and again the explanation is that the sense-organ is close to what it is like.

[37] *Sens.* 2 439a2–4.

ities.[38] So by being actually hot, the sense-faculty becomes potentially like its *primary* sense-object, the cold. Its organ's location near the heart ensures that the sense-faculty is actually hot. Similarly, both the sense-organs of smell and taste are located near parts of the body that make the sense-faculties potentially like their proper objects.

Aristotle in this way departs from his earlier claim at *De Anima* II.11 424a10–11 that the sense-faculty should be neither hot nor cold in order for it to be able to become either hot or cold. As we have seen, the departure is the result of focusing on one quality, the cold, as the primary object of touch. Methodologically, however, there is no departure from earlier claims insofar as the sense-faculty and its organ are still determined by the potentiality to be like their proper object. It is only that the proper object has here been narrowed down to one quality rather than a range of opposite qualities. The motivation for this narrowing-down is to explain the location of the sense-organ according to the same principle that explained its composition. That is to say, Aristotle is concerned to show which location is necessary for the sense-organ to provide the sense-faculty with the ability to be changed by its proper objects, just as he was concerned to show which composition of the sense-organ gave the sense-faculty this ability.

When discussing the location of smell and touch Aristotle focuses on the contrast between two qualities, hot and cold. What is potentially hot is actually cold. So the sense of smell is attached to matter that is actually cold but potentially hot, the potentially hot being potentially like the fiery odours. So by being attached to matter that is actually cold the sense of smell is appropriately attached to matter that, like the sense of smell itself, is potentially like the object of smell, the fiery odours. On the same principle, the sense of touch is located near matter that is actually hot, for the actually hot is poten-

---

[38] *Sens.* 2 438b30–439a1: τὸ δ' ἁπτικὸν γῆς, τὸ δὲ γευστικὸν εἶδός τι ἀφῆς ἐστίν. The genitives may cause confusion. The first genitive is an objective genitive, the second a partitive genitive. In other words, Aristotle is saying first that earth is something we perceive by touch and second that taste is a part of touch; cf. Ross (1955) 193.

tially cold, like earth. But we saw that the qualities of earth were first amongst the proper objects of touch. So by being attracted to warm matter, the sense of touch is appropriately attached to matter that, like the sense of touch, potentially has the qualities of earth. The sense of touch is therefore attached to matter that is potentially cold and actually hot. Given the alternatives, being attached either to the brain or to the heart and given that the brain is actually cold and the heart actually hot, the sense of touch must be attached to the heart.[39]

W. D. Ross finds Aristotle's argument objectionable and immature. 'It will be seen', he writes, 'that the organs of sight and hearing are brought into relation with water and air in one way, viz. as being composed of them, and those of smell and touch are brought into relation with fire and earth in quite a different way, viz. as perceiving them.' He concludes that 'the whole passage is not to be taken very seriously. It does not express Aristotle's mature view about the sense-organs.'[40]

However, Ross's description of the difference between Aristotle's treatment of sight and hearing, on the one hand, and his treatment of smell and touch, on the other, is not quite apposite. In the case of sight and hearing, as we saw in chapters 1 and 3, the organs are composed in such a way as to give the corresponding sense-faculty the potentiality to be changed by its proper sense-object, for sight colour, for hearing sound. This meant that the organ of sight had to be made of transparent matter, namely water, and that the organ of hearing had to be made of resonant matter, namely still air. In the case of touch, the organ is similarly composed of earthy flesh in order to be able to be changed by the proper objects of touch, for these include the hot and cold and the wet and dry. Aristotle's point, however, throughout is that the sense-organ

---

[39] Aristotle is generally careful to say that the sense-organ of touch is either near (as here: πρὸς τῇ καρδίᾳ) or in the region of the heart (περὶ τὴν καρδίαν) rather than to say that it is in the heart or simply that it is the heart. One reason *might* be that the extreme heat found in the heart itself is not conducive to accuracy of perception; cf. *PA* II.10 656b3–6. But the point is never explained.

[40] Ross (1955) 193.

has to have the properties potentially that the sense-object has actually. This is spelt out in slightly different ways for sight and smell, for example. For in the case of smell, the sense-organ must be potentially hot because the proper object of smell is actually hot. In the case of sight by contrast, the sense-organ must be wet because the wet (water) is potentially coloured. To be sure, Aristotle mentions the fact that the eyes are wet also because they develop from the brain. But this point only follows after the long argument in *De Sensu* 2 to show that the eyes are made of water because water is transparent. Transparency gave the eyes their ability to be changed by colour, the change that defined vision, so transparency refers to the form and function of the eyes, vision. It is for the sake of this form and function that the eyes develop as they do. So when Aristotle says that the eyes are liquid because they develop from the liquid brain he is not making an observation about the development of the eyes that can be read in isolation from the argument of the rest of *De Sensu* 2. He can rely on the argument that the eyes are made of water in order to be transparent so that we can use them in vision. Aristotle should not be read therefore as departing from the principle that the organs are explained by the potentiality to be like the sense-objects when he says that the eyes are made of water because they develop from the brain in order that they may become transparent and thereby also able to become coloured. So when Ross says that the location of the eyes is explained by their composition *rather than* by the object of sight it is misleading because the talk of the composition of the eyes refers back to the discussion of the eyes as transparent and therefore to the principle that the sense-faculty should be potentially what the proper object is actually.

This interpretation, of course, may not make us happier with the argument, because we may think that Aristotle is playing loose and fast with the principle that the sense-faculty is potentially what the sense-object is actually. He starts by saying that the sense-organ of smell is made of fire. But what this turns out to mean is that the sense-organ is made of fire in the sense that it is *potentially* hot which means being in a location that is *actually* cold and liquid. We shall see in the next chapter that Aristotle also argues that the sense of smell is potentially dry and that it is made actually dry by perceiving odours. We can understand now how he can also say (*De an.* III.1 425a5) that the sense-organ of smell is made of either water or air. Being made of water will make the sense-organ actually cold and wet and so potentially hot and dry: being made of air will make it actually hot and wet and so potentially cold and dry. Either composition will therefore make the sense-organ potentially dry. So either water or air would be suitable matter for the sense of smell.

Similarly, we can say about touch that by being composed of all the elements it will have all the tangible qualities potentially insofar as it actually has the qualities of a different element. For instance, the organ of touch will be potentially cold insofar as it is actually hot. So the organ of touch is potentially like earth, that is, potentially cold insofar as it actually is like fire, that is, actually hot.

However, it seems now that any description of the sense-organ as belonging to a certain element or as being made of a certain element needs disambiguation. Do we mean that the organ is actually made of the element in question in the way for example that the eye is actually made of water? Or do we mean that it potentially has the qualities that the element actually has, for example in the way that the sense-organ of smell is made of fire? Disambiguation is needed. For it now seems that at least touch, taste and smell can all be said to consist of any element according to whether we take the sense-organ to have the qualities of the element potentially or actually. We may complain that there is now a certain arbitrariness in whether we describe the organ of touch, for example, as being made of earth or as being made of fire. The organ of touch is fiery insofar as it is actually hot through its location near the heart, but it is also earthy insofar as its proper object is like earth, cold. And earlier we saw that it was earthy in yet another sense, for it was solid because it actually contained earth as well as the other elements.

Considerable confusion is thus possible when Aristotle says

that an organ is made of or belongs to an element unless we specify exactly what we mean. However, what is important to underline is something common to all these different ways of saying that the organ is composed of an element. In whichever way we describe the organ of touch, the organ is described in relation to the proper objects of touch. When the organ is described as fiery it is described as actually unlike *but therefore potentially* like earth, that is, potentially cold. When the organ is described as earthy it is described as potentially like earth.

We saw, then, that the location of the sense of touch near the heart, rather than in the head, is determined by one of the proper objects of touch, the cold. The sense of touch needs to be actually hot in order to be potentially cold. Aristotle's explanation of the location of touch, like that of the other senses, is functional in that it shows how this location is the right location for touch given the potentiality that defines it. The location of the sense of touch near the heart is right given the sort of sense-object that it is the job of touch to perceive, just as the location of the sense of smell near the brain was the right one given that we perceive hot odours by smell.

One final consideration also points to the heart as the location of touch. Touch is the sense that all animals must have *qua* animals.[41] An animal is a living being with perception. Perception is the potentiality that defines the animal *qua* animal. Touch is the basic form of perception. Not all animals need have sight or smell but they must all have touch. That is why the animal dies if its organ of touch is destroyed, whereas the animal need not die with the destruction of any of its other sense-organs. Now Aristotle believes that the heart is the part that the animal foetus develops first. Since the possession of touch is the minimum condition of being an animal, to have the organ of touch develop together with the heart as the first part ensures that the animal satisfies the minimum condition of being an animal from its conception. The sense-organ of touch is the first part that the animal needs to become an animal in the sense of a living being with the potentiality to

---

[41] Cf. *De an.* II.2 413b2–5, III.12 434b7–18 and 13 435a11–b19; *PA* II.8 653b19–24.

perceive. The location of the sense-organ around the heart thus ensures that the animal has the potentiality that defines it as an animal right after its conception.

8. Variations in the organ of touch

We have seen why Aristotle's considered position is that the heart rather than the flesh is the organ of touch. However, there are some animals that have no heart but nevertheless have touch. Bloodless animals are the prime example according to Aristotle.[42] Indeed, they in general lack the viscera of blooded animals. However, bloodless animals have something analogous to the heart because they are animals. As we have seen, animals must have a perceptual soul, and therefore there must be also a part of the body in which the perceptual soul is located. The heart in blooded animals is this part. Since the bloodless animals do not have a heart, they must have something analogous to the heart.

We are told nothing about the composition of this analogue apart from what Aristotle says at *De Partibus Animalium* II.2 647a27–31, that the heart must be composed of the simple parts (that is the four elements) since it is the origin/principle (*arkhē*) of perception and must be able to receive all the sensible qualities. In contrast, the heart is also the origin of motion and action. Aristotle says that it must therefore also be composed of *an*homoiomerous parts. The description of the heart applies equally to its analogue that must enable the bloodless animal to perform all the basic functions that the animal has *qua* animal just as the heart must enable the blooded animal to perform all the basic function that *it* has *qua* animal. The material composition of the analogue is not specified beyond saying that it must be both to a certain extent homoiomerous and to a certain extent anhomoiomerous to fulfil these functional demands.[43] Aristotle's interest in the

[42] Cf. *PA* II.1 647a30–1.
[43] Cf. *HA* I.4 489a25–6 which underlines that whether the organ of touch is flesh or something analogous it must be homoiomerous.

analogue of the heart is purely as the functional analogue of the heart.

Let us next consider the skin and the flesh. On reflection, I argue, we do not want to say that the skin and the flesh are the organ of touch. Nevertheless, they are still clearly important to touch insofar as they are the medium. Some animals, like the testacea (e.g. oysters) and crustacea (e.g. crabs) have their flesh inside a shell.[44] The shell is made of bone that serves to support the flesh, for the flesh is soft and therefore needs a hard structure such as bones to keep it in place. In other animals, such as man, the bones support the flesh from the inside, but in crustacea and testacea the flesh is supported by a shell outside the flesh because these animals have little body heat. By having the shell outside, the heat of the flesh inside is preserved. The shell is like the lid on a saucepan that keeps the food inside the saucepan warm.[45] There is an advantage, then, for these animals in having their protective part outside the flesh. Again, like a good housekeeper, nature has put the same part of the body to multiple uses.

However, there is also a potential disadvantage for the testacea and crustacea in this arrangement, for does the shell not prevent the flesh inside from responding to the tangibles outside the shell? Does their flesh not become insensitive to what the shell comes into contact with, just as when somebody puts on armour he becomes insensitive to what touches the armour? How, then, do these animals manage to perceive the tangible qualities? The answer seems to be: only with great difficulty. Aristotle is clear that accuracy of touch depends on the softness of one's skin and flesh.[46] Thus he says that because man has the most delicate sense of touch his flesh

---

[44] Cf. *PA* II.8 653b36–654a9.

[45] *PA* II.8 654a7–8.

[46] *De an.* II.9 421a20–6. Freeland (1992) 231 notes that Aristotle shows no interest in appendages such as the insect's antennae, the cat's whiskers and the octopus's feelers as playing a role in touch. These appendages might be thought to compensate for the lack of sensitivity of the flesh in these animals. Freeland's explanation is that Aristotle is being anthropocentric: he exclusively focuses on the role of the flesh in all animals because of its importance in humans.

is softer than that of any other animal.[47] We expect therefore those animals which like insects have no flesh but only a hard, sinewy body to have a reduced sense of touch. Animals with a shell would seem to count as an extreme case of hard-skinned animals.[48] Since, in general, an animal is more sensitive if its skin is thin and soft, having not only hard skin but also a shell around one's flesh must make for very poor sensitivity to tangibles.

We must of course assume that the testacea and crustacea do have touch since they are animals and all animals require touch. Also their behaviour insofar as they respond to objects that they come into contact with suggests that they have touch.[49] Yet it is difficult to see how these animals can have an adequate sense of touch given that their shells would seem to block out any tangible impressions. For example, just as the shell keeps the heat inside the flesh, so one would suppose that the shell isolated the flesh from heat or cold outside the shell. It is hard to understand, therefore, how the flesh could be sensitive through the shell to anything but extreme temperatures. Nor is it easy to understand how the softness or the hardness of an object could affect the flesh through the shell. The flesh, then, would seem to be protected from the impressions of tangible objects because of the shell.

However, we should notice here that it is generally not so easy to understand how the flesh even in soft-skinned animals reacts to a wet or a smooth object through the skin. The flesh of course does not go literally wet or smooth. The skin pro-

---

[47] *PA* II.16 660a11–13. Notice that Aristotle says that man's flesh is soft because his sense of touch is delicate rather than the other way around. The flesh is composed to serve one of man's characteristic functions, namely, delicate touch. It is not the case that man's flesh happens to be soft for other reasons and that the fact that his flesh happens to be soft accidentally enables him to have the most delicate sense of touch. On the contrary, having a delicate sense of touch is implied by being a man. It is one of the functions he has insofar as he is a man. His body is composed to serve those functions.

[48] Aristotle says at *HA* IV.2 525b12–13 that the shell of crustacea takes the place of their skin.

[49] Cf. *HA* IV.6 531a31–b7 where Aristotle says that sea-anemones, which are like testacea but have no shell, perceive and grab the things that come up against them with their hands.

tects the flesh just as much from getting wet as a hard shell would. Similarly, whether you are wearing armour or only a thin raincoat you are still protected from getting wet. The only case where it seems at all plausible to say that the flesh literally takes on the tangible quality through the skin is the case of the hot and the cold, where we can see how the skin literally could convey the temperature to the flesh inside. We shall look more carefully at this case in the final chapter (ch. 6). For now I note that this seems to be the *only* case in which it seems plausible to talk about the flesh literally taking on the tangible quality through the skin. In the case of other tangibles, both for animals that have a shell and for animals that have skin, the literalist interpretation seems implausible.

9. The sense-organ of taste

Let me turn now to the sense-organ of taste. We saw in *De Anima* II.10 that the dry and the wet interact to produce the tastable, the character of which determines how the sense-organ of taste is composed because the sense-faculty is potentially what the sense-object is actually. The sense-organ provides the material basis for this potentiality of the sense-faculty.

Since the tastable is moist it is necessary also that its sense-organ is neither actually moist nor incapable of being moistened. For the sense of taste is somehow affected [πάσχει τι] by the tastable *qua* tastable. So it is necessary that the sense-organ of taste is moistened, being that which remains potentially moistened but not actually moist. A sign of this is that the tongue does not perceive when it is very dry or too moist. For in that case there is a contact with the prior moisture [sc. the moisture already on the tongue] just as when somebody having tasted already a strong flavour tastes another flavour. And this happens also when everything seems bitter to sick people because it is perceived by a tongue that is full of such a moisture [sc. bitter moisture]. (*De an.* II.10 422a34–b10)

The organ of taste is the tongue.[50] The reason why the tongue has to be potentially moist but not actually moist is

---

[50] At *HA* I.11 492b27–8 Aristotle specifies that it is with the tip of the tongue that we primarily taste.

that it should be able to be changed by the tastable which is actually moist, for the tastable is liquefied flavour. Aristotle makes the same point about all the senses in his discussion of touch in *De Anima* II.11 423b31–424a10:

> For perceiving is a form of being affected; hence, that which acts makes that part, which is potentially as it is, such as it is itself actually. For this reason we do not perceive anything which is equally as hot or cold, or hard or soft, but rather excesses of these, the sense-faculty being a sort of mean between the opposites present in sense-objects. For the mean is capable of discriminating. For it becomes to each extreme in turn the other extreme. And just as that which is to perceive white and black must be neither of them actually, although both potentially (and similarly too for the other senses), so in the case of touch that which is to perceive such must be neither hot nor cold. (Hamlyn tr. with changes)

The sense-faculty should be potentially *and only potentially* what the sense-object is actually, for the sense-faculty cannot be changed by the sense-object if it is already actually what the sense-object is, and to perceive a sense-object is to be changed by it. By the same reasoning the sense-faculty is said to be a mean between opposites, for if it is a mean it can be changed by both extreme opposites. However, just as the sense-faculty would not be able to be changed by the extreme opposite if it itself was already characterised by that quality, so the sense-faculty cannot be changed by a mean quality since it is itself already characterised by that mean quality. That is why Aristotle says that 'we do not perceive anything that is equally hot or cold as the sense-faculty of touch. This was also his point when he said that our tongues should be in an intermediary state between being too dry and too wet if we are to be able to taste.

The phenomenon that we do not, for example, perceive by touch what is the same temperature as the sense of touch is commonly referred to as 'the blind spot' phenomenon. The phenomenon is sometimes mentioned in favour of a literalist interpretation.[51] For the fact that we do not perceive a temperature corresponding to the temperature that the sense-

---

[51] Cf. Modrak (1987) 58–60; Burnyeat (1992) 20–1; Marc Cohen (1992) 66; Sorabji (1992) 214–16.

organ already has seems to suggest that when we do perceive other temperatures then we perceive them because the sense-organ is able to change its temperature to the temperature of the sense-object. There is another explanation of the blind spot phenomenon, however, for the fact that I do not perceive a temperature equal to that of my sense-organ of touch need only mean that my sense-organ of touch is already stimulated by that temperature as an *object* of touch. In other words, the reason why I cannot come to perceive that temperature is that I am already perceiving it. Even when we are not particularly cold or warm we are generally aware of the temperature of our bodies. So if you put an object of the same temperature on my skin I will not perceive it as hot or cold, for its temperature is the same as the temperature that I am already perceiving because of my body's temperature. So I fail to notice the temperature of the object when it is put on my skin. The reason why I am not aware of the temperature of an object when it is the same as that of my body is not that my body's temperature literally needs to change in order to perceive something as hot or cold. The reason is rather that my sense-faculty needs not already to be exposed to that temperature if it is to become aware of it. The sense-faculty becomes insensitive to the temperature of other objects if the sense-organ itself has that temperature. For then the sense-faculty is already aware of the temperature and cannot become aware of it as the temperature of another object. There is nothing in this explanation of the blind spot phenomenon that lends support to a literalist interpretation.

Now there is still a disanalogy between taste and touch, on the one hand, and sight and hearing, on the other hand. For when Aristotle talked about transparency he talked about what has no colour but is able to receive colour and not about what has a colour which lies in between the two extremes of black and white. In chapter 1, section 11 (pp. 111–12) I used the example of a car with five gears. When Aristotle talked of transparency it was as if he was talking about an engine which had been put into neutral position, that is, into no gear. Now, however, when he talks about the intermediary state of the organs of taste and touch it is as if he is talking about an engine that has been put into the third position, the position in between the fifth and the first positions. For when he says that we do not perceive by touch what is neither hot nor cold he seems to mean that we do not perceive what is of middling temperature because the organ of touch already is of middling temperature.

In chapter 1, section 11 (pp. 96–8) I noted that there was an apparent difficulty in Aristotle's saying both that the transparent liquid in the eye was colourless and that it had a colour. The upshot of the discussion was that eye colour appeared only on the surface of the eye. The transparent was therefore still colourless to the person seeing through the eyes. The colour of a person's eyes did not interfere with her vision. Eye colour, however, was also indicative of the degree of transparency in the eyes. It was therefore indicative of the eyes' ability to function in different conditions of light. The best state was said to be the mean state of transparency such that the change of the sense-object was neither too strong nor too weak. The mean was here primarily understood as a functional mean rather than an absolute set state of the sense-organ. Different degrees of transparency could be preferable in different circumstances according to the degree of transparency that enabled you to see best in the circumstances. Thus less transparency was preferable by day, more by night. On a sunny day, even less transparency would be better and on a particularly dark night even more transparency would be better. It was in general preferable to have a degree of transparency that enables one to see reasonably well in all circumstances. Aristotle suggested that this degree of transparency coincided with a green eye colour, however, saying that this degree in general is a sort of compromise between the degrees of transparency that are preferable in all the different conditions of light in which we see. Sometimes it is best to have the lesser transparency of brown eyes; sometimes it is best to have the greater transparency of blue eyes; over all it is best to have the intermediate transparency of green eyes. To say when it is best to have which colour we have to consider what the conditions of light are and what sort of object (white or dark) we are using our eyes to see.

Eye colour, then, was indicative of a certain degree of transparency in the eye. Whether or not this degree could be described as the best and mean degree of transparency depended on the sort of object the eyes were asked to perceive and the sort of circumstances in which they were asked to perceive them. What decides what is a mean colour of the eyes is what is a mean or appropriate degree of *transparency* if one is to see well in different circumstances. Therefore the notion of a mean eye colour and a mean degree of transparency does not lead to the 'third-position' view, for the eye colour that would be described as best varies in different circumstances according to the degree of transparency that is favourable in those circumstances. The mean is not a mean state of the matter of the sense-organ *qua* matter; it is not understood in terms of eye colour; it is the best ability to function as an organ of sight in the circumstances; and it is understood in terms of the best degree of transparency, which may vary. There is therefore no fixed material state of the organ which can be described as 'the mean'.

For our understanding of the sense-organ of taste this is important. We are told that the tongue should not be too dry or too wet so that it should be potentially moistened. What the comparison with eye colour suggests is that the sense-organ of taste must be potentially moistened (but not actually moist) so that it can be moistened by the flavour. Whether the tongue is in a state where it can be moistened by a flavour depends on the kind of change that the flavour will set up in it. That the tongue is not actually moist but only potentially moistened means that it can become moistened by the change of that flavour, not that the tongue does not, in absolute terms, have a degree of moisture already. A mean state of moisture is the right state of moisture relative to the sort of flavour that you will be tasting. When the tongue is said not to be actually moist but potentially moistened, then that means that it is not moist in such a way that it cannot become moistened by the change of the flavour. It does not mean that the tongue does not absolutely have a degree of moisture already. A mean state of moisture is the right state of moisture to be in relative to the sort of flavour that you are going to be exposed to.

So the case of the sense-organ of taste is similar to the case of the eye. The mean of the eye is understood functionally in terms of a degree of transparency appropriate to a sense-object. Similarly, the moisture of the tongue is understood functionally in relation to flavour. The tongue is not moist insofar as it should be able to be moistened, be *made* moist, by the flavour. But this does not exclude that it has a degree of moisture already before tasting. From this point of view the question whether the sense-organ should be quality-less, the 'neutral' view, or have a mean quality, the 'third-position' view, is the wrong question to ask. The point is that the mean that Aristotle is talking about is a functional mean in relation to a sense-object. The sense of taste should be without the quality that it is to receive and be changed by in tasting.

In sum, the mean state both in the case of the eyes and in the case of the tongue is the state in which the sense-faculty is able to respond appropriately to a certain sense-object in the circumstances. The mean is properly described as a functional mean rather than as a material mean.

10. Variations in the organ of taste

In *De Partibus Animalium* IV.11 690b19–691a9 Aristotle compares two animals, the crocodile and the snake, in respect of their sense-organs of taste and their ability to taste. First, there is the crocodile which has no tongue, even though it has a space for a tongue. This is exceptional amongst blooded animals, which otherwise all have tongues. The exception is to be explained by the fact that the crocodile lives in water. Insofar as the crocodile is a water animal it has no tongue. However, the crocodile also spends some time on land. Insofar as it is also a land animal, it has a space for a tongue. 'The reason for this', Aristotle says, 'is that a tongue would be of little service to such animals [sc. as live in water], seeing that they are unable to chew their food or to taste it beforehand, the pleasurable experience that they derive from it occurring during swallowing' (690b26–9).

Water animals have no tongue or only a very short tongue because it is difficult to taste food in water. If the animal spends any amount of time extracting the flavour from the food, it will let in water. The point is perhaps that letting water into the mouth would also dilute the taste. It would make the environment around the tongue too moist for the animal properly to taste the flavour. However this may be, the short time, if any, that a water animal has to extract the flavour is reflected in its physiology. For such tongues as water animals have are very short just as the time they have to enjoy flavour is short (*PA* II.17 660b17–22). Contrast here the long and forked tongue of snakes, which allows snakes long and intense pleasure in tasting (660b7).

Since the tongue is the sense-organ of taste, and as such a necessary instrument of taste, there is no taste without a tongue. Whatever pleasure the crocodile derives from its food is therefore not gustatory. Instead its pleasure is exclusively tactile and experienced as the food passes the gullet. It is during this passage that the heat, oiliness, etc. of the food are enjoyed.

Aristotle says that the crocodile has a greedy character. The crocodile can be said to be greedy, that is intemperate in its pleasure of food, insofar as it excessively enjoys the passage of solid food down its gullet. But it cannot be said to be greedy insofar as it enjoys the flavour of food excessively. For it does not have the ability to taste flavour.[52] *Ethica Nicomachea* III.10 1118a23–b8 mentions as a case of intemperance (ἀκολασία) the gourmand who prayed that he might have a throat as long as a crane's.[53] He enjoys the feeling of the food passing down his throat but he does not enjoy the flavour of the food. He enjoys his food insofar as it is an object of touch, not insofar as it has flavour. The implication is that it is brutish to

---

[52] Cf. *PA* IV.11 691a2–5.
[53] Named in *EE* III.3 1231a17 as Philoxenus, son of Eryxis, a character from comedy; cf. Aristophanes *Ran.* 934.

enjoy food simply as an object of touch because the proper way for a human being to enjoy food is as an object of taste. 'Brutish' here means 'being like an animal', as opposed to being the way characteristic of a human being *qua* human. The crocodile nicely illustrates the brutishness of the gourmand.

The crocodile shows again how the sense-organs are composed in order to be serviceable for the animal given its natural environment. By contrast with the crocodile, the snake and certain oviparous quadrupeds such as the lizard have a forked tongue. A forked tongue increases the gustatory experience by being a sort of double sense-organ of taste.[54] A forked tongue gives, as it were, taste in stereo. Consequently, the snake is able to enjoy the flavour of tasty foods particularly well. It is appropriate that the snake should have this kind of tongue, for we understand the snake to be a particularly greedy animal. The forked tongue is teleologically geared to the greedy character (ἦθος) of the snake.[55] By 'greedy' we now have to understand 'greedy for flavour', not greedy just in the sense of the crocodile, which enjoyed the feel of the food.

Other variations in the organ of taste illustrate the point emphasised in chapter 3, section 8, namely, that the sense-organs often serve other functions in perception. This is a point that must frequently be taken account of to understand the composition of the tongue. For example, some of the features of the composition of the tongue in animals that communicate by sound are to be explained in terms of their contribution, not to taste, but to the articulation of sound. For example, the looseness and the breadth of the tongue in humans enable them to articulate sounds.[56] This is not just a fact about humans. Partridges cackle and nightingales sing. To be able to articulate sound the tongue must be broad and loose and not too thick.[57] That is why, for example, the dolphin, though it has a lung and windpipe with which it can

---

[54] *PA* II.17 660b9–11.
[55] For other references to character as an explanation, cf. *HA* IX *passim* and Sorabji (1980) 156.
[56] *PA* II.17 660a17–23.
[57] *PA* II.17 660a17–b2.

produce sound, does not articulate sound.[58] The dolphin's tongue is not loose.

Certain shellfish called *porphurai*, literally 'purple-fish',[59] and insects such as the gadfly use their tongues for yet another purpose besides tasting. Their tongues are particularly hard so that they can also use them as a bore. In this way the gadfly can pierce the skin of an ox and the *porphurai* can bore through the shells of other shellfish.[60]

Humans have the most highly developed sense of taste of all animals, the snake inclusive.[61] The explanation of this particular sensitivity to flavours is that our sensitivity to tangibles in general (including flavours) is the most highly developed.[62] Humans have the softest tongue, which enables them to register flavours more accurately than other animals, but this is because the human flesh in general is the softest. It is not just the flesh of the tongue that is soft; it is the flesh all over the human body. It is this general fact about human flesh that enables us to register tangibles more accurately than other animals. It is not a fact about the tongue alone.

The claim would be more difficult to understand if we had not already seen Aristotle reduce the tastable to a form of tangible. It is the fact, as Aristotle mostly sees it, that taste happens by direct contact that induces him to call taste a form of touch. But to this claim is added, as we have seen, an analysis of flavour that shows flavour to be a combination of two tangible qualities, the dry and the wet. And without this analysis there would be no way to understand why flesh that is particularly sensitive to tangibles should also be particularly sensitive to flavour. Because flavours are tangibles and because we are particularly sensitive to tangibles we are also particularly sensitive to flavours.

If there is this close connection between both the organs

---

[58] *HA* IV.9 536a3–4.
[59] Thus the colour of the dye that these shellfish secrete was called 'purple' (πορφύρα).
[60] *PA* II.17 661a12–30.
[61] Cf. *PA* II.17 660a20.
[62] Cf. also *Sens.* 4 441a2–3; *De an.* II.9 421a19–22.

and the objects of touch and taste, why is it that we only taste with the tongue and not with the rest of our flesh? Perhaps flavours are still sufficiently distinct from other tangibles to explain why it is only the tongue with which we taste. Aristotle suggests in *De Anima* II.11 423a17–21 that the tongue does yeoman's service: it perceives both all the tangibles that the rest of the flesh perceives *and* flavours. If, Aristotle conjectures, we could perceive flavours with the rest of the flesh, then it would escape our notice that taste and touch are separate senses. He is clearly presupposing here that flavours are a distinct group of sense-object which should not be reduced (away) to the other tangibles.

Perhaps a clue lies in the claim that flavours are only tastable when moist. Flavours are a special group of mixtures of the dry and wet. The flavoured had to be moistened by us before we could taste it. By contrast I can feel heat without coldness and dryness without wetness on the rest of my skin. The fact that flavours are only tastable in a liquid state seems to make the area around the tongue the appropriate place to perceive flavour. For example, when you put some salt on the tongue the liquid already on the tongue moistens the salt in such a way that the moistened flavour can act on the tongue's flesh. Though there is no statement to this effect, it may be that Aristotle thinks that it is necessary also for flavoured liquids to be mixed with the saliva on the tongue before they can properly speaking liquefy the tongue, that is before they can be tasted by the tongue. If so, a liquid environment is always required for the flesh to act as an organ of taste. We have wet tongues to fulfil this requirement.

How about putting salt on one's hands when they are wet? If the tongue as opposed to the rest of the body's flesh is able to perceive flavour simply because of its wet environment why can't I taste the salt with my hands if I make them wet? I see no obvious answer to this objection other than that it is probably significant that the liquid on the tongue is part of the perceiver's own body. Similarly, in hearing and smell it is not external air but the perceiver's own connate air that constitutes the sense-organ, though there is apparently no qualitative difference between the external and the internal air.[63] The point may be, therefore, that it is only if the water is part of the perceiver's own body that it can count as part of the sense-organ of taste. Generally, simply being continuous with my body, like the water on my hands, is not enough for anything to constitute a part of my sense-organs. For something to be part of my sense-organs it has to be a natural part of my body. The saliva on my tongue is a natural part of my body, the water on my hands is not. That may explain why the one enables me to taste and the other does not.

11. Conclusion

Taste is a form of touch both in the manner of its operation by direct contact and in having a proper object that is composed of the proper objects of touch. The fact, as Aristotle sees it, that taste is a form of touch is reflected in the composition of the organ of taste. Like the organ of touch, the tongue is made of flesh. Flesh is the right matter for an organ of touch. For flesh as a mixture of all the four elements is potentially all the tangible qualities, the hot, the cold, the dry and the wet. As with the other senses it is the proper sense-objects that determine the composition of the organ, for the organ must be potentially what the sense-objects are actually. The wavering in the location of the organ of touch was decided in favour of the heart also because of its objects. Amongst the proper objects of touch the qualities of earth, the dry and particularly the cold, stood out. This made the location of the organ of touch near the heat of the heart appropriate, again on the principle that the sense-organ should be potentially what the sense-object is actually. Finally, the variations in the organs of touch and taste showed that other functions than perception frequently have to be accommodated by the sense-organ. The sense-organs serve the functions of the whole animal, not just the function of perception.

---

[63] Thus Aristotle indicates at *GA* II.6 744a3–6 that the organs of hearing and smell, as opposed to the eyes, do not have their own body. For they, unlike the eyes, are composed of the same element, air, as the external medium.

5

SMELL

1. The difficulty in defining odour

The last of the five senses to be considered in this work is smell.[1] Aristotle examines smell in *De Anima* II.9. When we begin reading II.9 we expect Aristotle to start his account of smell by telling us what its proper object is. We expect that he will define the 'smellable' and then define smell as the potentiality to be like the smellable, just as he in II.7 defined what vision was by first defining the visible. The expectation is eventually confirmed at *De Anima* II.9 421b3–6 where Aristotle says that smell is of the smellable and unsmellable just as hearing is of the audible and inaudible and sight is of the visible and invisible. The claim links II.9 back to II.7–8 by emphasising that smell is to be explained in the same way as hearing and sight, namely, with reference to its proper object.

But before this he has argued that the smellable, that is odour, is difficult to define because we as human beings have an unclear sense of smell:

It is less easy to give a definition concerning the sense of smell and what can be smelt than concerning those we have talked about. For it is not clear what sort of quality odour is, in the way that it was clear what sort of quality sound or colour was. The reason is that our sense of smell is not accurate but worse than many animals, for man smells poorly. (421a7–11).[2]

---

[1] Secs. 1–4 of this chapter have previously appeared in Johansen (1996).

[2] Cf. *Sens.* 4 440b31–441a2; compare humans with the dolphin, for example, as it is described at *HA* IV.8 534b90; on the *endoxon*, see Plato, *Timaeus* 66d–67a; Diogenes of Apollonia, as reported by Theophrastus, *De Sensibus* 41; Theophrastus, *De Odoribus* 64. At *De an.* II.9 421a13–16 Aristotle compares the human sense of smell with the vision of the hard-eyed animals (cf. *PA* II.13). They do not perceive the differences in colour (421a14: τὰς διαφορὰς τῶν χρωμάτων), except insofar as they represent something to be feared or not. Similarly, we do not perceive differences in odour, apart from their being pleasant or unpleasant.

We have seen why the difficulty of defining the sense-object of smell should also make it difficult to define the sense-faculty, for, according to Aristotle's method, if we can define the sense-object, then we can define the sense also as a potentiality to be like the sense-object. But if, as we are now told is the case with smell, we find it difficult to define the sense-object, then we shall also find it difficult to define the sense. The definition of the sense stands or falls with the definition of its object.

2. The analogy between odours and flavours

One of the points that show human smell to be poor is that we do not have separate names for odours.[3] Instead we call them by the names of flavours;

Just as flavours are sweet and bitter, so are odours. But some things have a corresponding odour and taste (I mean, for example, sweet odour and sweet taste) while other things have an opposite odour and taste. Similarly too an odour may be pungent, bitter, sharp, or oily. But, as we have said, because odours are not very distinct, as flavours are, they have taken their names from the latter in virtue of a resemblance in the things; for sweet [odour] belongs to saffron and honey and bitter to thyme and such like, and similarly in the other cases. (*De an.* II.9 421a26–b3)[4]

The inaccuracy of our perception of odour means that we do not perceive the different species of odour. But the analogy with flavours introduces a way in which we *can* discriminate species of odours, *faute de mieux*. Odours are like flavours:

[3] Similarly at *Timaeus* 67a 'the varieties of smell have no name'.

[4] I agree with Torstrik on the interpretation of this passage. Sweet odours take their name, 'sweet', from a similarity between what it is like to smell such odours and what it is like to taste sweet flavours. That it is the fact that odours are called 'sweet' that we are trying to explain and not, as Ross ((1961) *ad loc.*) suggests, that odours are called 'saffron odour', 'honey odour', etc., is implied from the beginning of the passage: 'Just as flavours are sweet and bitter so are odours.' It is a similarity in the sense-experiences of taste and smell that gives rise to the similar names; it is not a similarity in the objects, saffron, etc., that bring about the sense-experience. That is also why a bitter odour from an object does not cease to be called 'bitter' even if the object also happens to taste sweet. If, as Ross argues, calling an odour sweet depended on the odour's coming from an object that also tasted sweet, then there would be a problem describing those odours that came from objects that tasted different. But Aristotle has just pointed out that some objects do taste and smell different.

pungent, bitter, sharp or oily. We can therefore acquire a sort of definition of odours by arranging them according to the species of flavour that they resemble.[5] This in turn will give us a sort of definition of the sense of smell as a potentiality to be like odour.

We should compare the quoted passage with *De Sensu* 5. Here Aristotle claims that there are two different classes of odour, a claim *De Anima* II.9 did not prepare us for.[6] The analogy between flavour and odour is now said to hold for one class of odour only, the odours that are affections of nourishment:

There is one class of odour which is ordered according to flavours and they are pleasant and painful accidentally. For because they are affections of nourishment, the smells of these are pleasant for those who desire [sc. nourishment]. But for those who are full and do not require [sc. food] they are not pleasant, nor are the odours pleasant for those animals for which the nourishment that has the odours is not pleasant. So these odours, just as we said, are sweet and painful accidentally. That is why they are also common to animals. But the other odours are pleasant in themselves, for instance, the odour of flowers, for they do not draw you in the least towards nourishment, and they do not contribute at all to desire, if anything, they do the opposite ... But this class of pleasant smell is peculiar to man, whereas the odours which are ordered according to flavours are perceived by the other animals, just as was said earlier. Because they are pleasant accidentally, the species of those odours [sc. those that are perceived by other animals] are divided according to flavours, but the species of this odour [sc. that perceived only by humans as pleasant] are not divided in this way because the odour's nature is pleasant or painful in itself. (*Sens.* 5 443b19–444a8)[7]

---

[5] There are eight species (τὰ εἴδη, αἱ διαφοραί) of colour: white, yellow, green, deep blue, purple, crimson, grey and black. Similarly, there are eight species of flavour: sweet, oily, harsh, pungent, astringent, acid, saline and bitter; cf. *Sens.* 4 442a17–25 with Ross (1955) note *ad loc.*; *Sens.* 6 445b21–32, 7 447b26–448a19; *De an.* II.10 422b10–14. *Top.* IV.3 123b23–7 confirms that the species of colour can be understood also as *differentiae* of the genus colour (cf. *De an.* III.7 431a24–5). Similarly the species of flavour can be understood as the *differentiae* by which one may define flavour.

[6] *Sens.* 5 443b16–18.; cf. Freeland (1992) 238. As noted by Ross (1961) *ad loc.*, Aristotle is polemicising against *Timaeus* 66d1: περὶ δὲ δὴ τὴν τῶν μυκτήρων δύναμιν, εἴδη μὲν οὐκ ἔνι.

[7] Aristotle uses the term εἶδος both for the two classes of odour, 'accidentally pleasant' and 'pleasant in itself', and for the species of the class of odours that are accidentally pleasant, i.e. sweet, bitter, etc.; cf. εἴδη at 443a16 with εἴδη at 444a6. To avoid confusion, I use two different terms, 'class' and 'species', for these two different uses of εἶδος.

This passage deepens the analogy between odours and flavours as it shows that some odours are also said to be 'pleasant' in relation to flavours. Odours are not just called 'bitter', 'sweet', etc. by analogy to flavours. They are also called 'pleasant' or 'unpleasant' according to whether the corresponding flavour is pleasant or unpleasant. Odours are pleasant whenever flavours are pleasant. Since flavours are pleasant when you would like to eat or drink the flavoured object as nourishment, odours too become pleasant whenever you would like to eat or drink the fragrant object. If you find a sweet flavour pleasant because you would like to eat something sweet, then you will find a sweet odour pleasant too.

The analogy between odour and flavours is thus deepened, but it is also narrowed down because the analogy is shown to depend on the perceiver's attitude to nourishment. The odour of something becomes pleasant or unpleasant to the extent that the corresponding flavour attracts you to some nourishment. Hence the analogy holds only when the fragrant and flavoured object is nourishment.

There is a number of things that smell good though we would not normally eat them. Aristotle mentions, for example, that we enjoy the smell of flowers though we do not, as a rule, eat them. He explains this by saying that the odour of flowers belongs to a different class of odours, odours that are pleasant whether we are hungry or not. Such odours, he says, are pleasant *as such* (καθ' αὐτάς, 443b27), that is not *relative* to the perceiver's being hungry.[8] Hence such odours are always pleasant.

The odours in this class are special also in that it is only human beings that always enjoy them. Though, presumably,

---

[8] At *Philebus* 51a–e Socrates distinguishes between odours that are always and truly pleasant and odours which are to do with food. Odours that are to do with food are mixed pleasures: they are to do with the pleasure you get from replenishment. (Contrast *Republic* VII. 548b–c where smells, without distinction, are said to be pure pleasures.) Replenishment presupposes want, which is painful. Though Aristotle does not share Plato's view of pleasure as a result of replenishment (cf. *EN* x.3), he retains the distinction between odours that are sometimes pleasant and sometimes unpleasant because of their relationship to food and odours that are pleasant as such.

other animals notice the odours, they will only enjoy them when they are hungry. So to them such odours will not be pleasant as such. Thus a cow may enjoy the smell of a buttercup. But it will only enjoy it when it is hungry and wants to eat, whereas I as a human being will enjoy the odour *as such* whenever I smell it.[9]

Let me summarise the argument so far. Aristotle defines the senses by their proper objects. In the case of smell it is difficult to define the proper object. We do not perceive odour accurately. Therefore we do not perceive the specific differences that we need in order to define odour. However, we can discriminate species of odour by analogy with the species of flavour. Hence we can define odour by analogy with flavour.

The analogy between odour and flavour is crucial, then, to our prospects of defining smell. So let us look at it in more detail. Simply borrowing terms from another sense-modality is of course not peculiar to smell. Shirts are 'loud' if brightly coloured or boldly patterned, sounds are piercing, and so on. As Aristotle points out, we make reference also across other sense-modalities to describe our sense-experiences.[10] The analogy between flavours and odours, however, is a much closer one than any analogy between other sense-objects. Let us see why.

The underlying reason why odours can be ordered according to flavours is given in *De Sensu* 5. The reason, as Simplicius points out, is that the same quality that produces odour also produces flavour.[11] Odour is produced by the

---

[9] *EN* III.10 1117b23–1118a25 makes the distinction ethically significant by saying that there can only be self-indulgence in relation to the odours of food, not in relation to odours that are pleasant in themselves. Just as the lion enjoys the lowing of the ox not for the sake of the sound but for the sake of the meal in store for it, so the self-indulgent enjoys odours of food not in themselves but for the sake of the food. *EE* III.2 1231a6–11, in addition, praises Stratonicus for introducing different terms for the pleasure one gets from the odour of food and the pleasure one gets from other odours. He calls odours to do with food 'pleasant' (ἡδύ) when enjoyed and odours which are pleasant in themselves 'fine' (καλόν).

[10] *De an.* II.8 420a29.

[11] κατὰ τὰ πράγματά ἐστι συγγένεια τοῖς ὀσφραντοῖς πρὸς τὰ γευστὰ διὰ τὴν τοῦ ἐγχύμου ἀπόπλυσιν ἐν τῷ κοινῷ ἀέρος τε καὶ ὕδατος ὑγρῷ (Simplicius quoted by Hicks (1907) *ad* 421b1, 392–3), supported by *Sens.* 5 443b6–8. Hicks (*ibid.*) curiously upbraids Simplicius for 'going too far afield' by bringing in *Sens.* 5 443b3–

same flavoured dryness which also produces flavour. Aristotle says in *De Sensu* 5:

For what the dry produces in the wet [sc. flavour], this the flavoured wet [τὸ ἔγχυμον ὑγρόν] produces in another class [γένει], in air and water equally. We were just saying that the transparent is common to these [sc. air and water], but it is smellable, not *qua* transparent, but *qua* being able to wash or cleanse the flavoured dryness [ἐγχύμου ξηρότητος]. For the object of smell exists not only in air but also in water. (442b28–443a3)

The passage has caused confusion. First we are told that odour is the result of 'the flavoured wet' acting on water or air just as 'the flavoured dry' acts on the wet to produce flavour. But then we are told that odour results from a washing or cleansing of the 'flavoured dryness' in air or water. So which is it? Does odour (A) arise by the action of the flavoured *dryness* on air or water or does it (B) arise by the action of the flavoured *wetness* on air and water? If we take line A, odour is the product of the same 'flavoured dryness' that produces the flavour that we taste. Odour and flavour are only to be distinguished insofar as the flavoured dryness can act *either* on air *or* water to produce odour but only on the wet (water?) to produce flavour. If we take line B, odour is produced, as W. D. Ross argued,[12] by a fully-fledged flavour, that is to say by a flavoured dryness that has already acted on the wet and then in turn acts on either water or air to produce odour.

So line A says that flavoured dryness can either produce odour or flavour; which of the two the flavoured dryness produces depends on whether it acts on the wet, in which case we get flavour, or on either air or water, in which case we get odour. Line B says that the flavoured dryness first acts on the wet, whereby we get the flavour that can be tasted. But the tastable then acts on air or water and produces odour. Ross explains the wobble between 'the flavoured dryness' and 'the

16; 'curiously' because Hicks himself at the beginning of his commentary on *De an.* II.9 rightly (cf. *Sens.* 3 439a6–9) enjoins us to compare the chapter with *Sens.* 5 442b27–445b2, 'which serves partly to illustrate, partly to supplement the present discussion' (390).

[12] W. D. Ross (1955) *ad loc.* 213. The interpretation goes back to Alexander, *in de Sensu* 185.2; cf. Rodier (1900) *ad loc.* (vol. II) 314–16, and Beare (1906) 152, n. 1, who both support it.

flavoured wetness' by saying that it is the flavoured dryness that acts throughout. Though the flavoured dryness first has to produce flavour in the wet before it can produce odour in air or water, it is the flavoured dryness throughout the production of flavour and odour which is the real agent. That is why Aristotle can still talk about the flavoured dryness as the cause of odour when it is washed or cleansed by air or water even though the odour-producing flavoured dryness must by that stage have been mixed with the wet.

So what is the relationship between flavour and odour and what is the relationship between the changes that generate flavour and odour? Some passages suggest that the washing of the flavoured dryness by water or air that produces odour is at least analogous to the wetting of the flavoured dryness that produces flavour.

For example, at De Sensu 4 441b15–19 Aristotle says that *flavour* arises when the wet percolates through the dry and earthy as happens when people wash away (οἱ ἐναποπλύνοντες) colours in the wet. The notion of washing away the flavoured dryness in the wet to produce flavour is admittedly only compared to people who wash dyes out in water. But the comparison stresses the difficulty of distinguishing what happens in the production of flavour and in the production of odour. For Aristotle talks in De Sensu 5 about the air or water's washing (πλυτικὸν, 443a1, πλύσις 445a14) the flavoured dryness in *odour*. At 445a14 we are told that odour arises from the washing of the dry in the wet and fluid. He concludes that, 'it is clear then that whatever flavour is in water, this odour is in air and water. And because of this the cold and freezing dulls flavours and makes odours disappear. For cooling and freezing make the hot that acts and creates [sc. flavour and odour] disappear' (443b12–16).

So the reason why we smell odours both in air and water is that air, like water, can wash the flavoured dryness, for both air and water are wet. Looking back at 442b28–9 ('For what the dry produces in the wet, this the flavoured wet produces in another class, in air and water equally'), 'equally' becomes the operative word. It seems to be the fact that odour arises both in water and in air that distinguishes odour from flavour, for flavour arises *only* in water. But this distinction between odour and flavour seems to become even more tenuous when we consider that the reason why odour can arise also in air is simply that air like water is wet.[13]

At the end one is left with two questions. First, why is there no flavour in air? If air like water is wet and the flavoured dryness needs to be mixed with something wet to make flavour is there any reason why flavour should not be produced in air? Second, what is the difference between flavour and odour for a water animal? If all that distinguishes flavour from odour is that flavour is perceived only in water whereas odour is perceived in air *and* water, why does that not imply that there is no difference between flavour and odour in those cases where the odour is perceived just in water, as it is by water animals? If there is no difference between flavour and odour in water, what is the difference between smelling odour in water and tasting flavour in water?

We cannot say that the difference between smelling odour in water and tasting flavour in water is simply that such animals smell odours with their gills and taste flavours with their tongues or some other organ.[14] This is no answer primarily because the sense-organs are understood as sense-organs of a sense-faculty. As the closing line (422a7) of *De Anima* II.9 makes clear, we should understand the sense-organ of smell in relation to the potentiality to be affected by odour. We need different definitions of flavour and odour before we can identify different sense-organs as sense-organs of smell and taste. Again Aristotle's method prescribes the priority of the sense-object.

Aristotle reminds us of the method again at *De Anima* II.9 421b19–23. He says the fact that bloodless animals do not

---

[13] Air at *GC* II.3 330a30–b7 is the 'hot and wet', water the 'cold and wet'.

[14] Sharples (1985) 194, discussing Theophrastus' theory of smell, sees the problem and the possibility of such a solution to it: 'It may be difficult to explain how smell and taste are different for fish, both being the sensing of particles in the water, except in terms of there being a different sense-organ, but that seems to be a problem, if it is one, for Aristotle's theory as well.'

inhale whereas we humans only smell when we inhale does not show that bloodless animals do not smell. For bloodless animals have perception of odour and perception of odour *is* smell.[15] So bloodless animals, if they have perception of odour, must also be said to have smell. Thus it does not matter how you perceive odour, by inhalation or some other way. As long as you can perceive odour you have smell.

The point applies also to the sense-organs. Whatever sense-organ it is that you use to perceive if you use it to perceive odour then it is a sense-organ of smell. If, on the other hand, you use the organ to perceive flavour, then it will be a sense-organ of taste. As with our understanding of the sense-faculties, so the sense-object determines our understanding of the sense-organs. The onus is therefore on identifying a difference between flavour and odour before we can identify the different sense-faculties and sense-organs that we use to perceive these sense-objects.[16]

We see therefore behind the apparently minor interpretative question of how to distinguish odour from flavour an issue of global importance to Aristotle's theory of the senses. What is at stake is the entire method of defining the senses by their proper objects. According to this method of definition a sense-faculty is identified as a potentiality to be like its *proper* object. Two senses are different if they have different proper objects and two senses are the same if they have the same proper object. We believe that smell and taste are different senses. But so far we have found no clear difference between their objects, odour and flavour. The account of odour is too similar to that of flavour for our method to deliver a definition of smell that is clearly different from our definition of taste. So far then the method has not been successful in our treatment of smell. This failure may in turn affect our faith in those definitions that the method has delivered in the case of other senses such as sight and hearing. The problem of differentia-

---

[15] Cf. *Sens.* 5 444b20–1.
[16] A further problem is that there are animals such as insects, some species of fish, and the dolphin that Aristotle knows to have smell but for which he cannot find an organ of smell; cf. *HA* IV.7 532a5–6, IV.8 533a34–b1 and 534b9–10.

ting odour from taste is therefore a problem, not just of local importance to the sense of smell, but of global importance to Aristotle's method of explaining the senses in Book II of *De Anima*.

We have seen that the evidence concerning odour is confusing. I suggest we turn to a passage we have not yet considered. At *De Anima* II.9 422a6–7 Aristotle says something that fits line A much better than it does Ross's interpretation B. He says that: '*Smell belongs to what is dry, just as flavour belongs to what is wet, but the organ of smell is potentially of such a kind.*' Odour belongs to the dry just as flavour belongs to the wet. This contrast between odour and flavour is difficult to combine with Ross's interpretation, for he holds that flavour has to be produced before odour can be produced. Odour arises at the second stage of a process whose first stage produces flavour. Odour arises out of the flavoured wetness which is already a tastable flavour. But in that case it is difficult to see why odour should belong to the dry rather than to the wet and why flavour by contrast should belong to the wet rather than to the dry. Odour on Ross's interpretation is, as it were, 'flavour plus', and there is no reason to think that odour should belong less to the wet and more to the dry than flavour.

What is particularly important to notice is that the difference between odour as belonging to the dry and flavour as belonging to the wet is supposed to give us different definitions of the sense-faculties (and sense-organs) of smell and taste. The sense-faculty of smell has the potentiality to become dry but the sense-faculty of taste has the potentiality to become wet. In actual tasting there is a liquefaction of the organ of taste in the tongue (*De an.* II.10 422a34–b10). That is why we do not taste anything if there is already too much liquid on the tongue. For then it is the flavour of the liquid already on the tongue that we taste rather than the flavour of what is put on the tongue. Nevertheless there should be *some* liquid on the tongue. The reason why there is saliva on the tongue seems to be that dry substances such as salt need to be mixed with liquid before they can act on ('liquefy') the organ of taste in the tongue. The saliva around the tongue makes the salt liquid so that the saline solution can act on the organ. By contrast, the organ of smell is made dry by the action of odour. The organ of smell should be potentially dry but not actually so, for only then can it be made dry by the action of the odour.

This difference between odour as dry and flavour as wet suggests that we should go with line A, for line A involves no liquefaction of odour. On this account odour can remain dry by contrast with the liquefied flavour. Perhaps this also fits how we actually perceive odours and flavours better. We certainly do smell herbs and other dry substances without mixing them with water first, but we do not taste them before they have at least been mixed with the saliva on our tongues.

We should say that there is one flavoured dryness which produces both flavour and odour. Perceiving odour certainly requires some sort of washing of the flavoured dryness. But, as I shall argue, this washing is different from the liquefaction that produces flavour.

Notice first that it is significant that odour is found in *both* air and water, whereas flavour is found in liquid, not in air. Odour is found in both air and water because both air and water have the ability to wash the flavoured dryness. Similarly, colour is seen both in air and water because they are both transparent. It is *qua* transparent that air and water mediate colour, not *qua* air or water. Similarly, odour is not perceived in water and air *qua* water and air but *qua* being able to wash the flavoured dryness (*De an.* II.7 419a32–5). It is significant that this is an ability that both water and air have, for if the ability was the same as the ability of water to became tastable when acted on by the flavoured dryness, then we would expect to find flavour in both water and air. The claim that we perceive odour equally (ὁμοίως) in water and air because they both have the ability to wash the flavoured dryness indicates that it is a different attribute of water (and air) that makes it a vehicle of odour from the attribute that makes water a vehicle of flavour. Whatever the washing that happens in air or water when I smell herbs is, it has to be different from the liquefaction that the salt undergoes on my tongue before

I can taste it, for the washing is the activity of a different attribute of water and air from the attribute that makes water a vehicle of flavour *just as* the mediation of colour is the activity of a different attribute of water and air from that by which air and water mediate sound.

Let me briefly return to the text that gave rise to the opposing interpretations. How, at *De Sensu* 5 442b27–443a2, could it both be the flavoured wet and the flavoured dryness that constituted odour? I have argued on philosophical grounds in favour of saying (interpretation A) that it is the flavoured dryness on its own that constitutes odour and against Ross's interpretation (B) that odour is constituted by the flavoured wet, as a byproduct of flavour. But the textual problem then remains for my interpretation. One solution is to accept Torstrik's emendation of ὑγρόν at 442b29 to ξηρόν. This reading is perhaps lent some plausibility by the immediate context. For manuscripts are divided between ὑγρῷ τὸ ξηρόν and ξηρῷ τὸ ὑγρόν already in the previous line. So confusion in 442b29 between ὑγρόν and ξηρόν would not be an isolated instance.[17]

However, there is an alternative. For one manuscript, L, omits τὸ ἔγχυμον ὑγρόν at 442b29. If we accept this reading, the text says 'for whatever the dry produces in the wet this it [sc. the dry] produces in another class, in air and in water equally.' This may be the more elegant solution and has the advantage of having at least some manuscript support.[18]

3. The medium of smell

It is an important difference between the two senses that smell is a mediated sense whereas taste is not. Smell, *De Anima* II.9

---

[17] Cf. also 443a10 with the variation ὑγρὰ καὶ ξηρὰ αὐτῶν (as opposed to ξηρὰ ... ὑγρά).

[18] Unease may be felt about following one MS against the joint verdict of the other MSS; but cf. Ross (1955) 67, 'None of the MSS cited in our apparatus can safely be neglected; any one of them from time to time, either alone or with little support from others, has a reading which is plainly right.'

421b9 says, happens through a medium such as air or water. Taste, by contrast, is according to *De Anima* II.9 421a19 a form of touch. For we taste by direct contact with the sense-object. But why are water and air suitable media of smell? At *De Anima* II.7 419a32–b1 Aristotle says that:

The medium of sounds is air, but the medium of smell has no name: for it is a sort of affection common to air and water, just as the transparent is for colour, so what is present in both of them [sc. air and water] is for what has smell. For it seems that the animals that live in water also have the sense of smell.

There is no name for the sort of affection that makes air and water media of smell. But it is clear from this passage that whatever affection it is its role is to be understood by analogy with the role of the transparent in vision. This analogy between 'the common affection' and the transparent enables us to identify the nameless 'common affection' of *De Anima* II.7 with the ability to wash out the flavoured dryness described in *De Sensu* 5 442b28–443a2. For Aristotle says there that odour, like colour, is found in both water and air. However, odour is found in water and air not *qua* transparent but *qua* having the ability to wash out the flavoured dryness. Since our main understanding of the transparent is as the medium of colour, the contrast and comparison with the transparent in *De Sensu* 5 implies a mediating role for the washing out of the flavoured dryness in odour. Taken together with the comparison of the common mediating affection with the transparent in *De Anima* II.7, this provides strong evidence that the washing out of the flavoured dryness corresponds to what happens in the transparent medium when a colour is seen through it. Odour, in other words, is 'in' air or water in the way that colour is in the transparent medium. Odour is in air and water as in a medium.

We should distinguish therefore the role of air and water in odour from the role of the wet in flavour. When the flavoured dryness is mixed with liquid it is made into a tastable flavour. In other words, the mixture creates the (potential) sense-object of taste. But when the flavoured dryness is washed out by air and water this is part not part of the creation of odour: it is part of the mediation of odour.

Let us at this point briefly rehearse Aristotle's reasons for saying that there is no mixture in mediation. This will help clarify the claim that the washing out of the flavoured dryness in odour is different from the mixing of the flavoured dryness in flavour. It will also help us understand better how odour is mediated. Mixture, for Aristotle, involves the mixture of both the form and the matter of the ingredients. The mediation of the sense-objects involves no mixture because there is no blending of the matter of the sense-object and the matter of the medium. The medium is only acted on by the form of the sense-object, not also by its matter. It receives only the form of the sense-object just as the wax receives the form of the signet-ring but not the iron of which the ring is made.[19] If there is no mixture in mediation in general, there is of course no mixture in the mediation of odour either. The washing out of the flavoured dryness in odour cannot therefore be a mixture such as the mixture of the wet with the flavoured dryness in flavour.[20]

More evidence against saying that there is a mixture in the mediation of odour comes from Aristotle's criticism of the Pythagoreans. They say that we are nourished by odour.[21] Aristotle argues against this idea as follows. Odours are simple; but we are nourished by composite bodies only; so we are not nourished by odours. This description of odour contrasts with the description of flavours as nourishing in De Sensu 4.

---

[19] The wax block analogy applies, of course, not just to the way in which the sense-object affects the medium of the distance senses but also to the way in which the sense-object affects all the sense-faculties; cf. De an. II.12 424a17–20.

[20] Cf. ch. 4, sec. 5.

[21] Sens. 5 445a16–29; cf. De an. II.3 414b10–11 and III.12 434b19–21. Alexander, in de Sensu 223.11–12 ascribes the belief to 'certain doctors' also. The idea that the odours of sacrificial animals nourish the gods occurs in Aristophanes, Av. 186–93 and 1516–24; cf. Lucian, Icaromenippus 27. The idea may have suggested itself from passages in Homer (cf. Iliad 1.317) and Hesiod (cf. Theogony 556–7); cf. also comments by Detienne (1981) 217–18 and Vernant (1981a) 15 and (1981b).

Aristotle there says that food nourishes *qua* tastable, and flavour is a mixture of the dry and the wet because neither the wet nor the dry on its own can nourish. It is only a composite of the dry and the wet that can nourish. Hence flavour has to be a mixture of these two if it is going to nourish an animal. Odour, by contrast, is not nourishing because it only consists of one quality, the dry. Notice also here that the fact that odour is not composite like flavour provides further evidence for line A above for on line A the flavoured dryness on its own constitutes odour without any admixture of liquid.

The point that there is no mixture in mediation also connects with Aristotle's criticism of the effluence theory. According to the effluence theory it is both some of the matter and some of the form of the sense-object that travel through to the perceiver. For example, when you smell an apple there are bits of apple, its effluences, travelling from the apple to the nose. But according to Aristotle it is only the form of the sense-object that acts, through the medium, on the perceiver, without travelling.

The point comes out clearly also at *De Sensu* 5 443b1–2. Here Aristotle argues against the theory that odour is a sort of smoky vapour or exhalation (καπνώδης ἀναθυμίασις). He objects that this theory is like the effluence theory of vision. His main complaint with the effluence theory is that it does away with the medium of vision because the theory implies that vision happens by direct contact between the sense-organ and the effluence. The theory is therefore accused of reducing vision to a sense of touch. For the important point about touch is that it happens by direct contact (cf. *Sens.* 3 440a16–21). Touch is so called because we perceive something with this sense by touching it (*De an.* III.13 435a17–18). Insofar as the vapour theory of odour is like the effluence theory, the problem with the vapour theory must be that it too does away with the medium of smell by stipulating that there are bits of the sense-objects that travel from the sense-object to the sense-organ and are in direct contact with the sense-organ. The vapour theory falters on the point that the medium of smell, like the medium of vision, does not operate by letting bits of the sense-object pass through to the perceiver.[22]

This does not rule out that odours may be mediated to the sense-organ, as Aristotle says, *by means of or amidst* a vapour (*Sens.* 5 445a25–7). For we need to keep in mind that humans, and other animals, smell by inhaling air. It is important also that it is through inhaling that those odours that are pleasant as such pass to the human brain and bring about their cooling, salutary effect (444a8–b2). What is ruled out is that the odour itself should be understood as a vapour or exhalation that we inhale. Even animals that do not inhale because they live in water and therefore do not smell through air can perceive odour, a point which Aristotle explicitly mentions as evidence against the vapour theory of odour (443a31–b1). But for human beings it is important that odours should be perceived through inhalation.

Notice finally how difficult it would be to accept a literalist interpretation of the mediation of odour. If the mediation consists in washing out the flavoured dry what are we to make of the mediation of odour in water? Aristotle insists that we should take account of the fact that water animals smell. We can see that they smell by the fact that they are attracted to food from afar because of its odour.[23] We cannot allow that the flavoured dry is washed out by the medium in the sense that it is mixed with the water of the medium, for then there is no difference between smelling the flavoured dryness in water and tasting it. But there can hardly be another way in which the flavoured dryness is *literally* washed out by the medium when the medium is water than by being mixed with the water. So it seems that we must understand the washing out of the flavoured dryness in a non-literal way. The obvious suggestion is to understand the mediation of the flavoured dry-

---

[22] At *Sens.* 2 438b24 Aristotle says that odour is a 'sort of smoky vapour' (ἡ δ' ὀσμὴ καπνώδης τίς ἐστιν ἀναθυμίασις), which but for the saving τις would appear to contradict 443a21–b2; cf. Rodier (1900) vol.II *ad* 422a6.

[23] *De an.* II.9 421b9–13.

ness along the lines of the mediation of colour.[24] The flavour is washed out insofar as it appears to the perceiver through a wet medium (air or water).

To summarise the argument so far, it makes good sense that odours are like flavours, for the flavoured dryness that constitutes odour also brings about flavour when mixed with liquid. This interpretation explains why smelling odours is like tasting flavours. The ingredients are almost the same, but only almost the same, for odour, unlike flavour, does not involve a mixture with liquid to be perceptible. As we saw, the washing out was not a mixture but part of the mediation of the flavoured dryness to the sense-organ. Thus the generation of odour is sufficiently similar to that of flavour for us to understand why odours should smell similar to the way flavours taste but is sufficiently different from that of flavour for these to be distinct sense-objects.[25] And this, as we saw, was the important point, for without different accounts of odour and flavour the distinction between smell and taste threatened to collapse. In the end Aristotle achieves the aim of defining the sense-faculty of smell by its object, odour, despite many difficulties.

4. Smell and Aristotle's mixed methodology

I have relied on the fact that smell is a mediated sense whereas taste is a contact sense to explain the difference between odour and flavour. But *De Sensu* 5 445a5–14 introduces a complication. Aristotle says here that smell occupies a place in between

---

[24] Theophrastus, according to Themistius, coined the term 'transodorant' (δίοσμος) to indicate the analogous role that the medium of smell plays to the role of the transparent medium of vision: just as in vision colour appears through air or water *qua* transparent, so in smell odour appears through air or water *qua* transodorant, *qua* the ability of air or water to be smelt through; cf. Alexander, *in de Sensu* 185.9: ἦν ἀνάλογον ἂν τις δίοσμον ὀνομάζοι. Philoponus uses the analogy between the transparent and the medium of smell to support the interpretation that the mediation of odour is incorporeal; cf. Ellis (1990) 296 with n. 26.

[25] This makes good sense of *Sens.* 4 440b29–30: 'odour and flavour are almost the same affection but they do not exist in the same circumstances'.

the contact senses and the mediated senses.[26] How are we to understand this claim?

The claim that smell is in between the contact senses and the mediated senses is a result of Aristotle's use of different criteria for defining the senses on different occasions. Up till now we have only seen one of these criteria in use, what we might call the 'object criterion'. According to the object criterion, two senses are the same if and only if they have the same proper object. So if two senses have different proper objects, they are also different senses.

On other occasions, as we saw in chapter 4, Aristotle uses what might be called the 'contact criterion' to define some of the senses.[27] On this criterion a sense can be defined as a form of touch if and only if it operates by direct contact with its object. When Aristotle talks about touch and taste he often focuses on the fact that they both operate by direct contact with their object and not through an external medium.

Taste appears to have a different proper object from the proper objects of touch. The object of taste is flavour; the objects of touch are the hot and the cold, the wet and the dry (cf. GC II.2). So on the object criterion, taste should not be a form of touch. Nevertheless, Aristotle maintains that taste is a form of touch because we taste things by putting them on our tongues, that is, by direct contact. So on the contact criterion taste qualifies as a form of touch. We see, then, in the case of taste a certain tension between the two criteria.

The tension is eventually resolved when Aristotle asserts that all the senses, including touch and taste, operate through a medium. The difference between the contact senses, so called, and the distance senses is that the medium of the contact senses is part of the perceiver's own body, whereas the media of the distance senses, air and water, lie outside the body. But there is no fundamental difference between the contact senses and the distance senses: they are both mediated in some way or other.

---

[26] Cf. *PA* II.10 656a31–2.
[27] Following Sorabji (1971) 86.

The tension between the two criteria is further diminished when we observe that even on the object criterion taste can be considered a form of touch. Aristotle says that flavour is a tangible object. Flavour is an affection of the wet by the nourishing, flavoured dry (*Sens.* 4 441b23–5). Since both the wet and the dry are proper objects of touch, flavour after all appears to be a proper object of touch.

Smell shows a similar tension between the two criteria. Smell can be considered a contact sense according to the object criterion. For odour belongs to the nourishing dry.[28] As we have just seen, the nourishing dry is a tangible. That was why taste too could be considered a form of touch on the object criterion. However, smell, as we have also seen, can be considered a distance sense too since odour, like colour and sound, is mediated by air and water (*Sens.* 5 445a10–11). So in terms of the contact criterion smell is a mediated sense, not a contact sense. It is because smell on one criterion appears a contact sense and on another a distance sense that Aristotle says that smell is in between the contact senses and the distance senses.

We saw that in the case of taste there was a move to reduce the tension between the two criteria. But in the case of smell there is no such move. Aristotle wants the tension, for he wants smell to act as a numerical mean between the two contact senses and the two distance senses.[29] As a mean it is ap-

---

[28] *Sens.* 5 445a8–13:

> That is also why the object of smell is a kind of affection of nourishing matters (but these are in the class of the tangible) and of the audible and the visible. Hence animals smell in both air and water. So the object of smell is something common to both of these [sc. the tangible and the audible/visible] which belongs to the tangible and the audible and the transparent.

There is an equivocation in the idiom of 'belongs to' (ὑπάρχει + dative) or 'is of' (genitive). (1) A can belong to B where B is A's medium or (2) A can belong to B where B is a constituent of A. It is clear that when Aristotle talks about the object of smell belonging to the audible/visible he means 'belonging as to a medium', whereas when he talks about the object of smell belonging to the tangible he means 'belonging as to a constituent'; cf. Ross (1955) *ad loc.*, who notes 'a certain confusion here'.

[29] *Sens.* 5 445a6–7.

propriate that smell should share features with both groups of senses.

5. The sense-organ of smell

If the detail of the physiology of the eye was vague, the detail of the physiology of the sense-organ of smell is all but non-existent. There is not a single extensive treatment of the sense-organ of smell in the Aristotelian corpus. Whatever evidence there is has to be pieced together from different passages, not all of which are concerned with perception.[30] In the case of smell we should be particularly sensitive to the point that not all the features of the sense-organ are features that the sense-organ has *qua* sense-organ. There are functions other than just perception that determine some of its features.

The sense-organ of smell is what is potentially dry. As I understand it, the sense-organ of smell has to be potentially dry in order to receive the flavoured dryness. But where is this sense-organ located? The proper sense-organ of smell in man seems to be the nostrils (αἱ μυκτῆραι).[31] At *Historia Animalium* I.15 494b12 Aristotle lists the sense-organs of sight, smell and taste as 'eyes, nostrils and tongue'. At *De Anima* II.9 421b16 he states again that there is no perception by direct contact with the sense-organ, which explains why we do not smell something that is placed against the inside of the nose.[32] At *De Generatione Animalium* v.2 781b7–10 the Laconian hound is said to have long nostrils, with the sense-organ of smell being set well *inside* the nostrils. This composition allows the changes from the sense-object to 'travel' straight through to the sense-organ and it shelters the changes from being dispersed. Hence the Laconian hound smells particularly well.

---

[30] Cf. *PA* II.16 658b33–659a36, which describes the elephant's nose, the trunk, from the point of view of its usefulness as a sort of hand.

[31] *Timaeus* 66d1 refers to the sense of smell as τὴν τῶν μυκτήρων δύναμιν.

[32] οὐδ' ἂν ἐπὶ τοῦ μυκτῆρος ἐντὸς τεθῇ could also be translated 'when placed inside on the nostril'. But 'μυκτήρ' in the singular usually means 'nose', whereas 'μυκτῆραι' in the plural usually means 'nostrils', see LSJ, *s.v.*

So the sense-organ of smell seems to be located not just in the nostrils but inside the nostrils. This, of course, is as we should expect by analogy with the other sense-organs, for Aristotle both in the case of the eyes and that of the ears has located the sense-organ somewhere inside the eyes and the ears and has explained their surface structures in terms of promoting the transmission of the sense-quality to the sense-organ inside, as well as in terms of protecting the sense-organ inside. This fits the evidence of the Laconian hound.

At *De Generatione Animalium* v.2 781b1–6 Aristotle says that accuracy of smell, as of sight and hearing, depends on purity of the sense-organ and of its surface membrane (τὸν ὑμένα τὸν ἐπιπολῆς). One might speculate that the surface membrane in the case of the organ of smell is the mucous membrane. But no further information is given about this membrane and it might well be that Aristotle postulates such a membrane simply by analogy with the membranes of the eye and the ear to account for different degrees of accuracy of smell.[33]

Then there is the 'nose-cover' mentioned in *De Anima* ii.9:

It would seem, again, that in man the organ of this sense [sc. smell] differs from that of other animals, as his eyes differ from those of hard-eyed animals. Man's eyes have, in the eyelids, a sort of screen or sheath and without moving or opening them he cannot see: while the hard-eyed animals have nothing of the kind, but at once see whatever takes place in the transparent medium. So, too, it seems, the organ of smell in some animals is unenclosed, just as the eye is, but in those which take in air the organ has a cover, which is removed in the process of inhaling, by dilation of the veins [τῶν φλεβίων] and the passages [τῶν πόρων]. And this is the reason why animals which breathe cannot smell in water. For it is necessary for them to take in breath before smelling and this they cannot do in water. And odour is of the dry, just as flavour is of the wet, and the organ of smell is potentially so. (*De an.* ii.9 421b26–422a7)

The cover in the nose provides a sort of protective shield around the sense-organ of smell. It is only when the cover in the nose is lifted that the smells are allowed passage through to the sense-organ inside the nose. The cover is lifted when we

---

[33] Cf. ch. 1, sec. 9; ch. 3, sec. 5.

inhale. So it is only when we inhale that we perceive odours. The cover in the nose corresponds to the eyelid in that it has to be removed in order for the odour to pass through to the sense-organ of smell inside. Similarly, in vision it is only when we open our eyes that the colour is allowed passage through to the transparent inside the eye. It is inhalation only which causes the 'nose-cover' to be opened. That is why we do not smell when we exhale or when we hold our breath.

One strongly suspects that the stipulation of the nose-cover is motivated by a wish to explain the fact that we only smell whilst inhaling. It is only humans that are explicitly said to have this cover. And the sense-organ of smell is in this respect said to be different from that of other animals. It is clear, however, from what Aristotle goes on to say (421b33–422a6) that other sanguineous animals that live on land must have a nose-cover too if we are to explain why these animals too smell only whilst inhaling. He introduces the nose-cover by saying that 'it is likely' (ἔοικε, 421b26) that humans have the cover. The likelihood is established simply by analogy with the difference between the eyes of hard-eyed animals and humans that have eyelids. If humans have eyelids and hard-eyed animals do not, why should not humans have a nose-lid which other animals do not have? No independent empirical evidence is brought in to support the stipulation of the nose-cover. The nose-cover seems simply to be stipulated in order to explain the peculiar way that the ability to smell in humans, and, as it turns out, in all inhaling animals, functions. The nose-cover does not appear to have much, if any, basis in empirical observation.

Nor is it even clear that Aristotle is consistent when he first compares the ability to smell in humans with that of the sight of hard-eyed animals and then, as we have just seen, compares the ability to smell with the ability to see in humans by contrast with that of hard-eyed animals. The comparison with hard-eyed animals is primarily a functional comparison on both occasions. But the comparisons highlight different aspects of the functioning of the human ability to smell. In the first case, the comparison shows the relative lack of discriminative power in the human ability to smell. In the second case it shows the human inability to smell when not inhaling. The two features of the ability to smell, however, would seem to point towards different material structures in humans. In the first case we would expect that humans had no cover for the nose, for if we perceive odours in the way that hard-eyed animals perceive colours then it is natural to think that it is because we, like the hard-eyed animals, have no cover over our eyes to protect them but instead have to see through a hard protective skin. Having hard eyes allegedly reduces the ability to discriminate colours, whereas having soft eyes increases this ability because it is easier for the changes of the colour to pass through in soft eyes. But hard-eyed animals also have no cover because they get sufficient protection from the hard skin. In the second case, however, we would expect that we *did* have a cover for the nose, for our ability to smell is here being contrasted with the vision of hard-eyed animals. It is only in the second case that the material structure pointed to by the comparison is actually stipulated by Aristotle. But the feeling is that the first comparison with hard-eyed animals could just as well have landed us with no nose-cover as no empirical evidence either for the nose-cover or for the alternative hard skin is taken into account.

The nose-cover might then be taken to confirm the thesis that Aristotle's attitude to the sense-organs is primarily determined by a wish to identify material structures that can accommodate the functions of the senses, as he sees them. When a species such as man displays a peculiar functioning, additional peculiar structures, such as the nose-cover, are brought in to realise the peculiar functioning. This is done, at least in the case of the nose-cover, without any apparent use of empirical evidence and in an *ad hoc* way that brings the nose-cover into potential conflict with other functional demands.

6. Variations in the organ of smell

In *De Partibus Animalium* II.16 Aristotle discusses the differences between the sense-organ of smell in different animals.

When Aristotle discusses by what means birds smell, he says that they use passages (πόροι) in their beaks instead of nostrils.[34] Fishes have no observable sense-organs, except eyes. They do not even have the passages that birds use for smell or hearing (*HA* II.13 505a33–5).

Again, as we saw in the case of the sense-organ of hearing, a difference in the composition of the sense-organ of smell arises between animals that live in water and those that live on land. Land animals are surrounded by air and they therefore use air rather than water as their medium of perception. So human beings as natural land animals see and hear through air, whereas fish see and hear through water. We saw how this difference between land animals and water animals resulted in their having different sense-organs of sight and hearing. Nature took the natural environment of an animal into account when devising the organs the animal needed in order to fulfil its characteristic functions.

The basic difference between water animals and land animals that is important to the composition of the organ of smell is that water animals do not breathe. Respiration, as we have seen, serves the purpose of cooling the animal. Water animals do not breathe because they do not live in air and there is no air in water.[35] Instead, they bring about the necessary cooling by drawing in water through their gills.[36] Though the basic distinction is between animals that live in water and those that live on land this does not leave us with the conclusion that all land animals are cooled by respiration and all water animals are cooled by taking in water, for there are two other possibilities. First of all, some water animals such as the frog or the seal do breathe. But Aristotle seems to think that this is because they reproduce on land and sleep either on land or with their mouth above the surface of

---

[34] Cf. *HA* II.12 504a21–2, IV.8 533a22–4 and, especially, *PA* II.16 659b13–14.

[35] Cf. *Sens.* 5 443a4–5. W. D. Ross (1955) notes *ad loc.*: 'It was not until the time of Boyle (1670) that it was known that water contains air, and not until the time of Bernouilli [sic] (1690) that it was known that fish cannot live in water from which the air has been expelled by boiling.'

[36] *Resp.* 10–16.

the water for breathing (cf. *Resp.* 475b26–476a1). So the frog and the seal are not pure water animals. Second, not all animals that live in air breathe, for example insects do not breathe because they contain relatively little natural heat and therefore do not need any cooling. Correspondingly, some water animals such as lobsters and crabs have relatively little natural heat so they are sufficiently cooled by the surrounding water (476b34–477a1). Not all water animals need to take in water to cool themselves. They therefore do not have gills.

Animals that do not breathe do not use inhalation as a means of smelling. Instead, some of them smell through their gills, the functional analogue to the respiratory system. Other animals, for example the whale, smell by means of a blowhole. Both the gills and the blowhole contain water. So it is reasonable to suppose that the proper organ of smell in these animals is composed of water.[37] As we have seen, the important point is that the organ of smell should be potentially dry. Both a watery and an airy composition would make the organ potentially dry, for both water and air are actually wet. A watery organ of smell would therefore be adequate for water animals.

Finally, insects smell through 'the middle part of their body'.[38] All the animals that do not inhale use the 'connate pneuma' (σύμφυτον πνεῦμα) instead of inhaled air. Aristotle says at *De Generatione Animalium* ii.6 744a2–3 with reference, it seems, to all animals that live in air that the sense-organ of smell is a *poros* which is full of connate air and in contact with the external air. We cannot therefore say that it is only insects that use the connate air in smell. Nor can we say that the connate *pneuma* plays no role in smelling for animals that breathe. Indeed, it may be exactly the *pneuma* that the inhaled odours directly cool down, thereby indirectly cooling down the rest of the body. However this may be, there is a difference between animals that inhale and which can therefore use the air coming from the outside to perceive smells and animals that do not inhale and which therefore, exclusively, use the air

---

[37] Cf. Sorabji (1992) 216.   [38] *PA* ii.16 659b16–17.

provided by their internal *pneuma*.[39] If you live in air and breathe, then you also smell through the inhalation. But in that case you will have respiratory organs adapted to smell, for example nostrils with membranes, nose-covers, etc. If, in contrast, you live in water, then your olfactory apparatus will be geared to that and you will smell simply by means of your connate *pneuma* or by means of gills or a blowhole.

7. Conclusion

In conclusion, the differences between the sense-organ of smell in different animals again illustrate the point that the composition of the sense-organs is determined by the natural environment of an animal. This environment is part of the animal's definition to the extent that animals can be defined as water animals or land animals. From this definition follow certain other characteristics. The environment is important to perception particularly in the case of the distance senses because it provides the medium through which the animal perceives. Since the manner of mediation of sense-objects differs in air from that in water different structures of sense-organ are sometimes preferable to others. Hence we can explain differences between animals' sense-organs with reference to the different conditions of mediation that their natural environment presents. Noting the differences between the sense-organs in different animals serves to confirm the thesis that the sense-organs are functionally determined.

---

[39] The animals must have this air anyway because it is by means of the internal πνεῦμα that they move; cf. *MA* 10 703a9–29.

THE ACTUALITY OF PERCEPTION

1. What is perceiving?

My analysis of the sense-organs has followed the same pattern. There are two central claims. (1) The sense-faculty is defined by its ability to be changed by the sense-object as such. This ability belongs to an attribute. For instance, the ability to be changed by sound belongs to resonance. (2) The attribute is present only in a certain sort of matter. This, for example, is why we have an ear whose inside is composed of still air, for it is only still air (or water) that is resonant. The sense-organ is here hypothetically necessary in the same way that iron is necessary if the saw is to have the ability to saw.

The sense-organ is in this way explained as a necessary material basis for the first actuality that defines the sense-faculty. The analysis shows that a material basis is necessary if the first actuality to be changed by a certain sort of sense-object is to be present. So far then the focus has been on the relationship between the first actuality and the matter or potentiality of the sense-organ. The analysis has not shown that a material basis is necessary because the first actuality can only be actualised in a material change. Suggestions have been made at various points to the effect that there need be no material changes in perception. However, I have made no attempt to argue this claim from the ground up. This is because the explanation of the sense-organs, on the whole, is neutral on the score.

But surprisingly neutral, for we might have expected a material basis that was functionally determined to be necessary because it was the basis of functions that were materially realised.[1] We might have expected that a theory that requires

---

[1] Cf., for example, Nussbaum and Putnam (1992) 38: '[S]ince we are dealing with embodied living creatures (and not, for example, the activities of god), we know,

perceptual changes to be explained with reference both to the form and the matter of the perceiver requires also that perceptual changes be explained with reference to material changes in the perceiver. This might be our expectation, if for no other reason, because it is our modern scientific preconception that perception is a physical change in a physical system. Whatever we think is the correct answer to the debate about whether material changes happen in the sense-organs when we perceive, the fact that the sense-organs in Aristotle can be explained without reference to such material changes must be considered a fundamental difference between him and our modern scientific view of perception.

I want now to consider whether in fact actual perception according to Aristotle is best thought of as necessarily realised by literal, material changes in the sense-organs. As I said in the Introduction, the subject may be too complex to reach any definite conclusion, certainly within the confines of the present work. So I want to pursue just one line of thought. This leads me to the conclusion that actual perception is not necessarily constituted by material changes. What follows will not directly affect my account of the sense-organs, for, if I am right, this account is neutral on the question. However, some view on whether actual perception involves material changes in the sense-organs might be called for, even though the answer to this question is not going to decide how we explain the sense-organs, as it will increase our understanding of the sort of actualities that the sense-organs are potentialities for.

I start with *De Anima* III.2:

The actuality of the sense-object and that of the sense are one and the same. But the being is not the same for them. I mean, for instance, the sound in actuality and the hearing in actuality. For it is possible for someone having the sense of hearing not to hear, and what has sound does not always make a sound. But whenever what potentially hears actualises its potentiality and what potentially makes a sound makes a sound, then the hearing in actuality and the sound in actuality occur together [ἅμα]. One might call the

too, that we will discover *some* physiological realisation for the psychological process in each case.'

first of them the process of hearing [ἄκουσις] and the other the process of sounding [ψόφησις]. (*De an.* III.2 425b25–426a1)

The argument is supposed to apply to all perception, not just hearing. But Aristotle chooses hearing as his example, for, he says, there happens to be a special word for making a sound which is actually heard (ψόφησις, 'sounding') as opposed to just a 'sound' (ψόφος) but there is no separate word for the actuality of colour when it is actually seen or for the actuality of flavour when it is actually tasted (426a13–15). So using sound as his example is convenient since there is a verbal difference that allows him to express the conceptual distinction that he wants to make, namely, the distinction between a sound that is actually heard and a sound that is only a potential object of hearing.

Let us follow Aristotle and use hearing as a case study of perception in general. He says that actual hearing and actually making a sound are one and the same, just as teaching and learning are said to be one and the same in *Physica* III.3 202a32–b22. That is to say, actual hearing and actual sound-making occur at the same time and in the same place, but they differ in that they are defined differently. If you were to say what it is to make a sound and what it is to hear, you would give two different answers because you would define them in different ways. But if you were to say where and when they occurred you would give the same answer. You would say that they both occurred in the sense of hearing for this is the patient of the change and the change always happens in the patient.[2] Just as teaching and learning both happen in the student, so actual sounding and actual hearing both happen in the listener. The actuality of the sense-object and the actuality of the sense-faculty are one and the same because they both happen in the same place.

L. A. Kosman[3] proposes the following interpretation of how

---

[2] Cf. again *De an.* III.2 426a4–5 with *Ph.* III.3 202a25–b22.
[3] Kosman (1975) 513–14.

the actualities and potentialities of hearing and sounding are related. It can be schematised as follows:

	Sense-object	Sense-faculty
Second actuality	Sounding (ψόφησις)	Hearing (ἄκουσις)
First actuality	Audible sound (ψόφος)	Power of hearing (ἀκοή)
Potentiality	Bell (having sound)	Ear

The right-hand side of the schema, the side representing the sense-faculty, is familiar from chapter 1, section 2. We now find added the same three levels of potentiality and actuality on the side of the sense-object. On the side of the sense-object, we find at the same level of potentiality as the ear what 'has sound', that is a smooth and solid object, a bell, to use Kosman's example. Next step up the ladder on the level of first actuality we find the sound being produced by the bell, corresponding with the sense of hearing. On the level of second actuality we find sounding (not sound), corresponding with actual hearing. The sense-object is at its highest level of actuality when it is actually heard rather when it just makes a sound which nobody hears. A sound that is not heard is no more actual (and no less, of course) than the sense of hearing when it is not exercised, for instance, when one is asleep.

Kosman's interpretation is geared to showing how perceptual awareness is not constituted by an extra act of apperception but is an essential part of actual perception at its highest level. The important point for Kosman's purposes is here that what coincides with actual hearing is not the audible sound, for this is only the first actuality of sounding. It is the sounding which is actually heard, a sound of which somebody is aware, for it is not possible to perceive without being aware of what is perceived.[4]

---

[4] Here Kosman brings in *De an.* II.12 424b17. This line should read ἢ τὸ μὲν ὀσμᾶσ-θαι αἰσθάνεσθαι, 'or is smelling perceiving?', that is, is smelling perceiving as op-

Kosman draws the conclusion from this that 'we cannot locate awareness outside the perception as an awareness of the perception different from an awareness of what is immediately perceived'.[5] I need not here go into whether this is right. What is important is to notice the new distinction between first and second actuality on the object side. There are two questions I would like to answer in this connection: does Kosman's distinction represent what Aristotle says about the sense-objects elsewhere? and how does our understanding of the actuality of the sense-objects affect our understanding of the actuality of perception, in particular the answer to the question about material changes? Let us begin to answer these questions by first looking at causal agency in general. We will then work our way towards the causal agency of sense-objects in particular.

Change (κίνησις), Aristotle tells us in *Ph.* III.1 201a10–11, is 'the actuality (ἐντελέχεια) of what is potentially as such' (i.e. insofar as it is potential). This definition of change allows Aristotle to distinguish the actuality of building in the sense of the process (κίνησις) of building from the actuality of building in the sense of the finished product of the process. The process of building is the actuality of the potentiality of something to be a building. It is the actuality of what is build*able*. The finished building, in contrast, is the actuality, not of what may be turned into a building but of what already is a building.

Contrary to what some scholars have argued,[6] we should translate 'ἐντελέχεια' here as 'actuality' rather than as 'actual-

---

posed to being affected. The alternative reading ἢ τὸ μὲν ὀσμᾶσθαι καὶ αἰσθάνεσθαι, 'or is smelling also perceiving?' suggests that smelling is perceiving in addition to being affected. Kosman argues persuasively against the alternative reading. The correct reading of this passage is particularly important since there is agreement on almost all sides that 'αἰσθάνεσθαι' for Aristotle has the implication of awareness. If smelling is already an awareness of smell, Kosman argues, no further act of apperception is required for awareness of smell; cf. also Sorabji (1974) 47, Burnyeat (1992) 25, and Marc Cohen (1992) 62–3. *Ph.* VII.2 244b10–245b2, and in particular 245a1–2, seems to make the point about awareness in perception explicit, οὐδὲν δὲ κωλύει καὶ τὸ ἔμψυχον λανθάνειν, ὅταν μὴ κατὰ τὰς αἰσθήσεις γίγνηται ἡ ἀλλοίωσις; cf. Kahn (1966) 5, and Ostenfeld (1987) 90, n. 204.

[5] Kosman (1975) 514.
[6] For instance, W. D. Ross (1936) 537; cf. Kosman (1969).

isation' for at least two reasons.[7] The first is that what Aristotle is defining is the process by which something becomes say an actual building.[8] The process might itself be called an actualisation. Mentioning 'actualisation' in the definiens of the process is itself a way of referring to a process, namely the process by which something becomes actual. What an actualisation is is part of what we are trying to define when we define a process. So it is circular to refer to an actualisation in the definiens of 'process'.

2. The reality of change

The second reason why 'actualisation' is infelicitous is that Aristotle defines process as the ἐντελέχεια of the potential as such in order to contrast it in a certain way with the ἐντελέχεια of the actual as such. The operative phrase in this contrast is 'the potential as such'. The ἐντελέχεια of the actual as such is of course not an actualisation since the actual is actualised already. To use the example of the building, the actuality of the actual as such is the finished product of the process, the house. It is what results from an actualisation but is not itself an actualisation.[9] The contrast between the ἐντελέχεια of the process of building and the ἐντελέχεια of the house is a contrast between two different sorts of the same kind of thing, two different actualities. It is not a juxtaposition of two different kinds of thing, an actualisation and an activity. So 'ἐντελέχεια' has to mean the same when we are talking about the ἐντελέχεια of the potential as such as when we are talking about the ἐντελέχεια of the actual as such. The ἐντελέχεια of the potential should be taken to be an actuality rather than an actualisation.

There is another reason why we should look at the two actualities in this way. It is to do with Aristotle's discussion

---

[7] On both points I am following Broadie (1982) 112ff.
[8] Cf. Kosman (1969) 41.
[9] Cf. Ph. III.1 201b7–15.

of the problem of change in *Physica* I. The problem is that change seems to imply that something can come into being from nothing. After the change you have something which you did not have before. So something comes to be out of something that was not. In order to show that such change is not *ex nihilo*, we need to show that there was something before the change. This we can do, as Aristotle does in Book I, by showing that there is something that underlies the change and that remains the same throughout the change. For instance, Socrates was pale, now he is tanned. The suntan was not there before the change but Socrates was. So it is wrong to say that the suntan came out of nothing. It came out of something, namely, Socrates.

However, it is not enough to say this if we want to say that the change is real, if by change we mean the *changing* and not the product of the change, for we could imagine that the suntan was acquired by a swap of attributes in which there was first Socrates pale and then Socrates tanned. First we would have the subject in one state, then the subject in another state. Both states would be real. We would have shown that one reality could follow after another. But the *changing*, the process of going from one state to the other, would not thereby have been shown to be real. It might still be said that change understood as changing was not real since it would still be mysterious what happened in between the two states when Socrates changed from the one state to the other.

Aristotle shows in *Physica* III that the process of changing is also a reality of a sort. He does this by saying that change is an actuality of something potential.[10] As we shall see in the next section, one of his strategies when arguing that something is real is to show that it can be described as an actuality or *at least* as a potentiality. It is a way of showing that change is not from nothing to say that the product comes from something that is potentially such. The product of the change did

---

[10] *Ph.* III.2 201b35–202a2: λείπεται τοίνυν ὁ εἰρημένος τρόπος, ἐνέργειαν μέν τινα εἶναι, τοιαύτην δ᾽ ἐνέργειαν οἵαν εἴπαμεν, χαλεπὴν μὲν ἰδεῖν, ἐνδεχομένην δ᾽ εἶναι. The description of change as a sort of actuality serves to show that it can exist.

exist in some way before change. It existed potentially. So the product did not come to be out of nothing. This is the alternative way of solving the problem of change, hinted at but not developed in Book I.8 191b27–9, the alternative, that is, to saying that there is an underlying continuant in change, for example Socrates remaining in the process of tanning. Describing the changing as an actuality of something potential therefore places changing within a distinction that Aristotle uses to establish the reality of something.[11]

If we translated 'ἐντελέχεια' as 'actualisation', then Aristotle's argument that change is real would fall to the ground. For an actualisation is itself a change. So if, on the one hand, we accepted the translation 'actualisation', we would have to ask again whether this actualisation as a change was something real. If, on the other hand, we translated 'ἐντελέχεια' as 'actuality', then we are given a direct answer to whether change is real, for calling something an 'actuality' is for Aristotle to say that it is real.

3. The reality of potentiality

In *Metaphysica* IX.3 Aristotle argues against those Megarian philosophers who claim that only what is actual is possible (δύνασθαι). Aristotle here takes 'possible' to mean potential in his sense. That is to say, the Megarian view is translated into Aristotelian terminology as the claim that only that which is actualising an Aristotelian δύναμις or potentiality has that potentiality. Aristotle gives as an example of the Megarian view the claim that only someone who is actually building is capable of building, is a potential builder. When the builder ceases to build he also loses his ability to build.

So will the builder, if the Megarians are right, reacquire his art every time he starts building? (*Metaph.* IX.3 1047a3–4) The question points to an explanatory deficit in the Megarian

---

[11] Cf. *Metaph.* IX.1 1045b34–5: being may be distinguished into potentiality and actuality.

view, for the view leaves unexplained the difference between a learning process and the exercise of a skill learnt. It is precisely this difference that Aristotle's distinction between a potentiality, a first and a second actuality is supposed to explain. Learning how to build develops a certain kind of potentiality that we all have as human beings into a first actuality to be able to build. Having a first actuality, as we saw in chapter 1, means that you can straightaway go and realise your ability. So the person who has learnt how to build can build whenever he wants, given the presence of the right materials and that nothing else interferes. So the ability once acquired can be immediately deployed given the right circumstances. For Aristotle it is only by seeing that the builder has this kind of potentiality, called a 'first actuality', for building that we can explain how the builder is able to start building at the drop of a hat, whereas I, the complete novice at building, am not able to do so.

It is to strengthen this argument for the presence of un-actualised potentialities that Aristotle brings in the sense-objects. On the Megarian view, 'neither cold nor hot nor sweet nor in general any sense-object will be when it is not being perceived (αἰσθανόμενον). So they will come to hold the view of Protagoras' (1047a4–7). Aristotle's argument here requires that we understand the hot and the cold, etc., essentially as sense-objects, that is to say, potentialities to be perceived, for only if they are understood as potentialities to be perceived will the Megarian premise lead to the conclusion that the hot and the cold do not exist when they are not actually being perceived. The corresponding conclusion is then drawn on the subject side of perception. Just as the Megarians do away with sense-objects by denying the reality of potentialities that are not actualised, so they do away with the sense-faculties, for the sense-faculties are potentialities to perceive. For instance, sight is the potentiality to see. The Megarians are saying that you cannot see if you are not actually seeing. But if you cannot see you are blind. So the Megarians will end up claiming in effect that when you are not actually perceiving you are blind. This conclusion corresponds, on the side of the subject of perception, with the earlier claim, on the object side of perception, that only what is actually perceived is perceptible. The argument against the Megarians is closely related to a discussion in *De Anima* III.2. In *De Anima* III.2 426a20–7, Aristotle is arguing against a group of earlier φυσιολόγοι, philosophers of nature, who claimed that 'there was neither white nor black without vision, nor flavour without taste'. This claim reiterates the conclusion we have just seen ascribed to the Megarians. The reference to the earlier φυσιολόγοι is vague, perhaps deliberately so.[12] In the *Metaphysica* IX.3 passage too we saw the claim attributed to Protagoras. But for Protagoras the claim does not, as it did for the Megarians if Aristotle is right, follow from a certain modal doctrine. It follows instead from the doctrine that 'man is the measure of everything', the so-called *homo mensura* doctrine. Protagoras, at least as he is presented in Plato's *Theaetetus*,[13] would say that there is no sense-object before actual perception. (Compare the wind that is cold to you but warm to me but neither cold nor warm in itself, *Theaetetus* 152a–b.) For if a sound existed before my perception of it, the quality of the sound would be something in itself independently of its appearance to me. But the theory is that I am the measure of all the things that appear to me as they appear to me. This implies that if the sound had qualities

---

[12] Gorgias is reported to have said that 'objects of sight and hearing are insofar as they are cognised in each case'; cf. Pseudo-Aristotle, *On Melissus, Xenophanes and Gorgias* 980a14–15. However, it is notoriously difficult in the context of this quotation to be clear as to what, if any, Gorgias' own views are; cf. Robinson (1973), Guthrie (1969) 193–200, and Kerferd (1955).

[13] W. D. Ross (1961) *ad loc.* thinks Protagoras must be excluded from the reference to the earlier φυσιολόγοι because he was not a φυσιολόγος. It is unclear what Ross's criterion of being a φυσιολόγος is and whether Aristotle would have shared it. However this may be, we can restrict our interpretation to the Protagoras that Aristotle would have met in the *Theaetetus*. This work seems anyway to be the most important source of Protagoras' doctrines for Aristotle. Compare, for instance, the discussion in *Metaph.* IV.6 of the view that all appearances are true. The main proponent of this view was identified as Protagoras back in IV.5 1009a6–8. The presentation of the view and the counter-examples that Aristotle gives follow *Theaetetus* 151e–164d closely. The *Theaetetus* tries to integrate Protagorean relativism into a theory of flux. The result is that Protagoras to the reader of this work would appear to be no less of a φυσιολόγος than Heraclitus. Ross's exclusion of Protagoras from the ranks of the φυσιολόγοι is therefore unnecessary; cf. also Hicks's illuminating note in (1907) *ad loc.*

prior to its appearance to me, then I would not be the measure of its being.

Let us call those who claim that the sense-objects have no independent existence outside perception 'anti-realists'. Aristotle's way with these people is to show that sense-objects are potentialities and to insist that potentialities are real. On the one hand, the anti-realists are right. For in a way a colour which is not seen is a colour only potentially. That is because a colour is essentially also a visible object, a potentiality to be seen. If it is not seen this potentiality is not realised. So to that extent the colour does not exist actually. On the other hand, the anti-realists are equally wrong, for the colour does exist as a potential sense-object even when it goes unseen.

Describing an unheard sound as a potential sound does not imply that the world is soundless when there is nobody around to hear it. The view implies only that insofar as a sound is something audible the sound is not fully realised until it is actually heard. We have to remember that the potentiality we are talking about already is an actual sound. There has to be actual sound before there is hearing. This is for general causal reasons, for if sound is going to act as the agent in hearing then it is has to be actual. In change, as we have seen, it is what is actually something that acts on what is potentially so. This goes for perception too. The sense-object actualises the sense-faculty's potentiality to be like the sense-object. It is no good then saying that sound only arises with hearing, for then it is unclear what causes hearing to arise in the first place. There has to be actual sound before there is actual hearing.[14]

Describing the sense-object before perception as in a way actual and in another way potential raises a question for Aristotle's account of causal agency. For on the one hand, the sense-object has to be prior in actuality to the sense-faculty in order to bring about a change in the sense-faculty. On the other hand, as we have seen, Aristotle says in *De Anima* III.2

---

[14] Cf. *Metaph.* IV.5 1010b30–1011a2. *De an.* III.5 430a16–17 says that light in a way makes potential colours into actual colours. This is consistent with my argument here, for something can be, or rather has to be, an actual colour in order to be a potential object of vision.

that the actuality of the sense-object is the same as the actuality of the sense-faculty in the sense that they occur together and simultaneously. The problem is to understand how the actuality of the sense-object can both be prior to the perception of it and yet only arise simultaneously with the perception of it. How is it that sound is actual before it is heard yet it is only when it is heard that it is actual?[15]

4. The sense-object as an active potentiality

To answer the question the first thing we should notice is that it is by no means a question that is specific to sense-objects. It is a question that can be raised about all agents of change. As often, it becomes clearer just what happens in perception when we place perception within Aristotle's general account of change.

What we need is the concept of acquiring a potentiality to act by acquiring an actuality. Compare the case of becoming hot. If the stove becomes hot it *ipso facto* acquires the potentiality to heat something else up. This potentiality is a direct consequence of being itself actually hot.[16] There is no further attribute required in order to be able to heat something other than being actually hot. Similarly, the water has the passive potentiality to be heated up simply insofar as it is actually cold.

What is required for the stove to *realise* its potentiality to heat is not a real change of attribute. The only real change it had to undergo was when it went hot in the first place. What is required now for the stove to realise its active potentiality to heat things up is simply that the stove be brought into contact with something that, like cold water, has the corresponding

---

[15] The problem is raised by Hartman (1977) 193–6; cf. Emilsson (1988) 170–1, n. 2.

[16] Cf. *Ph.* VIII.4 255a21–3: 'Some things are able to change things against nature. A lever, for instance, is not naturally able to move what is heavy. Other things are able to change things according to nature. For instance, the actually hot is capable of changing the potentially hot.' For a Platonic precedent, cf. *Republic* I. 335d2–13: it is the ἔργον of hot things to heat, of dry things to dry, and, by analogy, of just men to be beneficial.

passive potentiality to be heated up. That is to say, it requires the presence of a patient that is suitably disposed to be acted upon by the stove. It requires something that has the passive potentiality to be heated, matching the stove's active potentiality to heat. When those two are brought together the only real change that happens is in the water, in the patient, for the water does change attributes: it becomes hot from having been cold. The stove, the agent, does not really change.

Let us try and sum up the results schematically (Schema A). We have a hot stove that heats up some cold water:

Actuality   Hot stove   Hot water

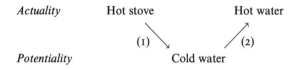

Potentiality   Cold water

Here the arrow from 'Hot stove' to 'Cold water' (1) represents the action of the hot on the cold. The arrow from 'Cold water' to 'Hot water' (2) represents the change that the water undergoes from cold to hot. Notice that the stove before the change is on a higher level of actuality than the water in terms of being hot, for the stove is actually hot, whereas the water is only potentially hot.

So far we have analysed what happens when something heats something up in terms of being hot. Let us now try another schema to show what happens *in the same change* in terms of heating up and being heated up, in terms of the passive and active potentialities involved (Schema B):

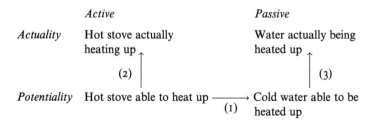

Here the arrow from the active potentiality to the passive potentiality (1) represents the action of the hot stove on the

264

cold water. The arrow from the active potentiality to the active actuality (2) represents the 'change' that the hot stove undergoes whilst heating up the water. The arrow from the passive potentiality to the passive actuality (3) represents the real change in temperature that the water undergoes by the action of the hot stove upon it. Notice here that before the change the agent and patient are on the same level in terms of active and passive potentialities. Before the change the stove is no more heating something up than the water is being heated up. They are both still potentially heating something up and being heated. During the change they are still on the same level in terms of active and passive actualities. The stove is now actually heating up and the water is now actually being heated. Contrast this with the previous schema (A) where before the change the stove was on a higher level of actuality than the water, for the stove was actually hot and the water only potentially hot. What is characteristic of the active and passive potentialities, then, is that before the change the agent and the patient are on the same level of potentiality (Schema B). The agent is no more actual with respect to its active potential than the patient is with respect to its passive potentiality. But if you look at the agent and patient from the point of view of the attribute (e.g. the hot) that the patient is going to acquire (Schema A), the agent is always on a higher level of actuality before the change.

Let us try to apply the analysis of heating to perception. What we get in hearing, corresponding to Schema A, is this:

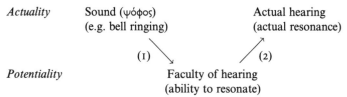

Actuality   Sound (ψόφος)   Actual hearing
                 (e.g. bell ringing)   (actual resonance)

(1)   (2)

Potentiality   Faculty of hearing
                        (ability to resonate)

Here the sound corresponds with the hot stove, the faculty of hearing with the cold water, and the actual hearing with the heated-up water. In hearing, our faculty of hearing changes from potentially having a sound to actually having one by

265

being first able to resonate but being soundless and then actually resonating. That is like the water first being potentially hot but actually being cold and then actually being hot.

Let us now try to apply Schema B and see how perception comes out in terms of active and passive potentialities:

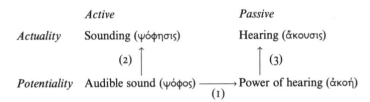

	Active	*Passive*
Actuality	Sounding (ψόφησις)	Hearing (ἄκουσις)
	(2) ↑	↑ (3)
Potentiality	Audible sound (ψόφος) ⟶ (1)	Power of hearing (ἀκοή)

Notice here that the important feature of Kosman's schema above has been reproduced simply by considering the sound as an active potentiality. The important feature of Kosman's schema was that there was a difference between a sound (ψόφος) *tout court* and a sounding that was actually heard (ψόφησις). Since this difference was understood as a difference between the first and second actuality of sound, the highest actuality of sound could be understood to be sound as an object of perceptual awareness. This was the conclusion that Kosman was interested in.

But if you are interested in how it is that the actuality of sounding can be said to coincide with the actuality of hearing whilst also causing the actuality of hearing, then here is your answer: sound is an active potentiality to cause hearing. The reason why the actuality of sounding coincides with the actuality of hearing is that hearing is the passive potentiality corresponding with the sound's active potentiality. That is just like the way in which the potentiality of the hot to heat up is actualised together with the potentiality of the cold to be heated up. There is nothing special going on in perception here.

Looking at sense-objects as active potentialities makes it possible to clarify Aristotle's answer to the anti-realists. You strike the bell. What happens? There is an actual sound before anybody hears the sound. Similarly, the stove is hot before it heats up the water. Otherwise the stove could not cause the water to heat up and the sound could not cause us to hear it. However, *qua* audible the sound is an active potentiality to be heard. So the sound has to make itself actually heard in order to realise this potentiality. This it does in actual sounding (ψόφησις) coinciding with actual hearing.

To see why sounding only occurs together with hearing compare the expression 'it sounds like'. Imagine that there is a tree at this moment falling in the woods of Alaska, which nobody hears the sound of. The sound is there.[17] But it is not going to sound *like* a falling tree, for sounds only sound *like* something when actually heard by somebody. Sounding is like that. It is something sound does only when it is heard. We can say the same thing about the other sense-objects. Colours *qua* visible are only actual when they look like something to somebody, smells *qua* smellable are only actual when they smell like something to somebody, tangibles *qua* tangible are only actual when they feel like something to somebody, and flavours *qua* tastable only when they taste like something to somebody.

So sounds can be seen as active potentialities that are actualised by affecting a perceiver. The perceiver has the corresponding passive potentiality to be acted on by the sound, that is to hear it. When the active potentiality of the sound *qua* audible and the passive potentiality of faculty of hearing come together, actual hearing and actual sounding take place together. But this does not imply that there is no sound before actual hearing, just as it was not implied that the stove was not hot before it heated up the water. This is Aristotle's reply to the anti-realists.

5. The sense-object as an irrational potentiality

In *Metaphysica* IX.2 Aristotle distinguishes between two sorts of potentiality, the rational and the irrational. A rational potentiality is, for instance, the potentiality that a doctor has to

---

[17] Contrast those who use *De an.* III.2 to make Aristotle an anti-realist about colours, sounds, etc. The anti-realist interpretation is discussed by Granger (1993) 165; cf. Modrak (1987) 29–30.

heal a patient. What characterises this sort of potentiality is that it is a potentiality for contrary results. The doctor can use his skill either to make the patient healthy or to make him sick. It is up to the doctor which result he will bring about. An irrational potentiality, in contrast, is a potentiality for only one result. For instance, heat has only the potentiality to heat other things. It does not also have the potentiality to bring about the opposite result of cooling things.[18] In *Metaphysica* IX.5 Aristotle picks up the distinction and argues that in the case of irrational potentialities 'when the agent and the patient meet in accordance with their potentialities then the agent must act and the patient must be affected' (1048a6–8). Whether or not the *rational* potentialities are actualised in these situations, however, depends on whether the rational agent so chooses or desires.

Heat has an active potentiality to heat. Because it is also an irrational potentiality it will necessarily realise its potentiality if it is brought near what has the potentiality to be heated. Put a kettle on a hot stove and the stove will necessarily heat up the kettle. Perception is just like that.[19] The sense-object has a potentiality to make itself perceived. Indeed this is what defines it as a sense-object. The sense-faculty has a corresponding passive potentiality to perceive. When these two are brought together the sense-object will necessarily act on the sense-faculty. Thereby it will make itself perceived.

Consider again the case of building. The agent in building is a builder. When the builder builds a house he imposes the form that he had in mind on some materials. There are some bricks, timber, etc., that acquire that form of a house. The materials change by realising their potential to become a house. There is, however, also a sense in which the builder

---

[18] *Metaph* IX.2 1046b4–9: καὶ αἱ μὲν μετὰ λόγου πᾶσαι τῶν ἐναντίων αἱ αὐταί, αἱ δ' ἄλογοι μία ἑνός, οἷον τὸ θερμὸν τοῦ θερμαίνειν μόνον, ἡ δ' ἰατρικὴ νόσου καὶ ὑγιείας. αἴτιον δὲ ὅτι λόγος ἐστὶν ἡ ἐπιστήμη, ὁ δὲ λόγος ὁ αὐτὸς δηλοῖ τὸ πρᾶγμα καὶ τὴν στέρησιν.

[19] The potentiality of the sense-object to make itself perceived must be an irrational potentiality, for heat, which is Aristotle's example of an irrational potentiality, is, after all, a sense-object.

'changes' when he is building, for in the act of building he 'changes' from being a potential builder to being an actual builder.

'Changes', however, is put in scare quotes to reflect the fact that Aristotle thinks that the sort of 'change' that the builder undergoes when building something is a rather different change from the change that the materials undergo. For like the knower exercising a knowledge that he already has, the builder when building exercises or manifests a skill that he already has. He cannot really be said to change by doing so, for he is not acquiring any new attributes. He is simply exercising the active potentiality that he has by being a builder. No new attribute is acquired by the builder when building. Similarly, no new attribute is acquired by the hot when it actualises its potentiality to heat things up.

In *De Anima* II.5 the distinction is made between a real change of attributes and the quasi-change of exercising an attribute one already has. Here Aristotle distinguishes again between (a) a mere potentiality for something, (b) a first-level actuality, and (c) a second-level actuality. He illustrates his distinction by describing three different characters. There is the man who is said to know because he has the potential to learn, that is given the effort and the opportunity, he will learn or would have learnt. Then there is the man who has actually learnt something but happens not to be exercising his knowledge. And finally, there is the man who both has learnt and is actually exercising his knowledge at this moment.

Aristotle introduces these distinctions to make the point that perceiving is like the change a man undergoes from possessing knowledge, but not using it, to having knowledge and actually using it. Perception is not like the change from being ignorant to coming to have knowledge. This is important because the second change is a different kind of change from the first. The difference between the two is that when one learns something from a background of ignorance one takes on the opposite of an attribute one had before. One comes to be knowledgeable about something from having been the opposite, ignorant. I can only change in this way by saying goodbye to one attribute in favour of its opposite. That is why Aristotle says that this kind of change or being affected (πάσχειν) is a sort of destruction of an attribute by its opposite (φθορά τις ὑπὸ τοῦ ἐναντίου, *De an.* II.5 417b3). There is an attribute of me that disappears in favour of another. So in that way I become different in the change.

Exercising what one has already learnt differs from this kind of change in that one does not become different in the exercise of what one already is. No new attributes are acquired in the process: only skills or abilities possessed already are realised. The exercise just shows that the faculty was already there. So the exercise is a manifestation rather than an acquisition of a skill. That is why Aristotle contrasts the destructive aspect of an acquisition, where one attribute disappears in favour of its opposite, with the preserving aspect of a manifestation, where an attribute that one already has is preserved.[20] Because a manifestation preserves rather than changes an attribute, it is difficult to justify calling it a 'change' (πάσχειν) if by this we mean 'becoming different' (ἀλλοιοῦσθαι).[21] Aristotle instead talks about a transition towards one's own states and nature.[22] For it would be wrong to say that using one's knowledge was a way of becoming different just as it would be wrong to say that the builder became different when he builds a house.

A perceiver perceiving is like the builder building. The perceiver does not really change, he manifests an ability already acquired, a first actuality. However, it is important to notice that there is a difference between perception and building insofar as the perceiver is the patient of perception whereas the builder is the agent. The patient in perception is the sense-faculty, in building it is the building materials. When the builder builds he does not really change but the materials do. The materials acquire the shape of a house. That means acquiring new attributes. So the materials, the patient of build-

---

[20] Cf. 'σωτηρία', *De an.* II.5 417b3.
[21] Keeping this literal meaning of 'ἀλλο-ιοῦσθαι' in mind helps us understand why a manifestation is not an ἀλλοίωσις; cf. Sorabji (1992) 221.
[22] 417b15–16: μεταβολὴν καὶ τὴν ἐπὶ τὰς ἕξεις καὶ τὴν φύσιν.

ing, undergo a genuine change. But in perception, the patient undergoes no such change of attributes. There is no real change in the sense-faculty in perception, for Aristotle says that:

The first change [μεταβολή] of what has perception takes place because of the generator [sc. the male parent] and when it has been generated it already has the ability to perceive in the way that one has knowledge. (*De an.* II.5 417b16–18)

We should compare the potentiality of the sense-faculty to the potentiality of the builder. As we have seen, the builder does not really change when exercising his ability. Similarly, the sense-faculty too should not really be said to change when we actually perceive. The peculiarity about perception as a change, then, is that both the agent, the sense-object, and the patient, the sense-faculty, undergo only a quasi-change in actual perception, for we saw earlier that the sense-object as an active potentiality could not be said to change when it actualises its potentiality. In other changes, however, like building and heating, it is only the agent that undergoes a quasi-change whereas the patient undergoes a real change. It gets some new attributes. On both the patient and agent side of perception actual perception only brings about a manifestation of a potentiality already acquired. This is also what Kosman's schema brings out. Before perception *both* the sense-object and sense-faculty should be understood as first actualities, and the realisation of a first actuality, as we now know, is no real change.

6. The effects of sense-objects

If the action of the sense-objects causes no real change in the sense-faculty, it makes sense to ask whether the action of the sense-objects causes any material change in the perceiver. This is a question raised at *De Anima* II.12, 424b3–19.[23] The passage begins by discussing the question whether anything that

---

[23] This passage is therefore particularly important for the functionalist debate; cf. Burnyeat (1992) 23–5.

does not have the sense of smell can be affected by a smell or, to generalise, whether anything that does not have a sense can be affected by its corresponding sense-object. Initially, Aristotle seems to want to deny that this is possible and he adduces two arguments to this end. But towards the end of the passage he seems to backtrack, for he accepts that tangible objects can affect bodies in general and that smell and sound can affect certain other bodies, for example air. So it is sometimes true to say that what does not have perception can be affected by a sense-object.

Let us consider the passage in more detail. Aristotle's first argument states that 'if the object of smell [τὸ ὀσφραντόν] is smell [ὀσμή], then if something affects the sense of smell [τὴν ὄσφρησιν] it is smell that affects it. So that none of the things that are unable to smell is able to be affected by smell' (424b5–8). The idea here seems to be this. Whatever is such as to affect the sense of smell (ὄσφρησις) is an object of smell (ὀσφραντόν). As their names suggest, ἡ ὄσφρησις and τὸ ὀσφραντόν are causal twins. An object of smell is by definition something that affects the sense of smell: the sense of smell is by definition something affected by objects of smell. But we identify the object of the sense of smell with smell (ὀσμή). So whatever is such as to affect the sense of smell is a smell. However, if something does not have the sense of smell, nothing is an object of smell for it. But if nothing is an object of smell for it, no object of smell affects it. And if no object of smell affects it, then no smell affects it.

I shall shortly return to this argument. But let me first consider the second argument against the proposition that senseless things can be affected by sense-objects. Aristotle says at 424b10–12:

Neither light nor darkness nor sound nor smell affects bodies in any way, but it is the things in which they reside that affect bodies. For instance, it is the air with the thunder that splits the timber.

The idea seems to be that it takes a body to affect another body. But as we know from Aristotle's criticism of Empedocles, light is not a body, nor is sound nor smell. However, the sense-objects reside in bodies. Light and sound reside in air.[24] Since this air *is* able to affect other bodies, it seems that it must be it and not the sound that resides in it which can affect other bodies. So when the thunderclap splits the timber, it would be the movement of the air that splits the timber rather than the concomitant sound.

However, Aristotle goes on to admit that at least some sense-objects affect some bodies:

> However, tangible things and flavours affect bodies. For if they did not, by what would soulless things be affected and altered? Will the other sense-objects then not also affect bodies? Or is it not every body which can be affected by a smell or a sound? For the things that are affected by them are indefinite and do not remain, such as air. For air smells just as if it was affected somehow. What then is smelling besides [παρά] being affected somehow? Or is smelling perceiving,[25] whereas the air becomes perceptible when affected quickly? (*De an.* 424b12–19)

So it seems that even in the case of the mediated senses there are examples of how a sense-object can affect a body that does not perceive it. For instance, if one fries some bacon then not only the bacon will smell but also the air in the room (because it is indefinite and does not remain) will smell of bacon long after the bacon is gone, having been eaten.

We need to remember here what is at stake for Aristotle in denying that the sense-qualities in general can affect non-perceptive bodies, for Aristotle's strictest definition of alteration is to affect something in terms of its sensible qualities. In *Physica* vii.3 245b3–6 he says that 'It can be seen from the following considerations that each thing that is altered is altered by sense-objects (αἰσθητά), and only in those does alteration occur which are said to be affected (πάσχειν) in themselves by sense-objects.' If it is true that it is only the sense-faculties that the sense-objects may affect, it follows

---

[24] Cf. ch. 1, sec. 9.
[25] Again reading ἢ τὸ μὲν ὀσμᾶσθαι αἰσθάνεσθαι.

therefore that there cannot be any alteration apart from perception, except accidentally.

But in fact, as the closing of the passage just cited suggests,
there is no need to draw this conclusion. The sense-qualities
may affect bodies without perception, *for the sense-qualities
may affect them so as to make them perceptible too.* The fried
bacon makes the air in the kitchen smelly, capable, in other
words, of being smelled. The bacon makes the air into a
potential object of perception. It is only, however, when the
smelly air affects the sense of smell that it becomes not only
smelly but also actually smelled. As we saw earlier in the example of the stove, being actually hot is to have the potentiality
also to heat something else up. One way of heating something
else up is to cause somebody to perceive heat. Another way is
to heat up a kettle. Aristotle's idea that acquiring an actual
sense-quality such as heat is also acquiring a potentiality to
act allows him to say that there can be chains of alterations in
nature outside perception where one body acquires a sense-
quality from another body and passes it on to a third body
without any of these bodies having the ability to perceive the
sense-quality. But every time a body acquires the sense-quality
it also acquires the potentiality to be perceived. The bacon can
make the air smelly, which can make my clothes smelly, which
can then smell of bacon to somebody.

7. Is perceiving a material change?

Now if this is possible, what is the difference between the way
the smell of bacon affects the air and the way it affects my
sense of smell when I smell it? What is the difference between
coming to smell *of* bacon and coming to smell bacon? We
started out with an argument to show that if a smell (ὀσμή)
affected anything, then it had to be the sense of smell (ἡ
ὄσφρησις), for smell was understood as being identical with τὸ
ὀσφραντόν, which exclusively affected the sense of smell. These
two were, as I put it, causal twins. Now it seems after all that
smell, that is odour, is not strictly identical with an actual
object of smell, for as in the case of the bacon-smelling air,

an odour sometimes affects something other than the sense of smell.[26] What, then, distinguishes the bacon-smelling air, that is the air that smells *of* bacon, from the sense of smell that smells the bacon? Are they not both cases of being affected by a smell? If so, are they the same affection?

The answer to this problem is contained in the final question of the passage: 'Is smelling perceiving, whereas the air when affected quickly becomes perceptible?' Becoming smelly, however, is not a case of perceiving. When Aristotle asks 'Is smelling perceiving whereas the air when affected quickly becomes perceptible?' he is drawing a contrast between what happens on the subject side of perception, what happens in the sense of smell when it perceives, and what happens on the object side when something becomes a sense-object. The object does not become perceived, it only becomes percept*ible.*

But not only is this a distinction between what happens on the subject side and on the object side of perception. As Kosman shows, it is also a distinction between what happens on two different levels of actuality. The smelling is actual perceiving. But when the air becomes affected by the smell it only becomes percept*ible.* The difference is here between the second-level actuality of actual perception and the first-level actuality of being perceptible but not actually perceived. For something to become actually smelly is one rung down the ladder of actuality from being perceived. Becoming smelly is to become percept*ible* (αἰσθητός), not to become actually perceived. So becoming smelly is not the full actualisation of a smell. The smell *qua* perceptible is only fully actualised when it is actually smelled.

Before Aristotle reaches the conclusion that there is a fundamental difference between the action of a sense-quality that makes a body perceptible and the action of a sense-quality that makes a sense-faculty perceive the quality, he suggests that at least tangible qualities must be thought of as being

---

[26] Cf. *DI* 2 460a29–32 where Aristotle says that oil and wine take on the odour not just of what is put into or mixed with them but also of what is placed or grows near to the vessels that contain them.

able to affect bodies that do not perceive them. It is indeed difficult to think that perceiving tangible qualities does not involve an affection of one's body. You put your hand on the hot stove and burn your fingers. Your fingers become hot when you feel the heat. Does that not show that you feel the heat because your fingers become hot? Or at least that you would not have felt the heat if your fingers had not become hot? Is it not clear that there is a heating process in your fingers similar to the one that happens in the water when it is heated up, that is, a literal, material change? We may speculate about whether there is a material change in the sense-organ of sight or hearing. But is it not plain to all that there must be a literal change of heating up the skin or flesh if we are going to feel the heat?

This was the question we were left with at the end of chapter 4, section 8, where I argued that a literalist interpretation seemed implausible for touch apart from the case of feeling temperatures. Let us now try to assess Aristotle's answer to this question. First of all we should notice that Aristotle located the proper sense-organ of touch in the area around the heart. So the fact that the skin and the flesh *may* get hot when you feel something hot does not show that the sense-organ of touch goes hot.[27] Nor of course does it show that the area around the heart does not get hot. At most the phenomenon suggests that a literal heating up of the flesh is part of the mediation of perceiving the hot. It does not show that the sense-organ goes hot. Again we should also remember the point argued in chapter 4, section 8, that the suggestion that the sense-organ literally takes on the tangible quality may seem initially plausible when the tangible quality is the hot or the cold. But it seems much less plausible when the tangible quality is the wet and the dry, the rough and the smooth, or the soft and the

---

[27] I say 'may' because it is quite possible to feel warm even if in fact one's skin is cold, for example when having been exposed to the cold outside one enters a warm room. Conversely, one sometimes feels cold even if one's skin is hot, for example when during an illness ones temperature is rising (as was noted in antiquity; cf. Sextus Empiricus, *PH* I.82; Diogenes Laertius IX.80).

hard, for it is difficult to believe that the heart literally goes wet when I feel the rain or that it becomes hard as stone when I touch a rock.[28]

Let us focus, then, on the literalist's strongest case, the perception of temperature. In *De Partibus Animalium* II.2 648b11– 649b8, Aristotle gives a list of the different meanings of 'hot'. He shows the different senses of 'hot' by showing the different ways in which one object is said to be hotter than another. For instance, one body is said to be hotter than another when it imparts a greater amount of heat to something than does the other body. But a body is said to be hotter *in a different sense* when it causes a stronger perception of heat when touched than does another body. There are more senses of 'hotter' and 'hot' than these two, the others being senses of hot in which soulless things can be said to be hotter than each other. What is important for our purposes is that one object

---

[28] Cf. Burnyeat (1992) 20–1; Freeland (1992) 231–2. Sorabji (1992) 222, in defence of the literalist interpretation, suggests that we think of the heart as undergoing a small-scale hardening when we feel the hardness of concrete. His evidence is *Mem.* 2 452b8–15. Aristotle here discusses how we measure the time-lapse between the present and the time of a past event which we remember. He uses the analogy of our knowing that we are perceiving a large object (cf. a long past event) rather than a smaller object (cf. a more recent event). We know this because the change that the smaller object sets up in us is proportionally smaller than the change that the larger object sets up. It counts against Sorabji's suggestion that there is no indication that Aristotle wants to extend this point about the perception of size to the perception of qualities. There is no indication that when we see red, for example, the eye does not go as red as the object but only say a paler shade of pink (what else could a small-scale version of red be?). Nor is it clear how this view would combine with saying that the sense-faculty and the sense-object are one in form in perception. If the eye goes pink when we perceive red would it not be more correct to say that the sense-faculty was one in form with a pink object rather than with the red object? Also, one of the advantages of Aristotle's theory is that because it says that the content of the perception is the same as the cause of the perception, e.g. the content of seeing red is the same as the red quality that causes us to see red (cf. ch. 2, sec. 3), he has an answer to the sceptic who asks: how do you know that the object that you perceive as red really is red? The answer is: we know it because (in normal conditions) it is red objects that cause us to see red. With the idea of small scale changes this answer is weakened, for we now seem to be inferring from the fact that our sense-organs go pink that the object that causes them to go pink must be red. But the sceptic can now come back asking: if it is a matter of *inferring* from the quality of the sense-organ to the quality of the sense-object, how do we know that we are making the right inference?

can be said to be hotter in a non-perceptual way but not hotter in a perceptual way. Thus A is said to be hotter than B if it cools down more slowly. Yet, Aristotle says, boiling water is hotter to the sense of touch than oil even though water cools down more quickly than oil.

This shows that the hot that acts on the sense of touch when perceived is different from the hot that acts on soulless things, for if the effects are different, the powers that bring them about must be different too. The hot is exercising different powers when it makes itself perceived from when it, for instance, heats up some water.

This passage does not in itself show that the difference between the exercises of the two powers is that the one is a literal alteration and the other is not. But we shall see that in conjunction with *De Anima* II.12 the passage makes life difficult for the literalist. There seem to be two possible interpretations of *De Partibus Animalium* II.2 open for the literalist. (1) She can say that the difference between the exercise of the power to heat up something like roast beef and the exercise of the power to cause a perception of heat is that they involve different kinds of literal alteration in the patient. In other words, the difference is not that the one exercise involves a literal alteration and the other does not, for they are both literal alterations. However, it is, as I noted in the Introduction, very difficult to find any relevant difference in kind between heating up roast beef and heating up the flesh or the heart if these are both literal alterations. In other words, there may be differences between heating up roast beef and heating up the organ of touch just as there are differences between heating up roast beef and heating up some water. But these differences do not seem sufficient to justify the introduction of two different *senses* of 'hot' in *De Partibus Animalium* II.2.

The other (initially) more plausible option (2) is for the literalist to say that the difference between the exercises of the two powers is that in the case of feeling heat there is both (a) a heating of the sense-organ of the sort that goes on when water is heated and (b) a perception of the heat, an alteration which only a sense-organ with the potentiality to perceive can undergo.[29] However, the problem here for the literalist is that *De Anima* II.12 does not, as Kosman showed, answer the question 'what is smelling besides from being affected in a certain way?' by saying that smelling an odour is being affected *plus* becoming aware of it. It says that smelling is being aware (αἰσθάνεσθαι) of odour. There is no implication that smelling is also (καί) being affected by it in the way the air is affected by it.[30]

De Partibus Animalium II.2 648b11–649b8, then, does not on its own require us to think that the difference between being and not being *literally* heated up is what constitutes the difference between perceiving heat and the other ways of being heated up. However, if we combine this passage with *De Anima* II.12's emphasis on awareness as what distinguishes the way in which the senses are affected and the way in which

---

[29] *Ph.* VII.2 244b10–245b2 is too hedged with qualifications to be of any help to the literalist; cf. ἀλλοιοῦνται γάρ πως καὶ αἱ αἰσθήσεις (244b10–11) and πασχούσης τι τῆς αἰσθήσεως (244b12).

[30] Sorabji, (1992) 219, attempts to make παρά do the job of καί:

> The implication is that exercising smell is partly a matter of being affected by odour, *but is also something else besides (para)* [my emphasis]. It is not only relevance that is decisive here, but also the word *para* (besides). The word implies that exercising smell has two aspects. If no physiological process were needed, as maintained by the alternative [sc. non-literalist] interpretation, there would be no room for two aspects. So that interpretation must reconstrue the *para* sentence. It might do so by taking the sentence in effect to be asking, 'What is exercising smell as opposed to being acted on in the way the air is?' But *para* does not mean 'as opposed to'; it means 'besides'.

Sorabji may be right that παρά should be translated 'besides'. But there is an ambiguity in Sorabji's argument without which it does not work. 'Besides' only clearly implies 'also' if we take 'besides' to be an adverb. This is the way Sorabji seems to take it when he says in the emphasised clause, '*is also something else besides (para)*'. That this is how Sorabji takes it also appears when, a few lines later, he says 'Aristotle's answer to the question, "what is exercising smell besides" may be to us disappointing.' In other words, Sorabji seems to be taking '*para*' as an adverb meaning 'as well'. However, at *De an.* II.12 424b17 παρά does not work as an adverb but as a preposition governing τὸ πάσχειν τι. 'Besides' as a preposition need not imply 'in addition to'. Both in Greek and in English it can mean 'next to' or 'apart from'. When used in this way, saying that X is something besides (*para*) Y does not imply that X is also Y. For example, at *EN* I.1 1094a16–17 Aristotle says, διαφέρει δ' οὐδὲν τὰς ἐνεργείας αὐτὰς εἶναι τὰ τέλη τῶν πράξεων ἢ παρὰ ταύτας ἄλλο τι, κτλ. The point here is not that either the ends are the activities themselves or they are the activities themselves as well as something else, but rather that the ends are either the activities themselves or they are something else, something apart from the activities.

bodies are affected, there seems to be no way out for the literalist, because *either* the change in the sense-organ is simply a literal change – but in that case the distinction between different senses of hot, in *De Partibus Animalium* II.2 seems unmotivated – *or* perception is simply the change of becoming aware of the heat. In the latter case, the distinction is motivated but the literalist interpretation is refuted.

We may of course still admit that whenever I do perceive an object as hot my skin and flesh are warmed by the object. It would obviously be wrong to say that this does not happen. However, the point is that (1) even if there always were a literal heating up of our bodies when we perceive heat, this would not enter into our account of perception. The perception is the awareness of the sense-object, that is what constitutes a change in relation to our senses. (2) Whether there is a literal heating up of my skin and flesh when I perceive heat says nothing about what happens in my sense-organ of touch, for the sense-organ of touch is the area around the heart. I conclude that the literalist's strongest case is weak.

CONCLUSION

To conclude, I wish to relate the various strands of the argument to the questions that I raised in the Introduction. In particular, I want to explore whether Aristotle's explanation of the sense-organs sheds any light on the functionalist debate.

I began this study by asking why we have sense-organs. Aristotle's answer was based on the idea that the sense-faculties are potentialities to be changed by certain objects. These potentialities are found only in certain sorts of matter. That was why we needed sense-organs. The sense-organs were the necessary material basis of perception. The matter had to be matter of a certain sort. For example, the ability to be changed by colours was known as transparency. But transparency was found only in certain sorts of matter, such as water. That was why the organ of vision was made of water. Similarly, the ability to be changed by sound was found only in matter that was resonant, such as air. That was why the organ of hearing was made of air. The ability to be changed by odours was found in water or air because both were potentially like odours, dry. So the organ of smell was made of water or air. The organ of touch consisted of all the elements, for it was only a mixture of the four elements that would make the sense-organ potentially like all the tangible qualities, the proper objects of touch. Finally, the organ of taste was said to be the same as the organ of touch, namely flesh, with the exception that it was only the flesh of the tongue that was sensitive to flavours. The reason for the exception seemed to be that flavours had to be perceived in a liquid environment, which was provided by the tongue.

It is correct, therefore, to say that for Aristotle the sense-

organs contain no *internal* structure,[1] For the proper organs
are either simple elements or, in the case of touch, a homoiomerous compound. However, we saw also that the sense-
organ *as a whole* often has different features. The eye consists
not just of transparent water inside the eye, for example. We
saw that the eye contained a membrane, an iris and a white
part, and was connected to certain passages, the *poroi*. But
we saw also that all these features were there to preserve and
promote the transparency. So though we can differentiate features of the eye they all refer to the potentiality of the transparent to be changed by colour. This means that when we
consider what happens in the eye in vision there is only the
actuality of one potentiality that we need to take into account,
the actuality of the transparent. There are no other 'changes'
in the eye relevant to the actuality of vision. As we saw in
the discussion of the medium in chapter 2, sections 5–6 and
chapter 6, section 5, the sense-object is sufficient on its own to
bring about perception in the perceiver if nothing else interferes. No more is needed to bring about perception than a
sense-object, a medium and a suitably disposed perceiver. But
a suitably disposed perceiver means a perceiver that has the
potentiality (first actuality) to be changed by the sense-object.
It is this potentiality that is provided by the transparent in
vision, the resonant in hearing and the equivalent attributes of
the other sense-organs. All the parts of the eye refer to transparency, and therefore to a potentiality for only one sort of
'change'. The situation is therefore not as in a modern scientific explanation of vision that there are various processes in
vision, chains of chemical and electronic impulses, in relation
to which different parts of the visual apparatus play different
roles. It is therefore not to accommodate different sorts of
process that the eye has differentiated parts. The eye has differentiated parts only to the extent that they are needed for
one 'change' to take place, the 'change' in the eye from the
first-level to second-level actuality of vision.

We have seen that there is considerable variation between

---

[1] Cf. Burnyeat (1993) 422–3; Lloyd (1991) 227.

the sense-organs of different animals. Both Sorabji and Marc Cohen argue that these variations are evidence in favour of the 'multiple realisability' of perception.[2] Sorabji points out that

for smelling, fish use their gills, dolphins their blow hole, and insects the middle part of their body, the first two of which contain water, not air. Indeed, it is a major theme of Aristotle's biological groupings that, in different genera, parts can be analogous in function but different in structure, and a case in point is the nostrils, the gills of fish and the middles of insects.[3]

Marc Cohen says, again in support of a functionalist interpretation, that

some psychic states are intimately associated with specific bodily parts, of course; sensation and the sense-organs are an obvious example. Aristotle discusses these in detail in De Partibus Animalium. His remarks strongly suggest a conviction that the same psychic state may have different material realisations. In animals made of flesh, for example, the organ of touch is the flesh; in other animals it is the part 'analogous to flesh' (PA 2,1 647a21). Sensations of touch occur in the flesh of humans, but in different (although analogous) organs of other species. Such observations, which abound throughout the work, suggest a sympathy for the compositional plasticity that is characteristic of functionalism.[4]

Both scholars thus point out that sense-organs of different material composition can serve the same perceptual functions. This study, however, has given reasons for not taking variation in sense-organs as evidence of compositional plasticity of the sort that the functionalists have in mind. It is true that Aristotle showed considerable interest in the variation in sense-organs. However, the reason why different animals had different sense-organs was that perception as the sense-organ's goal was more complex than at first appeared. The goal of the sense-organ was not just to enable the animal to perceive. It was to enable the animal to perceive given its natural environment. Thus fish had no external ear because it was not needed when hearing in water. Fish smelt using water instead

---

[2] Sorabji (1992); Marc Cohen (1992).
[3] Sorabji (1992) 216.
[4] Marc Cohen (1992) 59.

of air because the animal had to use the same part for refrigeration and smelling and water was what was available to
fish for refrigeration. This example also showed that the goal
of perception had to be negotiated together with the animal's
other goals. Thus birds had no external ears because it was
incompatible with flying. Perception was just one of a totality
of goals that determined the animal's body. The reason for
the variation in sense-organs was therefore not that perception was compositionally plastic, that the animal's sense-organ
could have had a different material basis. The reason was that
the animal had to have that material basis given other facts
about it. For example, the fact that for smelling fish use their
gills, dolphins their blowhole, and insects the middle of their
body is explained by the fact, as we saw in chapter 5, that
nature works out the organ of smell together with the animal's
organs of refrigeration. Fish, dolphins and insects have different organs of smell because they have different refrigeratory
organs reflecting their different refrigeratory needs and their
different natural environments.[5] The variations in the sense-
organs that Sorabji and Marc Cohen mention in support of
the compositional plasticity of perception no longer look like
evidence for compositional plasticity when we take this point
into account.

The functionalist interpreter may reply that though Aristotle does not give examples of how the sense-organs of an
animal could have been composed differently, it is consistent
with or indeed required by his general hylomorphism to say
that the sense-organs could have been composed differently.
In other words, it is a contingent fact about this world that
there is no other matter than water that can serve the human
eye. But in another possible world there might be some matter
other than water that would serve the eye as well as water. In
that case it would be right to say that the human eye *could
have been* composed differently.

---

[5] Cf. *PA* III.4 665b2–5: 'Just as not all animals have been provided with the use of the
same external parts, but each animal individually has been provided with the parts
useful for its life and the changes it undergoes, so also different internal parts belong
by nature to different animals.'

This study has emphasised that Aristotle determines the sense-organs by their potentiality as sense-organs. He is therefore interested in the sense-organs only to the extent that they can be shown to realise the potentiality that defines the sense-organ. Aristotle hardly ever shows any interest in the matter of the sense-organs as such. This was also the point of showing in chapter 1 how the various features of the eye were all determined with reference to transparency. Even where Aristotle apparently did show interest in the attributes of the matter as such, as in the case of eye colour, his interest revealed itself as an interest in the degrees of transparency coinciding with the different eye colours, that is, as an interest, after all, in the ability of the eye to function as a sense-organ. For the functionalist interpreter this is bad news because the functionalist interpretation requires that the matter of the sense-organ can be identified independently of the form or function. Otherwise, as I argued in the Introduction, it makes no sense to say that the same form could be realised by another type of matter, for that other type of matter if it had the same form would be the same type of matter.

The functionalist interpreter may respond by saying that multiple realisability is not to be found on the level of the matter of the form. It is not the so-called proximate matter that could be different, for that matter would obviously not be the same if it had a different form. Instead, we should try to find the matter that could be different at the next level down. For example, we cannot say that some other matter than the flesh could have served the function of medium/organ of touch if by flesh we already mean whatever part serves this function. But we should instead consider the flesh itself, the matter of the sense-organ, as a composite of matter and form, the matter being the four elements and the form being the ratio of their mixture. We could now say that other elements could have been mixed according to the same ratio as flesh. Thus we can describe another composite than flesh which has the same form or mixture as flesh but has different elements. We have described this composite independently of any role it might play as a sense-organ of touch. But since this composite has the same form as flesh, that is, its elements are mixed in the same ratio as the elements of flesh, it is reasonable to think that it might also serve as an organ of touch. If so, the argument concludes, we can say that the organ of touch could have had different matter, for the matter of the sense-organ's matter, where the sense-organ's matter itself is considered as a composite of matter and form, could have been different.

However, because of the point made in chapter 4, section 7, this response is unacceptable. The sense-organs of smell, taste and touch are defined according to the elementary qualities, the wet and the dry, the cold and the hot. For these are (in different ways) the proper objects of smell, taste and touch. We said, for example, that the organ of smell belonged to fire because odours, like fire, were actually hot and the organ of smell had to be potentially like its proper object. We said also that the organ of taste was potentially wet so that it could be made wet by flavour. Finally, we said that the organ of touch belonged to earth because the organ was potentially cold. In all these cases what it meant for the organ to belong to or to be composed of an element was understood in terms of the characteristic qualities of the element. What was important was that the sense-organ had a constitution that made it potentially like the elementary qualities that its proper object had actually. Now to say that the organ could have been made of a different element or belong to a different element in this context is to suggest that the sense-faculties could have had different proper objects. Aristotle understands the elements that the organ is composed of in terms of their characteristic qualities. The organ has those characteristic qualities that will make it potentially like the characteristic qualities of the sense-faculty's proper object. His argument for saying that the organ of touch is composed of flesh is that it is necessary for the organ to be composed of all the four elements because in this way the organ has all the tangible qualities potentially. This direct link between the proper object and the elementary composition of the organ means that you can only change the elementary composition of the organ if you change the sense-faculty's proper object. But that is impossible because the sense-faculty is defined in terms of that proper object. Smell, as we saw, is the sense of smells (cf. ch. 6, sec. 6). If it had some other object it would not be smell. So the elementary composition of the sense-organ is no more plastic than the sense-faculty's proper object, that is to say not plastic at all.

There is a further problem in the case of those sense-organs that are composed of simple elements. It is notoriously difficult to identify any matter underlying the simple elements. But even if we were to postulate something like prime matter this would certainly not help to establish compositional plasticity, for on the level of prime matter you will not find any other matter that the organ could have been made of. I conclude that for none of the sense-organs do there seem to be grounds for saying that the sense-faculty is compositionally plastic either on the level of proximate matter or on any other level of matter.

A recurring theme in this study has been that the sense-organs are composed according to the same functional requirements as the external medium. Thus the eye was not only transparent like the external medium. It was transparent for the same reason: to be able to be changed by colour and in turn enable something else to be changed by the colour. The sense-organ appeared to operate as an internal medium in relation to the seat of perception in the heart. Sometimes there seemed to be no difference between the medium and the proper sense-organ. For example, it was difficult to say what more there was to the organ of hearing in some animals than passages filled with resonant air (ch. 3, sec. 5). The inner sense-organ was a sort of inner medium protected from disturbances by its location inside a passage. In the analysis of hearing (ch. 3, secs. 2–4) I noted, as in the case of vision, how the conditions of the sense-organ recreated the conditions of the medium. Resonance was ensured in the inner ear just as you would ensure resonance in the medium by preventing the air from escaping and preserving its unity. It seemed that the organ of hearing, unlike the medium, was in the state of a permanent receptiveness to sound.

It is a good question why nature has given us sense-organs if the sense-organs are simply media. Why not have holes where the eyes are if such holes would be filled with transparent air anyway? The advantage of the sense-organs is that they, unlike the external medium, are always receptive to the sense-object. The animal therefore always has the potentiality to be changed by the sense-object. This is a potentiality that it requires because as an animal it must have perception. In some cases the sense-organ also compensates for the deficiencies of the external medium and improves the mediation. A tube-like protrusion from the sense-organ (long ears, deep-set eyes, etc.) prevented the change from the sense-object from being dispersed in the mediation. Soft, fluid and mobile eyes compensated the fish for the murky medium they live in. So the animal's need to be permanently receptive to the sense-qualities and the need to compensate for or improve on the external medium explain why the sense-organ is not always composed just like the external medium.

In chapter 2 I argued that the external medium does not literally take on the quality of the sense-object. Because of the analogy between the external medium and the sense-organ, this suggested that the sense-organ does not literally take on the quality either. In chapter 6 we saw that the effect of the sense-quality on bodies that could not perceive it was different from the effect of the sense-quality on a sense-faculty. I argued that the effect of the sense-quality on a body was best described as making the body into another potential object of perception, to make it percept*ible*. The effect of the sense-quality on the sense-faculty was to make the sense-quality itself an actual object of perception, to make it perceived. We could not say that both sorts of effect were involved in perception: that there were both a literal change of the sense-organ's matter and a perceptual change in the sense-faculty for, according to *De Anima* II.12, the perception was simply the change in the sense-faculty.

Sorabji sees this sort of interpretation as an attempt to 'dephysiologize' Aristotle's theory of perception. The interpretation is a product of a neo-Platonist history, which, he argues, is 'a history of distortions'.[6] To quote Sorabji, 'the result [of the history] was a theory in which, except for the case of the tactile qualities, hot, cold, fluid, and dry, the reception of form was no longer to be understood as a physiological process'.[7] However, the term 'dephysiologize' is unfortunately loaded for, as I hope to have shown, one can give a *physiological* explanation of perception in the sense of an explanation that mentions both its material and its formal/final cause without mentioning material processes in actual perception. For example, the sense-faculty of sight requires some transparent matter in order to have the first-level actuality of sight. But that does not imply that the second-level actuality of sight requires a material change in the transparent. Our explanation of sight is still physiological in the sense that it mentions both matter and form. Vision is still the actuality of the eye.

Nussbaum and Putnam's objection that 'the situation with perception, on Burnyeat's reading, seems to be exactly the situation we have for *nous* alone, on our reading – body providing necessary conditions without doing the functions' is unfounded,[8] for though *nous* for Aristotle in some way is dependent on the body (Nussbaum and Putnam say that it is 'housed' in the body), the sense-faculties are clearly related to their sense-organs in a different way. The sense-faculties are the first actualities of the sense-organs. Actual perception is the actuality of these sense-organs *qua* sense-organs. On Burnyeat's reading we do say that the sense-organ changes in actual perception, for we say that it 'changes' insofar as its actuality 'changes' from a first actuality to a second actuality. There is no equivalent sense in which we can say that the body changes when we use our *nous*, for *nous* has no organ.[9] Thinking cannot be described as the actuality of any organ in the way that seeing can be described as the actuality of the eye.

Finally, we should beware when we approach Aristotle for

---

[6] Sorabji (1992) 224.
[7] Sorabji (1992) 225.
[8] Nussbaum and Putnam (1992) 45.
[9] *De an.* III.4 429a27.

an answer to the problem: how are mental events related to physical events? We may try to answer the question by pairing off the two sorts of event. We may, for example, assert or deny that material events provide necessary or sufficient conditions for mental events. If so, whatever answer we give, we will present the *problem* by assuming there are two types of event involved. When I see a tree, for example, there is a material event in my eye, perhaps the emergence of a miniature picture of the tree on my retina. There is also an event in my mind properly described as 'being aware of a tree'. We assume that the two types of event both occur when I see the tree. We then ask how the material event in my eye is related to the mental event of seeing the tree. We receive different answers from the dualist, the functionalist and the identity theorist. The comparison with Aristotle breaks down not just when we get to these specific answers. It breaks down already with the presentation of the problem, for we have in Aristotle's theory to substitute 'event in the eye' with 'actuality of the eye' and 'mental event' with 'actuality of seeing'. So in Aristotle's theory our question amounts to asking what the relationship is between the actuality of seeing a tree and the actuality of the eye. For us the seeing of the tree and the actuality of the eye are distinct types of event. But for Aristotle there are not two sorts of event involved in perception. There is not a physical event in the sense-organ and a mental event in the soul. There is one event: the actuality of the sense-faculty.[10] It is never envisaged that the actuality of the eye could be anything other than the actuality of seeing. For my eye can only be actualised insofar as I am seeing. There is only an actuality of the eye to the extent that there is an actuality of seeing. In

---

[10] Cf. ch. 6, sec. 7. Burnyeat (1993) 431:

> According to the key doctrinal passage of [*De an.*] 3.2, the vibration or resonance in the ear (*psophēsis*) is identical with the hearing (*akousis*) of the sound. It is one single event that admits of two descriptions. But it is an event on the level of form alone. For us, a vibration or movement is a physical event, hearing a mental event. The fact that for Aristotle 'movement' and 'hearing' are two descriptions of one and the same event demonstrates how badly our categories, which emanate from Descartes, fit his philosophy.

modern parlance, it is never envisaged that the event in the eye could be anything other than the mental event, for there is only an event in the eye insofar as a mental event occurs.

The mental event can still *be described* or *explained* from two different points of view: that of the sense-organ and that of the sense-faculty. Thus we can describe seeing red as the sense-organ becoming red and we can describe it as perceiving or being aware of red. But the sense-organ becoming red is no other event than our becoming aware of red. By saying this we are not betraying Aristotle's hylomorphism, as Nussbaum and Putnam fear. We are insisting on hylomorphism. We are insisting on the place of perception within Aristotle's philosophy of nature, for we are insisting that perception is to be explained with reference to all the four causes. Form and matter are both involved in perception. They are not involved because perception involves both a formal, or mental, event and a material, or physical, event. Form and matter are both involved because perception is the actuality of a potentiality of matter. The matter provides the potentiality that becomes actual in perception. In this way perception is a *logos enhulos*, an account in matter. Aristotle's natural philosopher may not require matter to be involved in perception in the manner of a modern physiologist, but for him the sense-organs are still the matter necessary for perception.

BIBLIOGRAPHY

1. Editions, translations, commentaries

Aristotle

Balme, D. M. (1991) *Aristotle, History of Animals,* vol. III (books VII–X). Loeb edn. London/Cambridge, Mass.

Barnes, J., ed. (1984) *The Complete Works of Aristotle (The Revised Oxford Translation).* 2 vols. Oxford

Düring, I. (1961) *Aristotle's Protrepticus. An Attempt at Reconstruction.* Gothenburg

Hamlyn, D. H. (1993) *Aristotle De Anima. Books II and III (with passages from Book I).* 2nd edn. Clarendon Series. Oxford

Hett, W. S. (1957) *Aristotle On the soul, Parva Naturalia, On Breath.* Loeb edn. London/Cambridge, Mass.

Hicks, R. D. (1907) *Aristotle: De Anima.* Cambridge

Joachim, H. H. (1922) *Aristotle on Coming-to-be and Passing-away.* Oxford

Ogle, W. (1882) *Aristotle on the Parts of Animals.* London

Peck, A. L. (1953) *Aristotle, Generation of Animals.* Loeb edn. London/Cambridge, Mass.

  (1961) *Aristotle, Parts of Animals.* Loeb edn. London/Cambridge, Mass.

  (1965, 1970) *Aristotle, Historia Animalium,* vols. I and II (books I–VI). Loeb edn. London/Cambridge, Mass.

Rodier, G. (1900) *Aristote: Traité de L'Ame.* 2 vols. Paris

Ross, G. R. T. (1906) *De Sensu et Memoria.* Cambridge

Ross, W. D. (1924) *Aristotle's Metaphysics.* Oxford

  (1936) *Aristotle's Physics.* Oxford

  (1955) *Aristotle's Parva Naturalia.* Oxford

  (1961) *Aristotle's De Anima.* Oxford

Williams, C. J. F. (1982) *Aristotle's De Generatione et Corruptione.* Clarendon Series. Oxford

Empedocles

Diels, H. and Kranz, W. (1903) *Die Fragmente der Vorsokratiker.* 3 vols. Berlin

Wright, M. R. (1981) *Empedocles: The Extant Fragments.* New Haven/London

BIBLIOGRAPHY

Hippocratic corpus

Littré, E. (1839–61) *Œuvres complètes d'Hippocrate*. 10 vols. Paris
Withington, E. T. (1928) *Hippocrates*. Loeb edn., vol. III. Cambridge, Mass.

Plato

Archer-Hind, R. D. (1888) *The Timaeus of Plato*. London
Burnet, J. (1899) *Platonis opera*. 5 vols. Oxford Classical Texts. Oxford
Taylor, A. E. (1928) *A Commentary on Plato's Timaeus*. Oxford

Theophrastus

Stratton, G. M. (1917) *Greek Physiological Psychology* (containing the *De Sensibus*). London
Wimmer, F. (1831) *Theophrasti Eresii opera, quae supersunt, omnia*. (Greek with Latin translation) Paris

2. Ancient commentaries on Aristotle

Alexander of Aphrodisias. *In Aristotelis de Sensu*, in P. Wendland, ed. (1901) *Commentaria in Aristotelem Graeca*, vol. I. Berlin
John Philoponus. *In Aristotelis de Anima libros commentaria*, in M. Hayduck, ed. (1897) *Commentaria in Aristotelem Graeca*, vol. XV. Berlin
Simplicius. *In libros Aristotelis de Anima commentaria*, in M. Hayduck, ed. (1882) *Commentaria in Aristotelem Graeca*, vol. XI. Berlin
Themistius. *In Aristotelis de Anima*, in R. Reinze, ed. (1899) *Commentaria in Aristotelem Graeca*, vol. V. Berlin

3. Other literature

Please note that all page references in the text to works here mentioned as reprinted or renewed are to the reprinted or renewed version.
Ackrill, J. L. (1972) 'Aristotle's definitions of *psuchē*', *Proceedings of the Aristotelian Society* 73: 119–33, reprinted in Barnes *et al.* (1979)
Armstrong, D. M. (1962) *Bodily Sensations*. London
Balme, D. M. (1987) 'Aristotle's use of division and differentiae', in Gotthelf and Lennox (1987) 69–89
Barnes, J. (1979) *The Presocratic Philosophers*, vol. II. London/Henley/Boston
Barnes, J., Schofield, M. and Sorabji, R., eds. (1979) *Articles on Aristotle, Psychology and Aesthetics*, vol. IV. London
Beare, J. I. (1906) *Greek Theories of Elementary Cognition*. Oxford
Block, N., ed. (1980) *Readings in Philosophy of Psychology*, vol. I. London

293

Blumenthal, H. J. (1976) 'Neoplatonic elements in the *De Anima* commentaries', *Phronesis* 21: 64–88

Bonitz, H. (1870) *Index Aristotelicus*. Berlin

Broadie, S. (1993) 'Aristotle's perceptual realism', in J. Ellis, ed. *Southern Journal of Philosophy, Supp. Vol., Spindel Conference 1992: Ancient Minds* 31: 137–60

(Waterlow) (1982) *Nature, Change, and Agency in Aristotle's* Physics. Oxford

Burnyeat, M. F. (1992) 'Is an Aristotelian philosophy of mind still credible (a draft)', in Nussbaum and Rorty (1992) 15–26

(1993), 'Aristote voit rouge et entend un "do": Combien se passe-t-il des choses? Remarques sur "De Anima", II, 7–8', *Revue Philosophique* 1993: 263–80; reprinted as an additional essay as 'How much happens when Aristotle sees red and hears middle C? Remarks on *De Anima* 2.7–8' in the paperback version of Nussbaum and Rorty (1995) 421–34. Oxford

Byl, S. (1977) 'Les grands traités biologiques d'Aristote et la collection hippocratique', in R. Tolly, ed. (1977) *IV Corpus Hippocraticum, Actes du Colloque Hippocratique de Mons (22–26 September 1975)*, 313–26. Mons

Charles, D. (1984) *Aristotle's Philosophy of Action*. London

(1988) 'Aristotle on hypothetical necessity and irreducibility', *Pacific Philosophical Quarterly* 69: 1–53

(1991) 'Teleological causation in the *Physics*', in L. Judson, ed. *Aristotle's* Physics: *A Collection of Essays*, 101–28. Oxford

Cooper, J. (1982) 'Aristotle's natural teleology', in M. Schofield and M. Nussbaum, eds. (1982) *Language and Logos*, 197–222. Cambridge

(1985) 'Aristotle's hypothetical necessity', in Gotthelf and Lennox (1987) 151–69

Denniston, J. D. (1953) *The Greek Particles*. Oxford

Detienne, M. (1981) 'Between Beasts and Gods', in Gordon (1981) 215–28

Ellis, J. (1990) 'The trouble with fragrance', *Phronesis* 35: 290–302

Emilsson, E. K. (1988) *Plotinus on Sense-Perception: A Philosophical Study*. Cambridge

Everson, S. (1995) 'Proper sensibles and *kath' hauta* causes', *Phronesis* 40: 265–92

Frede, M. (1992) 'On Aristotle's conception of the soul', in Nussbaum and Rorty (1992) 93–107

Freeland, C. (1992) 'Aristotle on the sense of touch', in Nussbaum and Rorty (1992) 227–48

Freudenthal, G. (1995) *Aristotle's Theory of Material Substance. Heat and Pneuma, Form and Soul*. Oxford

Geach, P. (1969) *God and the Soul*. London

Gordon, R. C., ed. (1981) *Myth, Religion and Society*. Cambridge

Gotthelf, A., ed. (1985) *Aristotle on Nature and Living Things*. Pittsburgh

Gotthelf, A. and Lennox, J. G., eds. (1987) *Philosophical Issues in Aristotle's Biology*. Cambridge

Granger, H. (1993) 'Aristotle and perceptual realism', in J. Ellis, ed. (1993) *Southern Journal of Philosophy, Supp. Vol., Spindel Conference 1992: Ancient Minds* 31: 161–71

Gregory, R. L. (1966) *Eye and Brain, The Psychology of Seeing*. London

Guthrie, W. K. C. (1969) *A History of Greek Philosophy: The Fifth Century Enlightenment*, vol. III. Cambridge

Hamlyn, D. W. (1959) 'Aristotle's account of aesthesis in the *De Anima*', *Classical Quarterly* 9: 6–16

Hartman, E. (1977) *Substance, Body, and Soul. Aristotelian Investigations*. Princeton

Johansen, T. K. (1996) 'Aristotle on the sense of smell', *Phronesis* 41: 1–19

Kahn, C. H. (1966) 'Sensation and consciousness in Aristotle's psychology', in Barnes *et al.* (1979) 1–31

Kerferd, G. B. (1955) 'Gorgias on nature or that which is not', *Phronesis* 1: 3–25

Kosman, L. A. (1969) 'Aristotle's definition of motion', *Phronesis* 14: 40–62
(1975) 'Perceiving that we perceive: On the Soul III.2', *Philosophical Review* 84: 499–519

Lennox, J. G. (1983) 'Aristotle's lantern', *Journal of Hellenic Studies* 103: 147–51

Liddell, H. G., Scott, R. and Jones, H. S. (=LSJ) (1990) *A Greek-English Lexicon*. 9th edn. Oxford

Lloyd, G. E. R. (1962) 'Right and left in Greek philosophy', *Journal of Hellenic Studies* 82: 56–66; reprinted in Lloyd (1991) 27–48
(1966) *Polarity and Analogy*. Cambridge
(1968) *Aristotle: The Growth and Structure of His Thought*. Cambridge
(1975) 'Alcmaeon on the early history of dissection', *Sudhoffs Archiv* 59: 113–47; reprinted in Lloyd (1991) 167–93
(1978) 'The empirical basis of the physiology of the *Parva Naturalia*', in G. E. R. Lloyd and G. E. L. Owen, eds. (1978) *Aristotle on Mind and the Senses: Proceedings of the Seventh Symposium Aristotelicum*, 215–39. Cambridge
(1991) *Methods and Problems in Greek Science*. Cambridge
(1992) 'Aspects of the relationship between Aristotle's psychology and his zoology', in Nussbaum and Rorty (1992) 147–67

Long, A. A. (1966) 'Thinking and sense-perception in Empedocles', *Classical Quarterly* 16: 256–76

Marc Cohen, S. (1992) 'Hylomorphism and functionalism', in Nussbaum and Rorty (1992) 57–74

Maxwell-Stuart, P. G. (1981) *Studies in Greek Colour Terminology*, vol. I. Leiden

295

Modrak, D. (1987) *Aristotle. The Power of Perception.* Chicago

Nussbaum, M. C. and Putnam, H. (1992) 'Changing Aristotle's mind', in Nussbaum and Rorty (1992) 27–56

Nussbaum, M. C. and Rorty, A. Oksenberg, eds. (1992) *Essays on Aristotle's* De Anima. Oxford

O'Brien, D. (1970) 'The effect of a simile: Empedocles' theories of seeing and breathing', *Journal of Hellenic Studies* 90: 140–79

Ostenfeld, E. (1987) *Ancient Greek Psychology and the Modern Mind-Body Debate.* Aarhus

Owen, G. E. L. (1965) 'Inherence', *Phronesis* 10: 97–105; reprinted in M. C. Nussbaum, ed. (1986) *Logic, Science and Dialectic Collected Papers,* 252–8. London

Putnam, H. (1975) *Mind, Language and Reality, Philosophical Papers,* vol. II. Cambridge

(1988) *Representation and Reality.* Cambridge, Mass./London

Robinson, J. M. (1973) 'On Gorgias', in E. N. Lee, A. P. D. Mourelatos and R. M. Rorty, eds. (1993) *Exegesis and Argument. Studies in Greek Philosophy Presented to Gregory Vlastos, Phronesis, Supplementary Volume* I. Assen

Sedley, D. (1991) 'Is Aristotle's teleology anthropocentric?', *Phronesis* 36: 179–96

(1992) 'Empedocles' theory of vision and Theophrastus' *De Sensibus*', in W. W. Fortenbaugh and D. Gutos, eds. (1992) *Theophrastus, His Psychological, Doxographical and Scientific Writings. Rutgers University Studies in Classical Humanities* V, 20–31. New Brunswick

Sharples, R. W. (1985) 'Theophrastus on tastes and smells', in W. W. Fortenbaugh, ed. (1985) *Theophrastus of Eresus On His Life and Work, Rutgers University Studies in Classical Humanities* II. New Brunswick

Smyth, H. W. (1920) *Greek Grammar.* Cambridge, Mass. (renewed 1984)

Solmsen, F. (1961) 'Greek philosophy and the discovery of the nerves', *Museum Helveticum* 18: 150–67 and 169–97; reprinted in Solmsen (1968) *Kleine Schriften,* vol. I. Hildesheim

Sorabji, R. (1971) 'Aristotle on demarcating the five senses', *The Philosophical Review* 80: 59–79, reprinted in Barnes *et al.* (1979) 76–92

(1974) 'Body and soul in Aristotle', *Philosophy* 49: 63–89, reprinted in Barnes, *et al.* (1979) 42–64

(1980) *Necessity, Cause, and Blame. Perspectives on Aristotle's Theory.* London

(1991) 'From Aristotle to Brentano: The development of the concept of intentionality', in H. Blumenthal and H. Robinson, eds. *Oxford Studies in Ancient Philosophy, Supp. Vol.: Aristotle and the Later Tradition,* 227–60. Oxford

(1992) 'Intentionality and physiological processes: Aristotle's theory of sense-perception', in Nussbaum and Rorty (1992) 195–226

Stigen, A. (1961) 'On the alleged primacy of sight – with some remarks on *Theoria* and *Praxis* – in Aristotle', *Symbolae Osloenses* 37: 15–44

Taillardat, M. (1959) 'Le sens d' "amorgos" (Empedocle 84 Diels) et les lanternes dans l'antiquité', *Revue des études grecques* 72: xi–xii

Verbeke, G. (1978) 'Doctrine du pneuma et entéléchisme chez Aristote', in Lloyd and Owen, eds. (1978) 191–214

Vernant, J.-P. (1981a) 'The Union with Metis and the Sovereignty of Heaven', in Gordon (1981) 1–15

(1981b) 'Sacrificial and alimentary codes in Hesiod', in Gordon (1981) 57–79

Wardy, R. (1990) *The Chain of Change. A study of Aristotle's* Physics VII. Cambridge

(1993) 'Aristotelian rainfall or the lore of averages', *Phronesis* 38: 18–30

Wilkes, K. V. (1992) 'Psyche versus the mind', in Nussbaum and Rorty (1992) 109–27

Williams, C. J. F. (1989) 'Aristotle on Cambridge Change', *Oxford Studies in Ancient Philosophy* 7, 41–57

INDEX LOCORUM

'†' = spurious or dubious

GENERAL INDEX

actuality/potentiality, 24–5, 256–9
  active/passive, 263–7
  as form/matter, 26, 289
  first/second actuality, 26–7, 36, 255,
    260–3, 269–72, 275, 289
  irrational/rational, 267–9
affections, 101–2
air, 97, 150–1
Alcmaeon, 93
Alexander of Aphrodisias, 58, 65, 90
  n.104
alteration, 13, 126
  instantaneous, 143, 145
  perceptual, 74
animals,
  bloodless/blooded, 212, 220, 233–4
  definition of, 15, 211
  'dualizers', 166
  land/water 162–4, 165, 221, 249
  quadruped/biped 164, 166–8
  species of, 102
Armstrong, D. M., 21–2
art/nature, 28–9, 31–2

bear, 173
Beare, J. L., 15
birds, 159, 166–7, 170–1
blind spot phenomenon, 216–17
blood, 92
bones, 15, 213
brain, 79, 113, 205–6
breathing, *see* refrigeration
Broadie (Waterlow), S., 13–14, 129–31
Burnyeat, M. F., 3, 11, 12, 140, 289

change, 37, 268–70
  Cambridge, 136–46
  causal sequence, 122–3, 127
  kinēsis, 141, 256
  like by like, 70–2, 195–6
  material, 2, 10–11, 106, 253, 274–80
  'phenomenal', 127
  'quasi', 270–1, 289
  'travelling', 140–1, 245

Cohen, S. Marc, 283
colour,
  Greek terminology of, 100–1
  in *Timaeus*, 59–60
  limit of transparent, 98, 103
  proper object of sight, 38–9
  composition (*sunthesis*), 190
crocodile, 166, 220, 221

Democritus, 32, 44, 49, 94–5
  on reflection, 45–6
  on the medium, 118
Diogenes of Apollonia, 93
dolphin, 222, 226 n.2
dualism, 5

ear, 154–7
  external, 157–8, 160, 171
  inner, 154–5, 156–7
earlobe, 157
earth, 42, 205
efficient causes, *see* moving principle
effluences, 54, 240–1
elements,
  assigned to the senses, 40–2, 195, 205
elephant, 169–70
Empedocles, 32, 44, 51–7, 65, 68, 94, 95
environment, 18, 158, 161–5, 190, 222,
  249, 251, 284
  mixed, 165–8
eye, 18, 24
  actuality of, 290–1
  and hypothetical necessity, 105
  decay of, 52
  formation of, 112–13, 209
  hard, 247
  injuries to, 77–8, 81 n.98
eye colour, 95–115, 218
  and character, 110
  and material necessity, 103–5
  and the mean, 108, 219
  and transparency, 106–9
eyelashes, 166–7, 173–4
eyelids, 86, 163, 172

explanation,
  material, 32–5
  'mechanical', 125
  physical ('physiological'), 7–10, 53,
    289
  teleological, 16–18, 124–5, 176–7
  top-down, 32–7, 40–1

fish, 159, 163, 249, 283–4
flavour, 182, 216
  and mixture, 185–8, 189–92
  definition of, 186
flesh, 15, 42, 180, 185, 223, 285
  analogue of, 16, 199
  as medium of touch, 199, 213
  composition of, 193–9
foetus, 211
food, 221, 228, 239–40
form, 8–10, 19, 28–32, 289
  as end, 31
  sensible, 12
function
  and eye, 44–5, 115
  and form, 31, 36
  of simple bodies, 43–4
  of tools (organa), 32, 36
functionalism, 3–6, 10–13
  compositional plasticity in, 16, 283–7

Geach, P., 136–7
gills, 162, 249
Gregory, R. L., 1, 2
growth/decay, 73

hair, 173
Hamlyn, D. W., 38 n.21
heart, 78–9, 202–4, 211–2
  analogue of, 212
Hett, W. S., 85
Hippocratic writings, 56, 81 n.98
homoiomerous/anhomoiomerous parts,
  195, 201, 212
homonymy, 27–8, 50
'hot', meanings of, 277–8
hylomorphism, 6–7, 284, 291

independence, descriptive, 124–5
insects, 250
intemperance, 221
iris, 95

Kahn, C. H., 74
korē, 45, 51, 67, 82, 201
  as inner medium 87–8

as lantern, 52, 55, 84–5, 87, 90
as pupil, 56
in Empedocles, 52
Kosman, L. A., 254, 266, 275, 279

Laconian hound, 160, 245
light, 38, 65, 83, see also visual ray
limited/unlimited bodies, 97–8
literalist interpretation, 14, 146–7, 153
  n.5, 214–15, 217, 241–2, 276–80
lizard, 172, 222
Lloyd, G. E. R., 15, 18, 42 n.30, 51 n.46
  and 47, 74 n.84, 75, 112, 114
locomotion, 73, 143, 149

matter, 8–10, 16–17, 19, 28–32, 172–4,
  252, 285–6, 289, 291
  prime, 287
mean, perceptual, 110–12, 206, 219
medium/mediation, 67, 200, 249, 287–8
  and indirect contact, 118–19, 120–2,
    133–4, 191–2, 200
  change in, 134–6, 138–43
  of hearing, 148–9, 152–4, 243
  of sight, 83, 192, 243
  of smell, 237–42, 243
  of touch, 180, 185, 199, 243
  parts of, 140
  'phenomenal' account of, 120, 126,
    134
Megarians, 259–61
membrane of ear, 161
membrane (skin) of eye, 161
  in Empedocles, 61–2, 64
  transparency of, 62–4
membrane of nose, 246
mental events, 290
meteorology, 48
methodology, mixed, 242–5
mixture (mixis/krasis), 189–92, 239
  of colours, 100
mole, 75–6
moving principle, 102, 112

necessity,
  hypothetical, 34, 37, 102–3, 291
  material, 34, 102–3
night-blindness, 108
nose-cover, 246–8
nostrils, 160, 245
nous, 289
Nussbaum, M. C. and Putnam, H., 4, 6,
  13, 289, 291
nutrition, 22, 35